D0553629

THE ABC OF STYLE

BOOKS BY RUDOLF FLESCH

The ABC of Style

The Art of Clear Thinking

The Art of Readable Writing
(Revised and enlarged)

How to Write Plain English:
A Book for Lawyers and Consumers

Look It Up:
A Deskbook of American Spelling and Style

Rudolf Flesch on Business Communications

Say What You Mean

Why Johnny Can't Read—And What
You Can Do About It

THE ABC
OF STYLE

A Guide to Plain English

Rudolf Flesch

PERENNIAL LIBRARY
Harper & Row, Publishers
New York, Cambridge, Hagerstown, Philadelphia, San Francisco
London, Mexico City, São Paulo, Sydney

PUBLIC LIBRARY. PLAINFIELD. N. J.

808
F63A

A hardcover edition of this book was originally published by Harper & Row, Publishers.

THE ABC OF STYLE. Copyright © 1964 by Rudolf Flesch. All rights reserved. Printed in the United States of America. No part of this book may be used or reproduced in any manner whatsoever without written permission except in the case of brief quotations embodied in critical articles and reviews. For information address Harper & Row, Publishers, Inc., 10 East 53d Street, New York, N.Y. 10022. Published simultaneously in Canada by Fitzhenry & Whiteside Limited, Toronto.

First PERENNIAL LIBRARY edition published 1966.

Second PERENNIAL LIBRARY edition published 1980.

ISBN: 0-06-080083-6

80 81 82 83 84 10 9 8 7 6 5 4 3 2

00-3523

To my children

8706570

PREFACE

This is a new kind of book. It offers a word diet to those who are verbally overweight.

I know of no other book on style or usage that does just that. It's true that the best and most famous of them, Fowler's *Modern English Usage*, gives advice on how to avoid pomposities and circumlocutions. But this advice is mixed in with hundreds of articles on grammar, usage, spelling, pronunciation and dozens of other topics. Fowler doesn't focus on what Americans of today need most—the difference between natural English and ponderous jargon.

Other books on style and usage serve various other purposes. Bergen and Cornelia Evans' *Dictionary of Contemporary American Usage* concentrates on grammar and lists clichés to avoid; Theodore Bernstein's *Watch Your Language* tries to uphold traditional standards of usage; William Strunk's *Elements of Style* has good advice on basic points of composition and style, but isn't arranged for ready reference; neither is the excellent *Plain Words: Their ABC* by Sir Ernest Gowers.

Then there are the style books—the U.S. Government Printing Office *Style Manual*, the University of Chicago Press *Manual of Style*, the *New York Times Style Book* and others. These books are aimed at copy editors and printers and give more or less arbitrary rules on such matters as capitalization, compounding, spelling and punctuation. But they don't deal with style in the literary sense of the word, that is, with the choice of the best word.

Coleridge said, "Whatever is translatable into other and simpler words of the same language, without loss of sense or dignity, is bad." This basic principle of good style is what I tried to deal with in my book. I tried to give for every current pompous word, circumlocution or awkward expression a simpler way of saying it "without loss of sense or dignity."

The bad writer is like the overweight bad eater: he can't resist the fancy desserts, the extra snacks, the second helpings, the gravy, the candy, the fudge and the nuts; in the same way, the heavy-style addict lives on a steady diet of *prior to, subsequently, the latter, predominantly, underprivileged, in terms of, nonexistent, overall, transpire, involved, anticipate* and *institutionalization*. There's no other way of changing these bad habits than strict day-by-day abstention. Just as the dieter must learn to turn down pie à la mode, so the student of good writing must learn to avoid all those handy words that add up to poor English. He must replace *approximately* by *about* a hundred times until he has relearned the use of *about*; he must, if necessary, cross out a thousand *as to*'s; he must forswear the use of the word *pontiff* even though he's used the word *pope* in the sentence before.

Of course my book won't help you if you don't use it. Improving your style isn't an overnight affair; reading my book through once and then putting it on your desk or shelf will do little for you. What I hope you'll do is refer to it again and again while you're writing. When you've written *along the lines of* or *involved* or *viable* or *hospitalize* or *the question of whether*—interrupt yourself, look up what the book says on that point and choose among the listed replacements. I tried to be as generous as possible in my quoting of examples and give long lists of illustrations for the most common pompous words. Frankly, I didn't want to leave you an excuse; I don't think you'll find many places where I haven't listed *some* substitute word that will fit in with what you're writing.

Naturally, there are many pompous words I've overlooked. This is a one-man job and I can't possibly claim completeness. But if you've worked honestly on the words I *have* listed, others that might tempt you won't fit in any longer with your improved style and you'll get out of the habit of using them too. At least I hope so.

And now, I suppose, I should answer all those arguments

people always come up with. What's wrong with *thus*? Aren't there many situations where *abandon* is a better word than *give up*? Why *shouldn't* we build up our vocabularies and then use the words we've learned? Then follows an endless discussion that invariably winds up with neither side giving an inch. Well, there are incurable heavy-word and pompous-syntax addicts, just as there are incurable heavy eaters and calorie addicts, and there doesn't seem to be any way of breaking down the psychological defenses of either. All I can say is, if you're interested in improving your style, try my book and see.

And what about good grammar? you say. What about split infinitives, prepositions at the end of sentences, the use of *like* as a conjunction?

A few minutes of leafing through my book will show you that I am what is called a liberal in these matters. But I claim to be a reasonable liberal. I don't believe statistics of usage should decide every language question, and I'm unwilling to throw the advice of such people as Fowler out the window, just because he wrote before the scientific linguists took over. On the other hand, I don't feel that tradition should be followed to the bitter end against the overwhelming vote of the people for a new idiom. When I started writing this book, I was ready to defend and prescribe the use of the subjunctive with *as if*; but when I found dozens of examples showing that the subjunctive after *as if* is almost extinct, I changed my mind. If you follow my book, you'll learn to use current idioms rather than traditional usages whenever insistence on the older form would stamp you as a stiff, formal writer.

All my examples come from printed sources—most of them from newspapers and magazines. They seemed the most natural source. I could of course have excerpted well-known authors and literary figures, but then I'd have had to classify them and make rules on whose usage is best. If there's a difference in usage between J. D. Salinger and Arthur M. Schlesinger, Jr., who is the better model? I thought it was simpler and less confusing to collect thousands of examples from the *New York Times,* the *New York Herald Tribune,* the *New York World Telegram,* the *New York Post, Time, News-*

week, Life, the *New Yorker, Harper's,* the *Reader's Digest,* the *New Republic,* the *Scientific American,* and dozens of other newspapers, magazines and books that happened to come my way.

One more word. Most of the examples I used to illustrate a specific point are also examples of one or more other faults of style. To avoid confusion, I always corrected only the particular word or expression I was dealing with, leaving everything else unchanged. For instance, under UNNECESSARY WORDS you'll find this example: "Not having seen the stage production, this writer is unprepared to say how well it was translated or in what respects it was changed (*in transition*)." I hope it's understood that this sentence is poor not only because it contains the unnecessary words *in transition,* but also because it contains *not having seen, this writer, unprepared to say* and *in what respects.* What the author should have written is this: "I haven't seen the stage production and can't say how well it was translated or how it was changed."

R. F.

THE ABC OF STYLE

THE ABC
OF STYLE

A

a. The article *a* sounds unpleasantly snobbish when used with a proper name, as in "When you get into a row with *a* Noel Coward, you gotta know what the hell you're talking about." (The *a* implies the speaker is on intimate terms with dozens of people like Noel Coward and could drop their names too if he wanted to.)

Other examples:

Rare is the genius of *an Alec Guinness or a Peter Sellers* (better: of Alec Guinness or Peter Sellers) for disappearing within a character.

In many of the backward nations the critical determining factor may be the "historic force" of a commanding, but democratic and gradualist figure, such as *a Nehru or a Munoz Marin* (Nehru or Munoz Marin).

We may match or surpass the British in content, but in style we remain inferior. When one comes to *a Hemingway, a Faulkner, a Frost, a Thurber, or an E. B. White* (Hemingway, Faulkner, Frost, Thurber, or E. B. White), my generalization has no point. But in the case of the average American first novelist . . . .

See, also THE for the same device with the plural.

When the article *a* appears as the first word of a book title, fussy people insist on always using it, as in "Save $55.00 on Toynbee's Complete *A Study of History!*"

That's awkward. It's better to write "Save $55.00 on Toynbee's Complete *Study of History!*"

For problems with *an*, see AN.

a-. The old English prepositional prefix *a-* (meaning *on, in, at, in the act of*) appears in such words as *afire, asleep, ahunting*. It has a slightly obsolete flavor and often gives trouble to writers:

Oh, there was mischief *a-plenty* afoot that September night in New Brunswick, N. J., 41 years ago. (The hyphen is wrong; *plenty of mischief afoot* would have been better.)

A brief hearing was held in committee, no real discussion developed and the bill died even *before aborning*. (Wrong: you can't use the preposition *before* with the prepositional prefix *a-*. Better: *the bill died even before it was born.*)

The last faint hope for action on the bill went *a'glimmering* hours before he spoke. (The apostrophe is wrong; *went glimmering* would have been better.)

The morning after Kennedy had won the Presidential nomination, Johnson, the defeated candidate *lay abed* in his hotel suite. (The modern English phrase is *lay in bed.*)

Commander Alan Shepard announced that he and two Texas businessmen were putting up $1,300,000 for 1,800 shares in the First National Bank of Baytown, Texas, near the *abuilding* Manned Spacecraft Center. (Wrong: you can say *the Spacecraft Center is abuilding* but not *the abuilding Spacecraft Center.*)

aback. The phrase *taken aback* is common, but what with the slightly obsolete prefix *a-* (see above) it sometimes sounds odd:

The question *took him aback* and he looked startled, like someone found out. (The modern word for *taken aback* is *startled*, but the author shied away from it because he used it immediately afterward. *The question surprised him* would have solved the problem.)

The Texan ordered his car stopped and greeted the camel driver. "How do you do?" he said. Ahmed was *taken aback* (startled).

abandon is a good word in its place, but shouldn't be used instead of *give up* or *leave*:

Professor Black expressed the fear that the arrest might have been planned to induce the United States to *abandon* (give up) these negotiations.

Sensible Alsatians have long since *abandoned* (given up) the idea of promoting their wines as "Vins du Rhin."

The hermit's story and his meaning to the world he had *abandoned* (left) faded into nothingness.

abate, abatement are formal, old-fashioned words meaning *decrease, drop, cut down, end*. There are many other words that can be used instead:

The civil rights bill has increased, not *abated* (decreased) the demand for equal rights now.

Between these two specious contentions, smut continues *unabated* (unchecked).

The so-called "scandal" shows no sign of *abating* (dying down).

Political observers here fear that Dr. Erhard's position could be weakened by any sign of *abatement* (fading) of United States interest in European affairs.

ABBREVIATIONS. It's a superstition that abbreviations shouldn't be used in serious writing and that it's good style to spell everything out. Nonsense: use abbreviations whenever they are customary and won't attract the attention of the reader. In the sentence "One bright morning this week, there arrived in the Madison Ave. offices of Doubleday and Co. a brown package which looked as if it contained a decent time bomb, although its contents turned out to be not quite that good," your eyes hardly register the abbreviations *Ave.* and *Co.* Nor are you bothered by the abbreviations in "MCA is up there in entertainment the way AT&T is up there in telephones"—unless, of course, you happen to be unfamiliar with *MCA* and *AT&T*.

But shouldn't names and titles be spelled out when they appear in an article for the first time? Many publications have such a style rule and the results look like this:

Robert Service, president of the Bedford *Young Men's Christian Association,* says that too little is being done.

At the formal session on the Negro market, Roy Wilkins, executive secretary of the *National Association for the Advancement of Colored People,* pointed out that Negroes in the U.S. represent a consumer market estimated at as high as $20 billion annually.

A difference of opinion about the size and power of the Soviet Army has developed in the Pentagon and is being reflected in command circles of the *North American Treaty Organization*.

Securities and Exchange Commission Chairman William L. Cary said yesterday "the overwhelming preponderance of fraud cases in past years" has involved over-the-counter stocks.

Mr. Dodd himself at one time served in the *Federal Bureau of Investigation* under J. Edgar Hoover.

The American Federation of Labor and Congress of Industrial Organizations challenged the tactics of the *American Medical Association* yesterday in the continuing battle over methods of providing health care for the aged.

To my mind, these sentences look ridiculous and would have been better with *YMCA, NAACP, NATO, SEC, AFL-CIO* and *AMA* in their proper places.

See also FIGURES.

abet is an obsolete word meaning *help*. It still occurs in the legal phrase *aid and abet* and that's how it has been kept alive for the use of writers who like to fancy up their prose:

Electronic data processing, electric typewriters, teletypewriters, punch cards, duplicating machines and other modern office equipment *abet* (add to) the trend.

The soprano, *abetted* (accompanied) by mezzo Margaret Elkins and the London Symphony Orchestra, sang excerpts of her favorite roles.

abeyance is a formal word that can easily be spared in ordinary writing: "One of the reasons advanced for *holding the indictment in abeyance* (holding up the indictment) until Thursday, is that to have released news of it prior to the election might have had political connotations."

abide, abiding. Both the adjective *abiding* and the verb *abide by* are now too stately for everyday use:

One *abiding* (lasting) concern is the prospect of widespread unemployment posed by automation equipment his own company is developing.

They are shorn of the drive that spurred their predecessors, weirdly cut off from the middle-class culture their teachers *abide by* (belong to).

-able, -ability. The suffix *-able* is alive; if you want to, you can use it to form new English words. But it's risky business and I would advise against it. Consider these dubious examples:

Mr. Vidal's ambitious novel is a more balanced appraisal than any which Julian received in antiquity, and *arguably*, the best thing of its kind since *Count Belisarius*. (*Arguably* sounds pompous and strained; a simple *maybe* would have been better.)

The Manhattan Yellow Pages list some twenty hypnotists (excluding performers at smokers and nightclubs) in the New York City area alone; *expectably*, the California Association for Ethical Hypnosis claims 3,500 members. (What the writer meant was *predictably*; *expectably* isn't wrong but sounds odd.)

Hachette has exerted no depressing influence on the quality of the French press, which has *detectably* improved since the venal prewar period when the news columns of nearly any paper could be bought. (*Detectably* is just a fancy synonym for *visibly*.)

What we are watching is not the punishment meted on each other by two *dislikable* people, but war between Titans. (Yes, there is such a word; it's in Webster's Unabridged.)

Never mind; this isn't supposed to be reporting but appreciating, and no place looks more *appreciatable* than Provence. (Never mind the coyness; the only form is *appreciable*.)

The frightening but *unblinkable* truth is that, with certain qualifications it is a true picture of many a rural or small-town Southern court today. (*Unblinkable* sounds funny.)

Though often seeking to persuade, they rarely settle arguments. Their meat and drink is the *unsettleable*. (In his mighty effort to form a new word, the writer injected an unnecessary *e*.)

Inevitably, some of the poetry and the *unduplicatable* intimacy of Mr. Agee's particular expression was lost in this radical switch. (A poor word and wrong too: it should have been *unduplicable*.)

She is also a *non-foolable* virgin, which makes the contest more even, James Garner being wonderfully tall, charming and handsome. (Well, yes, we can see what is meant, but there must have been a better way of saying it.)

Finally, a shattering example of *-ability:*

No test of the *survivability* of a Minuteman silo could be conducted in the Pacific islands, because they are all sand, while our sites are encased in rock. (I'm happy to report that *survivability* is *not* in the 1961 edition of Webster's Unabridged.)

abode should never be used for *house,* as in "Couelle's *abodes* (houses) are influenced by flora as well as fauna, as, for instance, his staircases."

absence. Don't use *in the absence of* as a preposition instead of *without:*

The United States has generally granted this courtesy to the Soviet Embassy here, even *in the absence of* (without) an agreement.

Some lawyers use the word *absent* in the same ugly way; don't follow their example:

Nothing in New York's public policy prevents transfer, *absent settlor's contrary intent* (if settlor's intent isn't contrary).

ABSOLUTE CONSTRUCTION is the grammatical name for such sentences as "This being the origin of the rift, it will not easily be closed." The device was common in classical Latin and has been used in literary English for centuries. But that doesn't mean it is common in everyday speech. It is not, and I bet you can't remember a single instance when you heard someone use it in ordinary conversation.

In written English absolute constructions sound awkward and should be replaced by other ways of expression:

Although he has a contract through 1981 with NBC at a reputed $60,000 a year, the network was finding no outlet for his talents, *Berle's cheese sponsor having traded him in for Perry Como* (since Berle's cheese sponsor traded him in for Perry Como).

It seems both volumes were started two years ago, *the first inkling of another in the field coming* when the anthologists sought rights from a couple of the same poets. (It seems both volumes were started two years ago; the first inkling of another in the field came when. . . .)

Wagner, *his belief in fluoridation strengthened* by the 20-hour public hearing that ended yesterday morning, said the Board of Estimate would decide before the end of the year whether to set up the program. (Wagner's belief in fluoridation was strengthened by the 20-hour public hearing that ended yesterday morning. He said . . . .)

Lord Home did not kiss Queen Elizabeth's hand when he accepted her invitation to form a government, *the significance being that* he did not feel sure enough of success to accept formally. (A colon would be the best solution here: Lord Home did not kiss Queen Elizabeth's hand when he accepted her invitation to form a government: he did not feel sure enough of success to accept formally.)

See also -ING.

absolutely is apt to sound gushy:

The other night at a dinner, a happily married man I know was waxing *absolutely* rhapsodic over a temporarily single friend of ours.

Pictures of the period's glorious sculpture, on the other hand, were *absolutely* top rate.

ABSTRACT WORDS. "Students often find that an investigation of sentence patterns is a useful preliminary to the study of punctuation." What's wrong with this sentence? Too many abstract words. Stripped to the bone, it says that an *investigation* is a *preliminary* to a *study*—three abstract nouns piled upon each other, to express nothing more than that "students often find it useful to study sentence patterns before punctuation."

Abstract words are the most common disease of modern writing. Unfortunately this disease can't be cured by simply replacing abstract words by concrete "synonyms" (usually there aren't any), but only by rebuilding whole sentences so that the thought is expressed more simply and directly. This needs a constant effort of sticking to the pattern of who-is-doing-what.

Here are some examples:

The *inability* of "Spoon River" to attract sufficient customers despite highly enthusiastic notices from all of New York's drama critics has become a *puzzlement* as well as a *source* of theater *conversation* along Broadway. (Theater people are talking and wondering why "Spoon River" doesn't attract more customers despite . . . .)

A *willingness* to discuss the question, *recognition* by both sides that their competitive wooing of the Germans must end and a *more positive French view* on the future of European unity have *encouraged a belief* that relations between Paris and Washington may be improving. (Relations between Paris and Washington may improve since both sides are willing to discuss the question and recognize that their competitive wooing of Germany must end; besides, the French now think more highly of the future of European unity.)

The *apparent lack of liquidation* in securities assets by investors and businessmen should also bolster confidence that was shaken by the frightful events of a week ago. (Investors and businessmen seem not to have cashed in their securities. This should bolster confidence . . . .)

The *varying interpretations* in Western capitals last week about both the pattern and motives of current Soviet policy *underlined one of the chief problems for effective Allied response:* unity on tactics and strategy. (The pattern and motives of current Soviet policy were interpreted differently in Western capitals last week, which shows how hard it is for the Allies to get together on tactics and strategy.)

What an *awareness* of the *ambiguity of events* thus *subtracts* from the *optimistic view of progress* is the *luxury of believing* that progress is a simple pyramiding of success. (If you think about how ambiguous most events are, you may still be hopeful about progress but you won't consider it simply a matter of piling one success upon the other.)

It should be emphasized that the alternative of a political settlement that would enable us to reduce drastically our military involvement in Vietnam *exists so far only in the realm of theory.* (There's no political settlement in sight that would permit sharp cuts in our military aid to Vietnam.)

Exposure of the vulnerability of the Communist system cannot be *accomplished by isolation* but only through working relationships. The *limited opportunities* for our people to contact their people in functioning relationships have already *borne fruit in appreciation of other concepts.* (Communists can be shown the flaws in their system only through working contacts with Westerners. Even in the few contacts they've had so far they've learned something about Western ideas.)

See also -ABLE, -ABILITY; -ATE, -ATION; -ION, -ITY, OF.

accelerate is just a long word for *speed up*.

ACCENT MARKS. Most newspapers now drop accent marks in such words as *communique, resume, fiancee, nee,* etc. It's a good rule of thumb for writing to use only foreign words so familiar to English readers that they don't need an accent mark. If you want to use words like *raison d'être, élan, arrière-pensée,* think twice—and then use an English word instead.

accomplish is often used as a fancy synonym for *do,* as in "If the Attorney General is really serious about helping, there is a great deal he could *accomplish.* By using the powers of the Department of Justice he could turn the tide overnight. Here are some of the things he could do." (*Do* in both places would have been better.)

accord (verb) is much too formal for everyday use: "The magnitude of the swindle now being lovingly wrought by the organized World War I veterans can be plainly discerned in the light of the skinflint treatment the nation *accords* (gives) its truly deserving veterans and their widows and orphans."

according to, in accordance with are two of those awkward compound prepositions that clutter up sentences. They can be replaced in various ways. Sometimes the best word is *under:*

According to (Under) the dictionary definition of *soft,* Soft Whiskey should be a whiskey having a soothing or quietly agreeable taste.

According to (Under) the agreement, the banks' commitments are extended and the interest rates on the companies' debts are reduced.

Sometimes *in accordance* can be left out:

In accordance with (With) this aim, Britten has composed in about every manner extant except all-out "atonalism" of the Arnold Schoenberg sort.

Sometimes the best replacement is *by:*

But the polls name him front-runner and if he is going to

run, *according to* (by) his own estimates of the situation, he must get about it soon, build a staff, and show his intent.

Most often *according to* is used to refer to the source of information. Such sentences should be rewritten with *say:*

In February, 1960, *according to* (says) Mrs. Novak, Bobby Baker borrowed $12,000 from the Novaks to buy 3,600 shares of stock of the Mortgage Guarantee Insurance Corporation of Milwaukee.

According to these sources, (These sources say) Sir Robert was strongly influenced by the results of a poll taken last August.

According to one survey proudly publicized here, (One survey proudly publicized here says) the Netherlands has just passed West Germany as the most overweight country in Europe.

McCann was dipping his bait net in Los Angeles harbor last weekend, *according to wire service reports* (wire services report).

According to a prospectus filed with the Securities and Exchange Commission, Prudential plans to sell group variable annuity contracts geared to the Smathers-Keogh Act of 1962. (In a prospectus filed with the SEC, Prudential said it plans . . . .)

Last Friday was the beginning of Susan Stovall's world, and mother and daughter, both doing "just fine," *according to the new father,* are expected to come home to their new four-room apartment in Brooklyn on Wednesday. (Last Friday was the beginning of Susan Stovall's world, and mother and daughter are expected to come home to their new four-room apartment in Brooklyn on Wednesday. Both are doing "just fine," said the new father.)

See also SOURCE ATTRIBUTION.

accordingly is a cumbersome conjunctive adverb that can easily be changed to *therefore, so, thats why:* "He charged that The Times had 'distorted this thing beyond belief.' *Accordingly* (Therefore), he said, he would not discuss the matter further with a Times reporter."

accrue is sometimes misused as a pompous synonym for *come:* "Being barred from participation they are denied the income that *accrues* (comes) to participants."

ACCURACY. *See* WRONG FACTS.

acerb, acerbity. The adjective *acerb* comes from the Latin and means *bitter, sharp, harsh*. There's no reason why any of those words shouldn't be used instead:

> Not long ago Malcolm Muggeridge, that *acerb* (bitter) critic of British morals and manners, laced into the holier-than-thou hand-wringing that has gone on over the Profumo scandal.

> With some *acerbity* (sharpness), Keating therefore asked Rockefeller just what the devil he had meant by saying that the polls showed a sure win.

> *See also* EXACERBATE.

achieve, like ACCOMPLISH, is often abused as a synonym for *do*, as in "This is *achieved* (done) by using special high-gain antennas pointed toward the Hartford transmitter."

Sometimes *achieve* can simply be left out: "Numerous restrictions were adopted to (*achieve*) this end."

acquire shouldn't be used as a pompous synonym for *get*.

ad. Don't hesitate to use a shortened word like *ad* that is used and understood by everyone. And when you do use it, don't apologize for it with quotation marks, as in

> BRING THIS "AD" (better: BRING THIS AD)

> *See also* SHORTENED WORDS.

A.D. Use this abbreviation only when there's a possible confusion over whether a date is A.D. or B.C. Otherwise *A.D.* sounds pompous.

addition. *In addition to* is a cumbersome preposition meaning *besides, aside from; in addition* is an equally cumbersome adverb meaning *besides* or *also*. Make it a habit to replace *in addition* and *in addition to* by simpler words:

> *In addition to* (Besides) the Medal of Honor, the highest award for valor, he also received the Distinguished Service Cross, the second highest, and the Distinguished Service Medal.

> *In addition to* (Besides) all the other health routines Johnson has learned to follow, he also does a fairly creditable job now of controlling what used to be a hot temper.

In addition to (Aside from) the 10 House members, the American entourage to the Paris conference included eight wives, three congressional staff workers and the widow of Sen. Estes Kefauver, D-Tenn., who reportedly was there as an "observer."

In addition, he is (He is also) on the board of Prince Littler's Associated Theater Properties, which operates 11 West End theatres.

In addition, there was (There was also) a barely discernible tendency to hasten soft legato passages.

address shouldn't be used as a pompous synonym for *speech*.

adjacent is just a longer word for *next:*

If the land *adjacent to* (next to) our self-defense military installations is open to trained military men, questions inevitably arise . . . .

Frederick Barghoorn occupies an apartment in New Haven *adjacent to* (next to) that of his 80-year-old mother.

ADJECTIVES. The English language lets you make any noun into an adjective—as in *kitchen cabinet*—but there are limits to this, which are often disregarded by headline writers and others.

In the first place, a noun adjective can easily look odd or funny, like

CHARLES R. HOOK, RETIRED *STEEL HEAD*

Second, don't use a noun as an adjective where there already is an English adjective that does the same job:

CITY HONORS *BOLIVIA* (BOLIVIAN) CHIEF

ITALY (*ITALIAN*) COALITION HELD UP

FINN (*FINNISH*) BARITONE'S WELCOME
RETURN

He told his *industry* (industrial) audience that the American people seem to want government control of the makers of health products.

Third, it's poor style to use a noun adjective where the normal English idiom calls for a prepositional phrase:

The Ruth and Augustus Goetz play (The play by Ruth and Augustus Goetz), produced on Broadway in 1954, is based on André Gide's autobiographical novel . . . .

Because of the date, *the Diamond composition* (the composition by Diamond) had to be performed.

This Johnson performance (This performance by Johnson) was all the more remarkable because this sort of thing has never before been the new President's long suit.

One of the worst writing habits is the stuffing of all kinds of information into one sentence until it bursts at the seams. Often this is done by using adjectives that give added information on people's appearance, eyes, hair, beard and whether they wear glasses or not. For instance:

Traveling by jet from London via Montreal and Toronto as "Mr. and Mrs. Hayman and child," the *violet-eyed* actress and *jut-jawed* actor talked to reporters at both Canadian stops.

A *graying* Californian of 38 years, Hoppe joined the Chronicle after graduating from Harvard and the Navy, soon progressed from copy boy to reporter, with twin specialties: humor and executions.

Besides running the world's seventh largest ad agency (1962 billings: $135 million) and serving as a candid industry spokesman, the *graying, soft-spoken* Cone has found time to sit on the Chicago Crime Commission, the Committee for Economic Development, and the Chicago School Board, a post he resigned last month to step in as chairman of the University of Chicago's board of trustees.

It was the first of 100 or more questions which Morris Ravin, attorney for receiver Daniel F. DeLear, planned to put to the *pudgy, bespectacled* president of Allied, which lurched into bankruptcy last week after failing to meet $18.6 million worth of margin calls by Ira Haupt & Co. and J. R. Williston & Beane.

The world's biggest baker of cookies, as well as a pantryful of other goods from arrowroot biscuits to zwieback, Nabisco has increased its sales 27% in the past five years, to $526 million in 1962, and *white-thatched* president Lee Smith Bickmore, 55, has reported that sales for 1963's first three quarters are a cracking good 7% ahead of last year's.

Sitting in the lounge of the Lunt-Fontanne while a preview performance was being played upstairs, the *mustached* native of Budapest smilingly admitted that for a Hungarian to translate a German play into English was somewhat un-usual.

An operation was set for 10 A.M. Saturday but at 3:40 the aneurysm burst and death came swiftly to the *soft-voiced* campaigner who made the coonskin cap his folksy symbol in two bids for the Democratic presidential nomination.

See also HYPHENS, SENTENCE STUFFING, UNNECESSARY WORDS.

adumbrate is a formal Latin-root word meaning exactly the same as the simpler English word *foreshadow:* "Mrs. de Peyster determined to go one better, and in a demure interview she *adumbrated* (foreshadowed) the kind of occasion that reaches its zenith when Mr. Hellman, once again consulting an oracle four years later, gives an April Fools' Day party exactly according to the recipe of Baroness d'Erlanger."

advert to is obsolete; the modern word is *refer to:* "In reaching this conclusion, he was much helped by an interview with the candidate—in which Mr. Kennedy spoke appreciatively of Mr. Mailer's books, *adverting to* (referring to) ' "The Deer Park" and the others.' "

advise. In business jargon, *advise* is regularly used for *write, tell, inform.* This is an ugly usage—on a par with *same, said, such, beg to acknowledge* and *contents noted:*

I *advised* (told) him that I will discuss this with him upon his return to the city.

Weissman moved out of the apartment three years ago, *advising* (telling) the landlady that he was going back to New York.

The lawyer went on to explain that on his return to court the next day, he wore a bow tie again and that Judge Saypol called him to the bench and inquired of him if he had not been *advised* (told) of the "proper attire."

advisement. *Under advisement* is a phrase perhaps suitable to writing about the Supreme Court: "The Supreme Court took *under advisement* today one of the most important international law cases to come before it in recent years." But when you're writing, say, a business letter, *under advisement* is much too haughty a phrase—particularly if it's used to cover up a polite brushoff.

ae. It's simpler and more modern to spell such words as *esthetic, archeology, anesthesia* with *e* rather than *ae*. The same is true of such plurals as *formulas* instead of *formulae*.

See also LATIN PLURALS.

affirmative. Don't use the long word *affirmative* when you mean *yes:*

Affirmative (Yes) answers mark you as a wet blanket and a sponger.

The answer was an easy *affirmative* (yes) to all three.

This led to the conclusion here that the Senator's answer will be *affirmative* (yes).

afford (verb) sounds pompous when you mean *give:* "Oddly enough, the praise and blame my book has received *afford* (give) almost equal satisfaction."

aforementioned, aforesaid. These legalisms should be utterly taboo in ordinary writing:

But, *as aforesaid* (as I said), a trend against the party in office could affect any of these combinations.

Here the reviewer blunders—if he had bothered to check he would have found complete biographies on three of *the aforementioned* (those) gentlemen.

The action of the play takes place in a Greenwich Village apartment, where *the aforesaid* (that) bastard is living in sin with a doxy better looking than most . . . . (Of course the writer used the word *aforesaid* to be funny; but I don't think it is.)

afoul. *To run afoul* is musty English: "His ethical behavior (cheating, lawbreaking) can be punished when it *runs afoul* (is against the rules of) the community."

age. The phrase *years of age* is unnecessary and should be left out:

My cousin is 40 (*years of age*). She is attractive, well-edu-cated and . . . .

Almost seven million Algerians were theoretically entitled to vote—men and women older than 19 (*years of age*).

aggravate, aggravation. For years purists have been railing against the use of *aggravate* in the sense of *irritate* or *annoy*.

(The dictionary says *aggravate* means *sharpen* or *make worse*.) However, there seems to be something in the words *aggravate* and *aggravation*—perhaps it's the *ggrr* sound—that appeals to people who want to express a feeling of irritation. So I wouldn't worry too much about this:

> It's amazing how celebrities are drawn to appear on interview programs when they know they'll be exposed to controversial questions; the shows don't pay enough to make the *aggravation* worth while.

> She considers the typical, over-crowded Washington cocktail party "the biggest *aggravation* in the capital."

ago has the treacherous old English prefix *a-* built into it (*see* A-) and doesn't go with some words you might feel like putting in front of it. Here it is with a wrongly used *forever:* "It was really only yesterday that we were hearing about the silent generation and how it was concerned only with security as opposed to opportunity, but it's beginning to seem like *forever* (ages, an eternity) *ago*."

AGREEMENT (grammar). *See* ARE, IS or ARE, ONE OF, THEY.

aide, aid. An aide-de-camp—or *aide*—of an army or navy officer is his personal assistant. Headline writers seized upon the neat, short word *aide* and began to use it for any kind of employee. Later some of them shortened it to *aid*. Still later *aides*—or *aids*—began to show up everywhere:

> The Assistant Secretary of Agriculture, Dr. James Ralph, and his *aid* (assistant) William Morris, had to be fired for accepting gifts from a man doing dubious business with the government, Billie Sol Estes.

> It was Mr. Baker's interest in Serv-U and the company's extraordinarily rapid expansion among aerospace firms doing government contract work that focused attention on the Senate *aid's* (majority secretary's) business involvements.

As you see, *aid* is usually shorter than the word it replaces; unfortunately, it simply isn't part of civilian English.

ain't is the most famous "unacceptable" word in English. The rule is that you must never use *ain't* in print or writing; if it happens to slip out in conversation, you're supposed to feel ashamed for having used bad English.

But things are changing. More often than not when conversational talk of educated people is reported in print, you see *ain't* whenever the speaker felt it was the right word to use:

> "I'll give you a clue," he added. "All that stuff on TV about the Cosa Nostra—that *ain't* fairy tales."

> "My definition of a celebrity," Mr. Amory said in an interview, "is a name which, once made by news, now makes news itself. The real test is, if you have to say who someone is he *ain't* one."

> "Famous," remarked a lady I know, "I'm glad I *ain't*."

> "They'll come sliding in here on their vests and tell you over and over again that the President is a smart man, smarter than anyone else. Now Harry, you and I know he *ain't*." Amid laughter and applause, Mr. Johnson added, "And you all know he *ain't*."

Even outside of reported speech, you find *ain't* in headlines:

> ### HARVARD STUDENTS: IT *AIN'T* SO!

and in regular text:

> People either love me for my stand, or absolutely loathe me. There just *ain't* no in-between.

> It *ain't* easy, as one gathers from the train-and-bus crowds, to live without a job.

In short, *ain't* is on its way in.

-al is sometimes tacked on to a word unnecessarily: "Such *behavioral* (behavior) similarities as are observed can be explained largely by a certain apprehension felt by a person who receives an inactive substance he thinks is a drug."

alas comes from Middle English and that's exactly what it sounds like in a modern English sentence:

> Dorothy wanted to love the family life they had invented in the Vermont farmhouse, with all the simple good things of American life, but she, (*alas,*) must cable her love from international arenas.

> Can good ideas guarantee a good performance of this opera? *Alas, no.* (No.)

albeit. H. W. Fowler, in his *Dictionary of Modern English Usage,* wrote, "Archaic words thrust into a commonplace context to redeem its ordinariness are an abomination." He mentioned *albeit* as one of those archaic words, but couldn't possibly have foreseen that 40 years later *albeit* would spread through American writing like wildfire:

> Mr. Needles, quavering and fussing and staunchly defending himself as a man of the spirit, brings a sudden warmth to the stage and draws, *albeit* (though) briefly, upon our credulity.

> This is a good Buddhist statement, *albeit* (though) one of a popular, untutored Buddhism.

> John F. Gallagher has reconstructed the original and edited the whole five volumes with many notes, *albeit* (although) somewhat haphazardly.

> There have been strong, *albeit* (though) inconclusive signs in the last two weeks that the long-awaited business boom may really be getting started.

> Mr. Saunders resorts to the fashionable quota of quips about Catholicism, sex and scatology, *albeit* (though) in dull rather than offensive terms.

> We know from the start the husband's secret; midway everyone but the wife knows it—and she gets the message in no uncertain *albeit* (though) antique terms.

> George Kleinsinger's score was superb, *albeit* (although) solemn and remote.

alibi is a prize example of a word that doesn't mean what it's supposed to mean. In the original Latin it meant *elsewhere;* therefore the classical English meaning is a defendant's proof he was elsewhere at the time of the crime. But nowadays, nine times out of ten, *alibi* means something entirely different—a trumped-up excuse for having fallen down on a job:

> Instead of those responsible for their education being made to teach them, all sorts of *alibis* are provided.

> To them, he may sound like a "cry baby" who is building up an *alibi* for the future.

> At the same time, because they are less dependent on Moscow, they cannot use Moscow as an *alibi* for their own failure.

> Chatham's President Eddy frets that "youth is beginning to retreat behind excellence" to what he calls "the permanent *alibi* of scholarship."

COLLIER WON'T *ALIBI* DEFEAT

Does this mean you shouldn't use *alibi* with this newer meaning? Not at all. The spirit of the English language has found the word *alibi* to express in a single word what can't be expressed as clearly by any other word or phrase—the lameness of the excuse, its seeming plausibility and its essential phoniness. If you mean *alibi*, don't hesitate to use the word.

all but is a literary, ponderous substitute for *almost:*

Changes in the Soviet Defense Ministry, perhaps even including the dismissal of the Defense Minister, Marshal Rodion Malinovsky, were considered as *all but* (almost) inevitable.

Installment buying has long been accepted as one of the cornerstones of the U.S. economy, but in Nebraska that cornerstone has been *all but* (almost) crushed.

all of. A good writer or editor automatically changes *all of* to *all:*

All (of) the works in the first show were either sold by Curt Valentin, a well-known dealer who died in 1954, or by artists whose works he handled.

The embassy reported that *all (of)* Mrs. Nhu's bills were being returned to the senders.

Dr. Wilson conceded that the fact that *all (of)* the nation's 2,100 colleges and universities come under the provisions will mean that the money involved will have to be spread a little thin.

Mr. Gilpatric acknowledged *all (of)* this, but dismissed it as unimportant.

all right or **alright?**   The spelling *alright* is now the most popular misspelling in the English language, but what with our well-trained editors and proofreaders it hardly ever appears in print. Still, I've found one example: "Rice, a young magician, does some startling things, such as pulling decks of cards or several lighted candles out of the air. So *alright*, it's illusion, but try it."
    In the long run, I'm sure *alright* will win out.

allege is a handy legal word if you want to write about an *alleged* murderer (who is thought to have done it by the police but hasn't been indicted yet). For most ordinary purposes *allege* is much too formal a word and should be changed to *suppose, claim,* etc.: "As parents, she *alleges* (claims), we focus too much attenton on our children and allow them to influence too much of our thinking."

ALLITERATION is the ancient poetic device of using words that begin with the same sound. There may be a point in using alliteration in political oratory, but in everyday prose it sounds pretty silly:

Goldwater charged that Kennedy's term thus far "adds up to nearly a thousand days of *w*asted spending, *w*ishful thinking, un*w*arranted interventions, *w*istful theories and *w*aning confidence."

*B*rave *B*anker *B*eckhardt has also gone all out for instinct.

But it was in Europe that her *f*lair *f*or the *f*lamboyant *f*lowered into *f*ame.

ALLUSIONS are a temptation to be resisted. Consider this sentence: "Despite increasing evidence of wall-to-wall mink in the United States, still, there is vastly more affluence in my own, my native land than I had dreamed, Horatio."

Where does the reference to "my own, my native land" come from? From Sir Walter Scott's *Lay of the Last Minstrel:* "Breathes there a man with soul so dead, Who never to himself hath said . . . ."

Where does Horatio come from? From Shakespeare's *Hamlet,* Act I: "There are more things in heaven and earth, Horatio, Than are dreamt of in your philosophy."

And why did the writer of this sentence decorate it with those messy, irrelevant scraps from English literature? Because many people just can't resist the temptation to fill their writing with vague literary allusions whether they have anything to do with the matter on hand or not.

Here are some more warning examples:

Such literary snipers as Lord Alfred Douglas, Kate Stephens, Hugh Kingsmill and Vincent Brome will be invoked to put the finger on Harris: that he misrepresented Oscar Wilde, contrived the story about Carlyle's impotency, never really met Ralph Waldo Emerson while in America, etc., etc., and the irony is that the *J'accusers* are probably factually right in two-fifths of their charges but inherently wrong. (*J'accusers* refers to the pamphlet *J'accuse* the French writer Emile Zola wrote in the famous Dreyfus affair; it has nothing to do with what the writer is talking about here.)

The architectural and decorative effects of "*conspicuous wealth*" are visible in many areas throughout the land. (The phrase coined by Thorstein Veblen is "conspicuous waste," not "conspicuous wealth." The allusion creates the opposite effect from what the writer meant.)

A horrible example of *how not to succeed by hardly trying at all* is in stockpiling. (The title of the musical is "How to Succeed in Business Without Really Trying." The change in the wording makes the reference utterly pointless.)

It is a truth universally acknowledged that most English political leaders write much better than most American political personages. (You'll never guess where the phrase "It is a truth universally acknowledged" comes from. It's in the opening sentence of Jane Austen's *Pride and Prejudice:* "It is a truth universally acknowledged, that a single man in possession of a good fortune, must be in want of a wife.")

See also NAME DROPPING.

alma mater.   The best advice on Latin words is to leave them strictly alone—or at least to avoid monkeying with them, as in "Some old grads give their *almae matres* football stadiums, but Van Cliburn gives his a concert." (The English plural of *alma mater* is *alma maters*. It's true that the Latin plural is *almae matres,* but the sentence happens to call for the dative case, which would be *almis matribus.* As I said, you better stick to English.)

alright. *See* ALL RIGHT.

alter is a pompous synonym for *change:*

MAO MAY GO—BUT CHINA WON'T *ALTER* (CHANGE)

On Wednesday, 14 Asian members met privately to discuss how they could *alter* (change) that situation.

Liberal Democrats are quietly organizing a new effort to *alter* (change) what they call the power structure of the House of Representatives.

alternative is often used where the simpler word *choice* would do: "Advertising performs a socially and economically useful function in so far as it educates the consumer to the broad range of product *alternatives* (choices)."

ambivalent, ambivalence.   These fad words were brought into the language by the Freudians. They mean exactly the same as what you and I would express by the phrase "mixed feelings": "Mr. Albee said yesterday that he was looking forward to it with *a kind of ambivalence* (mixed feelings). 'It's fascinating and frightening at the same time.'"

ameliorate is just a long word for *improve*.

amid, amidst. The preposition *amidst* (or *amid*) is a purely literary word not used in ordinary English. However, since it's short and can replace several different words, it has been taken up as a space- and thought-saver by professional writers and now appears in print a thousand times a day. If you want to improve your style, avoid *amid* (or *amidst*) and substitute *among, with, under, in* or *from*:

> I've never felt so deeply moved by the National Anthem as I was standing in the alien corn *amid* (among) all those Englishmen.

> Scattered *amid* (among) stores advertising wares in Spanish, English and Yiddish are Hasidic butcher shops and wine and dairy produce stores.

> The doctor was ushered into the room *amid* (with) extensive rituals and chanting of hymns.

> How, *amid* (with) the pressing demands of family, business, and extracurricular life, do the Renaissance Executives find time to fit in everything?

> MARSHALL FIELD THRIVES *AMIDST*
> (UNDER) COMPETITION

> Do you ever ask yourself: "Is there any way to retain my peace of mind *amidst* (under) the stresses of modern life?"

> We must find time *amid* (in) the tumult and tension of a cold war, to encourage those pursuits that might inspire a cultural revolution.

> A FAMILIAR VOICE *AMID* (IN) A NEW SETTING
> ETHEL MERMAN SINGING IN
> NIGHT CLUBS AGAIN

> The problem is to enable that initiative to surface *amid* (from) ambiguous human relationships.

Sometimes *amid* is used to glue two parts of a long, information-stuffed sentence together. Those *amids* should be replaced by a period, semicolon or colon:

American and foreign shipowners spent yesterday reviewing their sailing schedules *amid* optimistic reports from Washington and Mid-West grain centers that Russia had agreed to buy American grain. (American and foreign shipowners spent yesterday reviewing their sailing schedules: optimistic reports from Washington and Mid-West grain centers said that Russia had agreed to buy American grain.)

amount. *In the amount of* is almost always unnecessary. Strike out *in the amount* and say *of* or *for*.

an. The article *a* changes to *an* when the next word starts with a vowel. There's no problem about that, except that you have to watch out for words that look as if they started with a consonant but don't, like "an $8 billion-a-year business" or "an S.P. (Special Progress) class." The other way round, it is "a utopian mood" because the spoken word *utopian* starts with the sound of the consonant *y* rather than the vowel *oo*.

So far so good. Thee trouble comes in with words like *hotel, heroic, hospital, historic*, that once started with a silent *h* but now are pronounced with the *h* sounded. Many writers still write *an* with such words, but it always looks like an affectation:

Dr. McNeill is *an* (a) historian with a quest for adventure.

Mrs. Jacqueline Kennedy has purchased *an* (a) historic 169-year-old Georgetown house with 14 rooms.

An (A) historic declaration absolving the Jews of blame for the death of Christ will be presented today to the Second Vatican Council.

analysis. *In the last* (or *final*) *analysis* is a long, awkward phrase, beloved by pompous writers. Usually the sentence is better without it:

A comparison of the Soviet and American psychiatric system makes one wonder whether (*in the last analysis,*) the medical and public health approach (so often advocated in the United States) is a suitable one or an exclusive one for this range of phenomena.

In the final analysis the (The) success of these efforts will depend not on the theoretical points of contact and difference between science and the law but on the willingness of the individual behavioral scientists and lawyers . . . .

anathema is a long, formal word meaning something cursed or detested. It doesn't mean the person who is doing the detesting, as the writer of this sentence mistakenly thought: "*Anathema* (Firmly opposed) to illegal gambling, which he regarded as the basis for almost all organized crime, Mr. Kennedy also was the implacable foe of police who, in the language of the force, were 'taking.' "

and. Don't fall for the old superstition that *and* should never be used at the beginning of a sentence. Sometimes no other way of writing will do:

> The sentences in the Everest article are short. The paragraphs are short. *And* the style is intimate.

> Juicy, juicy, thought reporters at London Airport as they penetrated the dark glasses, collar-up disguise of many-faced Funnyman Peter Sellers, 38. *And* they clicked away as he greeted a *femme mystérieuse*.

> The proportion of our population represented by those over 65 is growing at the rate of 1,000 people a day. The cost of medical care for each of them has been estimated at $226 a year as opposed to $103 a year for those under 65. *And* the income of most persons over 65 is much lower than of those under 65.

> "You left 'Maverick,' " the boy said. "My favorite TV program. *And* you left it."

When you use *and* at the start of a sentence, don't put a comma after it as in "They perform brilliantly where other makes fail. *And, they are priced* (And they are priced) far below what you'd expect for such excellence."

The word *and* also often leads to the mistake Fowler's *Modern English Usage* calls "bastard enumeration." Here are a few illustrations:

> Italians generally pay small heed to Dolci because he is non-violent, nonpolitical, *and gets* his money from friends abroad.

> Alexander has a beautiful voice, easy production *and is* good looking.

> "The Securities Market and How It Works" is a standard text in its field; it's now been completely revised, brought up to date, *and new chapters added*.

You see the trouble? The second item in each of these examples fits the verb before the first item (*he is nonpolitical, he has easy production, it's been brought up to date*), but the third item starts with a new verb (*and gets, and is, and added*). So the *and* ties together a three-part series of items that don't match.

The easiest way to fix such misbegotten sentences is to insert *and* between items 1 and 2 (*nonviolent and nonpolitical, beautiful voice and easy production, completely revised and brought up to date*). However, this method doesn't always work. Some sentences have to be rewritten from scratch:

> Right about noon, maybe, the realization set in that nobody knew exactly what the significance was of the grand jury investigation, who would comprise the jury, *and the fact that* steel companies have almost a month to report their pricing data.

> She must also have a high-school education or its equivalent, be not less than 18 years old, unmarried, have no dependents *and in good health.*

> But the entire program was a joy in terms of dance, in pageantry, in costuming (breathtaking describes it best), in decor, musically *and of fascination to the pursuer of the ethnic or the seeker of theatrical diversion.*

Then there's the ugly habit of headline and news magazine writers of leaving out *and* and replacing it by a comma:

> SEN. NEUBERGER THROWS BOOK AT *SMOKING,* *U.S. AGENCIES* (SMOKING AND U.S. AGENCIES)

> Mosher has had his eye on Barrett for 15 *years,* (years and) particularly admires its president, Harry Wetzel, 43.

> It was a hugh *success,* (success and) became a key first step in the Dillingham family's development of the islands.

> A brief dispatch said the brothers escaped custody at the Presidential palace, sought church *asylum,* (asylum and) were recaptured.

> It *hops, skips, jumps* (hops, skips and jumps) along at a jerky pace which disturbs the viewers.

For the question of a comma before *and* in a series, *see* COMMAS.

and/or. In law and regulations there are many sentences of this type: "The misdemeanor charge carries a maximum penalty of one year in jail *and/or* a $500 fine." The word *and/or* was invented as shortcut for such legal sentences because otherwise you'd have to write "one year in jail or a $500 fine or both."

And/or has spread outside of legal prose and is now used by many as a sort of fancy synonym for *or*. Look at the following sentences and you'll see that the thought in each one of them could have been fully expressed by using *or* instead of *and/or*:

When Sears goes into the mutual fund business, it will be as an investment adviser *and/or* (or) underwriter.

Many prosper because it is the critical fashion today to hail as "art" any book that abundantly contains clinical *and/or* (or) psychological details of sex.

She is usually a housewife who prepares by equipping herself with an extra-large pocketbook, *and/or* (or) by wearing a double girdle, stretch socks, oversize undies, or a a many-pocketed coat.

Positions require strong project *and/or* (or) product engineering experience including analytical and creative design of precision electro-mechanical components.

To designate as worthy of preservation buildings and other works of historic *and/or* (or) esthetic importance, as well as groups of buildings and districts . . . .

The motorist deposits coins *and/or* (or) paper money in any combination up to $7 in the control console, then pumps the gasoline he has just bought into the car's tank.

There are also rare cases where the writer meant *and*, but weakened his sentence by using *and/or*: "For special regimens—*and/or* (and) good eating . . . get Cream of Rice at your grocer's"

See also IF AND WHEN, UNLESS AND UNTIL, WHICHEVER.

and which is always awkward and usually wrong. My advice is simple—cross out *and*:

One of the most elegant dinners to be given this season, (*and*) which followed the classic pattern, was a gala affair offered by a group of American chefs and restauranteurs to a distinguished delegation of restaurant owners from France.

The law police were upholding—(*and*) *which* the Negroes want repealed—requires segregation in any establishment selling alcoholic beverages.

All you have to do is suggest something the company might adopt (*and*) *which* would increase sales from $6.6 million to $60.8 million in seven years.

There are rare sentences where the method of crossing out *and* doesn't work. In these, cross out *which*:

> It does not balk at displaying the shocking violence which broke out on both *sides, and which* (sides and) went further than either the Indians or the British could possibly have expected or planned.

and who works much the same way as *and which*. Again, cross out *and*:

> The nation requires a succession law that will give reasonable assurance that the post of Chief Executive will always be filled by men of broad experience and sound judgment (*and*) *who* enjoy the confidence of the country.

> This is the Mortgage Guaranty Insurance Corp., a firm organized in 1957 (*and*) *whose* stock rose from $1.50 a share to $54 when it became known in late 1959 that seven top officials of Federally-chartered savings and loan associations would be added to its board of directors.

angle sounds slangy in such sentences as "Minute Maid is now taking over as a substitute for the morning tea and the breakfast approach—a big do on the health *angle* of Vitamin C." However, it's easy to condemn this use of the word, but hard to find a substitute that will have the same meaning and the same, slightly sarcastic connotations.

animadversion is old-fashioned and pompous. Example: "A good many of the gloomiest *animadversions* (comments, thoughts) on what all this means to unions, workers, and our industrial society have come from The Center for the Study of Democratic Institutions in Santa Barbara, Calif."

antecede is obsolete; the current word is *precede*: "Heinrich Johann Franz von Biber, the German composer who *anteceded* (preceded) Bach by some forty years, is not precisely on everyone's tongue these days."

anti-. Yes, you can use *anti-* as a live prefix, but there are obstacles. For one thing, *anti-* doesn't fit before a word with an Anglo-Saxon root: "*Antifouling* properties of potential use to shipping have been found in the weeds of the Sargasso Sea."

Second, it's a poor idea to use *anti-* before a very long word: "Among the *anti-flouridationists* who appeared before the Board of Estimate last week was Dr. Edwin Langrock, consulting obstetrician of Beth Israel Hospital."

anticipate. There's no long word that means exactly the same as *expect* or *await,* so lovers of long words hit upon *anticipate* which originally meant *do in advance.* But the long-word addicts don't care; they use *anticipate* as a synonym for *expect, foresee* or *wait for* anyway:

> These trends, which had been widely *anticipated* (expected) were bad news for the Kennedy Administration.

> It has long been *anticipated* (expected) that the schema's chapter on Jews would be met by strong resentment among Arab political leaders.

> Some of her brushes with death were *unanticipated* (unexpected).

> The forces of tradition and conservation in the use of English have been weakened, and the forces of disintegration strengthened, to a degree which Logan Pearsall Smith could not have *anticipated* (foreseen) a mere thirty-five years ago.

> There is no hope it will be ready for voting before the present session ends Dec. 4, but Council Fathers *anticipate* (expect) it will be the first order of business when they convene next fall.

> There is every reason to *anticipate* (expect) that the similarities of Mr. Johnson's policies to the late President's will be more striking than the differences.

> Once more, as in many pre-Presidential years in the past, politically minded citizens along with many writing pundits are *breathlessly anticipating* (waiting breathlessly for) the New Hampshire Presidential preference primary.

antipathy is a fancy word for *dislike.* You can feel antipathy *to* or *toward* someone, but hardly *for* him: "Privately Cavanagh has a deep antipathy *for* (toward) Romney whose self-righteousness, particularly irks him."

anxiety means vague fear. It is one of the greatest fad words of our time—"the age of anxiety." Among hundreds of examples of the current use of *anxiety* I've picked just one, which shows up neatly the weakness of the word:

> He said this fits in with other findings "that some *anxiety* may increase achievement drive—and hence learning—but that too much *anxiety* may cause deterioration of learning.

For finicky writers who feel that *anxiety* has already become too trite, there's always the original German word *angst*:

Pollock, de Kooning, Kline, Guston have invested their their canvases with too much freedom, too much *angst*.
See also FAD WORDS.

anybody, anyone. *See* THEY.

anyplace. Purists object to the use of *anyplace* (or *any place*) for *anywhere*, but most Americans seem to prefer it:

You got a better chance here than *any place* in the city.

In the 19th century great powers didn't put up with the mistreatment of their nationals *any place* in the world.

Yesterday, after Johnson finished his second round trip, he was met on the platform at 205th St. and asked why anybody with a daughter earning $8,500 a week would be found *anyplace* except on a barge on the Nile.

apogee is much too fancy for ordinary purposes: "But in fairness it must be said that their only offense is that they have reached *an apogee* (a peak) of success that is denied to all but the most expert in their fields."

apologia is a fancy synonym for *apology* that sometimes tempts literary snobs into sentences like this: "Prof. Farley's *A Study of Goethe* is by far the most reasonable *apologia* for his greatness."

APOSTROPHES. It's a good style rule to use as many apostrophes as possible. This is not because apostrophes are specially pretty (they're not) but because they're an outward sign that you're using many contractions like *it's, I've, he's, we're,* etc. And the more contractions you use, the more your writing will resemble idiomatic, spoken English.

In fact, the spelling out of usually contracted words is sometimes downright unidiomatic and wrong. Here are two examples:

Let us (Let's) face it: There are some problems in our society which simply won't respond to solution except by trial and grief.

Since he is an adroit politician and a popular personality, why *is he not* (isn't he) more successful?

So let yourself go with contractions and put words down the way they're actually spoken. To encourage you, here are some unusual examples of *it'd, there've, who'd* etc.:

The New York Mirror was a sorry newspaper, heaven knows, but *it'd* be alive today if it could have produced a Hall-Mills case every year or two.

BRITISH LABOR CONFIRMS *IT'LL* YIELD A-POWER

There've been rumors for a long time.

Although discrepancies in his papers revealed the ex-convict's masquerade, after he'd been teaching a month, up to then *there'd* been no complaints.

There'll be the fullest coverage of the events of two or three weeks, and then there may be nothing else for a couple of years.

"The hell of it is," said Capt. Don Toth (Penn Argyle, Pa.), "when you come back they say, '*Where've* you been?' and you say, 'Vietnam,' and they say, '*Where's* that? What state is it in?'"

But the real professionals, the ones *who've* been responsible for some of these so-called highs in the market still can get as much money as they want.

Can women *who've* been stifled for long years by the mystique come out from under?

BAKER PROBERS BUTT HEADS OVER *WHO'LL* RUN SHOW

But what really hurt them was the chislers *who'd* eat a big meal and just pay for a cup of coffee.

Joe bought me the prettiest ring. But it's too small. He thinks my *finger's* the same size it was when he bought me the first ring.

The *cops'll* say they need more money, and the Youth Board will complain about its appropriation, and the others will say they need more money, and *everybody'll* deplore the situation. But *nobody'll* do anything about it.

But don't go overboard: contractions can look phony and artificial when you use them for words you would *not* contract in saying the particular sentence out loud.

See also DECADES, 'S, WAY.

apotheosis, apotheosize. *Apotheosis* means "exaltation to the rank of a god." It isn't a word to be used casually, as in "He *apotheosized* the conversation pit."

apparatus is a long, cumbersome word, so why drag it in where it doesn't belong? "This development manifests itself in a proliferation of institutions needed to 'support' the increasingly dependent individual and in the rise of *bureaucratic apparatuses* (bureaucracies) needed to control the technological machinery itself."

appareled. *See* ATTIRED.

apparent, appear. There's a school of writing that says every statement must be qualified by "it appears" or "it seems" unless you can prove each detail to a hostile jury. This timidity has led to millions of sentences that never quite say what they're supposed to say. Here's a prize example of triple qualification: "The decisive vote on the second day of business *appeared to indicate* (showed) that the second Council session *might* move at a brisker pace than the first."
See also SEEM, WOULD SEEM.

appellation. You wouldn't think that *appellation* is still used as a fancy synonym for *name*, but it is: "The comics (and the nostalgia motivates the *appellation*) bumble about listlessly and their single entendres are dragged out with dreary inevitability."

append is an overformal word that should always be changed to a simpler one: "In 1956, the Senate *appended* (added) to a House bill a provision reversing two court decisions and sparing an Oklahoma City contractor the unpleasantness of paying hundreds of thousands in back taxes and penalties."

appreciate is vastly overused as a synonym for *thank for*.

approach is a popular fad word. It's so vague that it may mean almost anything. What, for instance, does *approach* mean in this sentence?: "From the Book of Knowledge, to Field's World Encyclopedia to Britannica's Britannica Jr., the *approach* reaches to lure the young reader." (The best I can offer is that *approach* here serves as a sort of pronoun, vaguely referring to encyclopedias.)

appropriate as an adjective can and should almost always be replaced by *proper*:

Appropriate (Proper) officials in the government well knew that this particular journey by this particular attaché was going to be made exactly when it was made.

"Indeed," he declared, "some price reductions would seem *appropriate* (proper) as the expansion proceeds."

approximately. Don't say *approximately;* say *about:*

Should the *approximately* (about) 10,000 high-rent apartments be decontrolled, it would represent the first effort since 1957 to remove any apartments from controls by administrative action.

The Tobacco Industry Research Committee has allotted $800,000 for 1963, *approximately* (about) one half of one per cent of the industry's intended outlay for advertising.

In Virginia, *approximately* (about) three-quarters of the state's counties qualified for feed grain assistance.

In 1960, as in the 1956 election, men and women cast *approximately* (about) the same number of votes.

Approximately (About) 1,000,000 earthquakes occur in the world every year (most of them under the ocean).

arch- is a prefix meaning "chief"; *arch* is an adjective meaning "cunning, sly, roguish." If you confuse the two words, you may get a sentence like this: "It also served to rebuke Los Angeles' *archly* conservative cardinal, J. Francis A. McIntyre." (Cunningly conservative?)

ARCHAISMS. Many writers think it's cute or pretty or interesting to revive obsolete words or expressions. They're wrong; for readers of today, use the language of today. Don't write things like *"Thus spake* Mayor Wagner yesterday at the abrupt decision of Edward N. Costikyan to quit as leader of a sadly disrupted Tammany Hall."

See also ALBEIT, AUGHT, BEHEST, ERSTWHILE, ESSAY, ILLUME, SAVE, SURCEASE, TO WIT, WAX, etc.

archetype has recently become a fad word. It's pronounced AR-ke-type and means "the original model or first form of a thing," which is also the exact meaning of *prototype,* the word used before *archetype* took over. Now we have *archetypes* everywhere:

All three of these books mention Cardinal Mazarin, who is perhaps the *archetype* of any great collector.

Bobby is an *archetype.* In a culture rapidly being consumed by various unlovely anaerobic bacteria, he is the typical success story.

are. The usual problem with *are* is simple sloppiness. If you don't watch out, a plural noun next to the verb will trick you you into writing *are* instead of *is*:

"Billy Liar" is a teen-age Walter Mitty—and the stuff that adolescent dreams are made on in this British film *are* (is) universal and funny and ironic.

Dr. Chew, with Drs. Murray Gell-Mann of the California Institute of Technology and Arthur Rosenfeld at the Berkeley campus, *are* (is) trying to bring order out of the chaos of particle physics.

The irony of it is that Goldwater's following, which must have a largish proportion of people who regard Jews as foreigners and perhaps even as Communists, *are* (is) quite ready to swallow his Jewishness and like it.

No single terrible event or coincidental combination of stresses *seem by themselves* (seems by itself) to cause mental illness but piling stress after stress on top of one another is directly correlated with the amount of mental illness.

See also IS or ARE?

area is now the fashionable word for *field*. The best thing to do with *area* is to leave it out:

Personalities as well as issues can develop *new areas of involvements* (new involvements).

They propose that government press itself into every (*area of*) decision.

The transcript contains some valuable background on the Soviet leader's thinking, especially *in the area of* (about) increased trade with the West.

Chiefly, "integration" enters the public dialogue *in two areas of real demand*: *schooling and housing* (in schooling and housing where there is real demand).

Area is also overused in the literal sense of *region* or *section*:

I have been making a swing through some American *areas* (regions, sections) from Boston to Chicago, from Chicago to Indiana. . . .

as. The little word *as* is responsible for more stilted, artificial writing than almost any other word in the English language.

First, it is often used unidiomatically instead of *since* or *be-*

cause to tack a long reason or explanation to the end of a sentence:

> The series of contemplated demonstrations and marches in Southern cities should be halted, *as* (since) they would not lead to a cooling of passions but rather to an intensification of bitter feelings among whites and Negroes."

Second, it's the preferred means of quotation-happy writers to tie quotes into the text. I suppose this is meant to make quotations seem casual; but all it does is make them look artificially dragged in:

> *As Chemical and Engineering News pointed out last week,* space contracts have become an important part of the political pork barrel. (*Chemical and Engineering News* pointed out last week that . . . .)

> *As the* (The) lanky, 47-year-old Tishman says: "Sure, the market is a little soft, but the vacant space is being taken up nicely."

> For culture, that over-fingered and self-conscious word, can often, *as Archibald MacLeish has warned us, creep like an East wind into the soul* (to quote Archibald MacLeish, "creep like an East wind into the soul").

Third, the word *as* is a favorite tool of the sentence-stuffers. They take two long swatches of information, tie them together with *as*, and serve you a double helping of overloaded prose:

> The Guardsmen, some of them called up three months ago, to enforce integration at the University of Alabama, were not needed *as* 20 Negroes entered white schools and broke a new deadlock between Gov. Wallace and the Federal Government.

> The Commerce Department approved the sale of another 1.4 million bushels of corn to Hungary yesterday *as* U. S. and Soviet officials appeared to mark time in negotiations on American wheat shipments to Russia.

> Elizabeth Taylor and now-unhitched Richard Burton plan to marry early next year with Jan. 14 as the tentative date, it was learned today, *as* attorneys for Liz and Eddie Fisher met here to complete arrangementes for her Mexican divorce.

> Texas A. & M. jolted Rice University's bowl game hopes by striking for 10 second-half points yesterday for a 13–6

come-from-behind Southwest Conference upset *as* student
groups provided halftime fist fight entertainment.

Australia's Herb Elliot, previous outdoor recordholder at
3.54.5, Beatty and Jim Grelle have run faster winning miles
outdoors than O'Hara did last night *as* Bill Bonthron, Glenn
Cunningham and Gene Venzke, celebrating a 30th reunion
of the 1934 Baxter Mile, looked on.

as against is a compound preposition that can usually be reduced
to *against* or replaced by a simpler phrase:

The Russians boast 8.4 psychiatrists per 100,000 population
as against (against, compared with) the U.S. figure of 6.4

What does a costume cliché matter *as against* (against,
when it comes to) pounds and pounds of excess baggage?

as far as . . . concerned is sheer wordiness and should be cut out:

As far as he is concerned, (He says) retailing is being hurt
because the management is engineering rather than mer-
chandising-minded.

I've turned down Caseys and Kildares and all that on TV,
until I found just what I wanted, and I'll do it *as far as
Broadway is concerned* (on Broadway).

as if. "The second act sets out *as if it means* to sustain high
spirits Miss O'Shea and her friends have released." Look into
any composition textbook and you'll find that this sentence
is supposed to be incorrect; the textbooks insist the right form
is *as if it meant.*

This form is called the subjunctive. Grammarians tell us it
is gradually dying out, but still being used for "conditions
contrary to fact." The conjunction *as if,* the grammarians say,
introduces such a "condition contrary to fact"; therefore *as if*
is followed by a subjunctive.

Well, it isn't so. The subjunctive after *as if* seems to be extinct. Why? Because a writer uses *as if* when he wants to picture
an imaginary situation as an actual fact. For this purpose the
subjunctive is no good.

Here are some examples of *as if* as it is used today—without
the subjunctive:

It was hush-hush, *as if somebody was* (not *were*) zeroing
in on the combination to the big vault in Fort Knox.

Lobeline dulls the urge for cigarettes, he said, "because

it's *as if you've* (not *you had*) already smoked a lot of cigarettes."

He urged them to fight the President's medicare program. "Thank God," he said, "it looks *as if that is* (not *were*) dead."

"Well, Vladimir," we said to him the other day, "it looks *as if your system has* (not *had*) failed."

A spokesman for Abraham & Straus noted that "it looks *as if it will be* (not *would be*) a record day for Election Day."

The funny thing about the undeclared Goldwater candidacy is that in some respects it looks *as if* the junior Senator from Arizona *really has* (not *had*) not made up his mind.

The most controversial shocker movie ever made in Britain looks *as if it is* (not *were*) going to have the final curtain pulled on it before it even gets into a movie house.

The real sin of the Ngo brothers was that they acted *as if the war was* (not *were*) just the trimmings, and that the heart of the matter was their ability to maintain their war power and keep out potential rivals.

Individual Senators lunge at others for "conflict of interest" and then disdainfully condone their own violations of "conflict of interest," *as if* rules for ethical conduct *do not* (not *did not*) apply to elected officials.

It is almost *as if* Supreme Court justices and laymen alike *are* (not *were*) resigned to the letter of blue laws living forever, although their spirit has long been dead.

There is a feeling of frustration among the detectives who have been working day and night on the case, *as if they know* (not *knew*) they will be unable to break through the wall of silence of those who have the answers to some of the puzzles.

The only exception to this current usage is an *as if* clause that expresses disbelief in the thing supposed: "But included within these operating expenses were the costs incurred in extending credit services. Service charge revenue was then added to this 'operating profit' *as if it were* an independent, cost-free source of revenue." (The writer argues that service charges are *not* an independent source of revenue and attacks those who say they are. The subjunctive *were* means "it isn't so.")

See also AS THOUGH, BE, LIKE, SUBJUNCTIVE, WERE or WAS?

as many shouldn't be used to avoid repetition of a number. It's better to repeat the number: "The reason that he came to write so well about the city was that he had the perceptive vision, absorptive capacity and creative stamina which it took to produce his four triumphs in *as many* (four) years' time."

as of are two words that are usually superflous:

In every group one meets people who say that (*as of*) a few years ago they instinctively thought of themselves as political liberals—and so voted.

As of now (Now) the great progress that Goldwater has made is that people are willing to consider him as a probable nominee, where a year ago they would have scoffed at it.

as the saying goes. Some people get self-conscious when they use colloquial words or trite sayings and try to apologize for them by using quotation marks or the awkward phrase *as the saying goes*. Both devices are silly. When you feel like using a certain word phrase, use it; when you're ashamed of it, don't use it; but *don't* use it with a written apologetic cough:

Money talks, too, (*as the saying goes*,) and salaries range from $19 to $24 a day plus free transportation and an allowance . . . .

The easiest night of the week, decision-wise, (*as the saying goes*,) is Monday night.

The phrase *as the saying goes* itself has become hackneyed now and some writers are paraphrasing *it* apologetically:

This, however, is, (*as the cliché goes*,) only skin-deep.

Nature abhors a vacuum, (*or so goes an old wives' tale*,) but T-formation quarterbacks can't get enough of it . . . .

See also CLICHÉS, QUOTATION MARKS, RARE WORDS, SLANG.

as though is used exactly the same way as *as if*, but it's a little more colloquial. Like the subjunctive after *as if*, the subjunctive after *as though* seems to be thoroughly extinct:

It looks *as though* Otto Preminger *has* (not *had*) missed the boat again in attempting to make a motion picture on a vital contemporary theme.

It looks *as though* Thomas Dunn *is* (not *was*) giving the LP record catalogue a run for its money.

Due to hurricane damage to the sugar crop, it looks *as*

though Russia *will* (not *would*) have to shop for sugar as well as wheat in America.

So many offers have come my way it looks *as though* I *may* (not *might*) play "meanies" the rest of my life.

It almost seems *as though* the trial *is* (not *was*) only an annoying, out-of-context chapter in the life of a man who's really most likely to succeed.

The idea of anybody's being in an ivory tower seems to have a stigma on it these days (*as though* any withdrawal from the everyday world *is* [not *was*] unbusinesslike). We don't see it that way.

Every so often you feel *as though* you've (not *you had*) been kicked in the stomach by a heifer.

When you finish an autobiography you feel *as though* you *have* (not *had*) been remaindered.

See also AS IF, BE, SUBJUNCTIVE, WERE or WAS?

as to, like *as of,* is usually unnecessary, particularly in the common phrase *as to whether.* Look at these examples and see how they're improved by leaving out *as to:*

Inevitably, speculation has already begun (*as to*) whether he will be Lyndon Johnson's running mate in next year's race.

For several months now, the American people have been puzzled (*as to*) whether anyone in the government of the United States may, on a formal or official occasion, ask people to pray to God.

There seems to be some confusion in the minds of the state's lawyers and jurists (*as to*) whether Mississippians must obey the law of the land as interpreted by the Federal Courts.

The question arises (*as to*) whether the recent agitation and series of demonstrations hasn't produced a racial consciousness that didn't exist before as widely as it does today.

The chances are good that 1964 will come and go without any sharp decision (*as to*) whether these were wise or unsophisticated acts.

Mr. Cook said he was investigating (*as to*) whether any state law had been violated by the marriage.

"You would be surprised (*as to*) how close the appraisals are in most cases," Mr. Colin said.

When we then turn to these specific challenges, there is no doubt (*as to*) which one first draws our attention.

Last week Attorney General Robert Kennedy finally indicated he was concerned (*as to*) what was happening to the Washington Redskins football team.

When the method of leaving out *as to* won't work, you can at least change *as to* to *of, for, on, in* or *about:*

It provides a $100 monthly pension to virtually all honorably discharged veterans of the first World War, with no requirement *as to* (for, of) need or disability.

The book contains a number of inaccuracies *as to* (of, about) dates and places.

In announcing plans for the citizens' group, he said that no decision had been reached *as to* (on) its composition.

A very considerable body of information now exists *as to* (on) why we have so many millions unemployed.

There was considerable discussion *as to* (on) what chance he had to defeat the incumbent.

No clear picture has emerged *as to* (of) who can speak for world Jewry.

Authority for every type of action or decision is spelled out clearly in the management manual, along with guides *as to* (on) who should be consulted for advice in different situations.

The law is unclear in New York State *as to* (on) what precisely a citizen may do, should do, or should not do, when he witnesses other citizens being attacked in the streets.

It is probably the largest contract in the nation's history, *both as to money and number of workers involved* (in money and number of workers).

I have received many queries *as to* (about) my position on off-track betting.

See also OF, QUESTION OF WHETHER.

as well as doesn't mean *and;* it means *like*. This sometimes leads to trouble: "Mr. Aumont *as well as* most of the spectators as the ice rink *were* visitors to the city." (Mr. Aumont, *like* most of the spectators at the ice rink, *was* a visitor to the city.)

ascendancy is a long, big-sounding word that's used much too indiscriminately:

> Despite Clorox's *ascendancy* (lead), competition has never been wholly absent from the liquid bleach field.

> Leinsdorf's *ascendancy* (leadership) was exactly what this fine old orchestra needed.

> Here visitors seek to recall the lavish entertainment and hospitality of the newspaper magnate *in the great days of Hollywood's celluloid ascendancy* (in Hollywood's heyday).

ascertain is a formal word meaning *find, find out, make sure:*

> The survey would *ascertain* (make sure) whether the bridge is really needed and what its impact would be in the Eastern seaboard highway network.

> The doctor waited in his hotel while monks and Sikkimese astrologers *ascertained* (found) through extensive consultations the most auspicious hour for a meeting between the Maharaja and the physician.

> Mr. Ross, whose company has five subsidiaries and includes a real estate department, said he had encountered so much difficulty in *ascertaining* (finding) the true ownership of the tenements that he had decided to go ahead with his plan without the permission of the landlords.

assist, assistance are much overused as synonyms for *help:* "I was joined in front of the cameras by a group of children— some from homes for neglected and dependent youngsters—who had been brought in *to help dramatize the need for assistance* (to dramatize the need for help)."

associated with. This pompous phrase is abused in two ways.

First, it often means that someone is *employed by* or *works for* a certain company: "The Technicolor company *with which he is associated* (he works for) is headed by Patrick J. Frawley . . . ."

Second, *associated with* is sometimes used to express a statistical correlation; in such sentences it can be replaced by *match, go with,* etc.: "Either a higher or lower weight increment *was associated with* (matched, went with) an increased prematurity and mortality rate in the four weeks after birth."

ASTERISKS are out of style now. Don't use them for any purpose, particularly not to mark words left out of a quotation. Use three periods instead (four at the end of a sentence).

-ate, -ation are the most common endings of abstract words; they're warning signals showing that it may be better to replace the word or recast the sentence to express its meaning in a different way. Here are a few examples:

> He was Will Rogers, characteristically *capsulating* (boiling down) a large idea, inflation, in a single pungent sentence.

> All of this, however admirable, seems to *exsanguinate* (drain the blood from) the man of flesh and bone.

> This—and a pseudo-sophisticated *derogation* (disdain) of the audience itself—may be humility on Mr. Sanders' part but it's of the sort that only a very slick, bright and perceptive playwright can get away with.

> What was needed in more generous quantity was *oral substantiation* (spoken examples) of the diversity of the Greek commitment to the intellect, something to enrich the ear as well as the eye.

Sometimes *-ate* can be simply left out:

> Watson was *orientated* (oriented) towards a practical applied psychology and despised theoretical hairsplitting.

> When a semester ends, the two *novitiates* (novices) trade places. *See also* ABSTRACT WORDS, RARE WORDS.

attain shouldn't be used as a fancy synonym for *gain* or *win:* "To those who sincerely, or for personal political considerations, have made a fetish of nonrecognition of East Germany, the Senator offered statistics of West-East-German trade that show the high degree of *de facto* recognition already *attained* (won)."

attempt. When you mean *try,* say *try:* "After the conferences, the scientists have *attempted* (tried), with varying degrees of success, to communicate to their political leaders the ideas that have been discussed."

attend. Avoid the archaic use of *attend,* as in "One particularly sophisticated school would emphasize intangible horrors, such as those which undoubtedly *attend on* (accompany) the one or two meals a year that Nero Wolfe is forced to take outside of his own home."

attired is a poor word to use instead of *dressed:*

> *Attired* (Dressed) in semi-military uniforms, they were firing live ammunition . . . .

> *Attired* (Dressed) in the nondescript clothes of a London fish-and-chips monger, she sang four songs and did some beguiling steps.

attractive. When newspapermen can't think of anything else to say about a woman, they say she's *attractive:*

> In Marseille, where Deferre lives with his *attractive* wife Marie-Antoinette in a villa overlooking the harbor, politics can be as rough as in Chicago.

> The *attractive* blonde Mrs. Boyer has apparently found one secret of holding a husband.

Sometimes *attractive* is used in the general sense of *nice:*

> I never believed King Hussein was enthusiastic over the idea of trying to seize the *attractive* new nation in the Sahara.

attributable is a five-syllable word. I haven't found a single instance where the one-syllable word *due* wouldn't be better:

> These revisions are *attributable* (due) to a variety of factors.

> The collapse of the New York Mirror, with 1,600 employees, is *attributable* (due) to some extent to Power's strike.

> The rise in deaths, it was reported, is *attributable* (due) largely to widespread outbreaks of acute respiratory disease in the early months of the year.

> Estimates for the period from February through April of this year are 57,000 excess deaths from all causes, of which 12,000 were directly *attributable* (due) to flu or pneumonia.

> The toy mania that has the republic by the throat is, of course, directly *attributable* (due) to the oily hucksters of television.

Sometimes *attributable* can be left out altogether: "The defendant in this case, the Judge pointed out, was Wohlgemuth, and if any evil intent was involved, it appeared to be *attributable to Latex rather than to him* (that of Latex rather than his)."

ATTRIBUTION. *See* SOURCE ATTRIBUTION.

aught is the word people used 200 years ago when they meant *anything*. It doesn't fit into a modern sentence like this one: "It is equally unthinkable that he would set down *aught* (anything) in malice, whatever his personal position."

augment is an old-fashioned formal word meaning *increase* or *enlarge*. Some writers use it to fancy up the simple word *and:* "But the real telltale signs of imminent marriage were his having shed 16 pounds on a diet *augmented* (and) by hiking to and from jeweler David Webb's and the Park Avenue home of Doris Warner Vidor."

augmentation is just a long word for *increase:* "The liberal arts are threatened by the speed-up, by the rapid *augmentation* (increase) and fragmentation of knowledge, and by society's urgent demand for trained specialists of all kinds . . . ."

augur, augury. The ancient Romans had official soothsayers, called *augurs,* whose job it was to interpret omens and signs. It's better to use a more modern word when you mean *predict, sign* or *omen:*

This *augurs well* (is a good omen) for the future of art with the new administration.

The point is that no unlikely *augury* (prediction) should be rejected simply because it imposes a strain upon the imagination.

author (verb). It sounds mocking or degrading when you say that someone *authored* a book:

Kirst wrote the famous trilogy about "Gunner Asch" which was translated into 20 languages; and also *authored* (wrote) the best-seller "The Seventh Day."

A former member of the Rand Corp. think factory, where he *authored* (wrote) a classic study on transport planes for the Air Force in 1953 . . . .

authoress. *See* -ESS.

auto shouldn't be used as a substitute word whenever you want to avoid the normal American word *car:*

Pope Paul already has several cars, including a black limousine given to Pope Pius XII by American Catholics, and a German-made car presented to Pope John XXIII by German Catholics. One of the Papal *autos* (cars), a tiny Italian-made *car* (one), was carried into an audience for Pope John.

avatar is a far-fetched word, meaning the incarnation of a Hindu god. Even if used correctly, as in the following sentence, it's a poor choice since it might puzzle some readers: "The *avatar* (reincarnation) of Kreuger in this affair is a dubious Rumanian who is endlessly loquacious and such a cad that he is ready to tease a homosexual financier with the charms of his illegitimate son."

aver is just about the most pompous of all the synonyms for *say:*

Judging by past performance, I have no confidence that there will be "strict control" of Federal expenditures which Secretary Dillon *avers* (says) can be anticipated.

Every face and beard is different, it *avers* (says) and it is betting to the tune of a money-back guaranty that its blade will give more shaves than any other.

How long shall we continue pompously to *aver* (say) that the chief contribution of Jesus was simply a rehash of all that has been said before by his Jewish ancestors?

averse to is sometimes abused as a pompous synonym for *against:* "Mr. Black and Mr. Osborne are inherently *averse to* (against) Government's financial entry into the private sector of the economy."

avid. Forty years ago Fowler wrote that the use of *avid* instead of *eager* was an example of "escape from the obvious"; he predicted that *avid* would some day become hackneyed. Well, that day has come:

He was an *avid* (eager) photographer early in life, participated in recording sessions before 1920, experimented with television . . . .

Dorothy Thompson was the last of the profoundly serious, intellectually equipped journalists, before the debutantes *avid* (eager) for new kicks danced into the city rooms.

awful, awfully. The use of these colloquial words in writing is condemned in some of the more old-fashioned textbooks, but they're now common in academic and literary prose. One example: "The argument took on added force because Mark Schorer's biography of Lewis had just appeared, and I thought it was an *awful* book."

awhile. There's a fine distinction between the adverb *awhile,* written as one word, and the article-plus-noun *a while,* as in *for a while* or *once in a while.* However, people like to run words together, and the compound *awhile,* like *alright,* is generally taking hold:

> John said they probably would remain in Des Moines "for *awhile.*"

> It seemed right to sit on Thanksgiving Day and put out butts in a coffee cup and, every once in *awhile,* have an attendant in white shirt and slacks reach past your shoulder and take crumpled napkins from the table.

B

background is something of a fad word and greatly overused: "Adjustments and relaxations (in East-West relations) which occur from time to time must be evaluated *against a background of totalitarian controls* (with totalitarian controls in mind) if their significance is not to be optimistically exaggerated."

badly. *See* FEEL BADLY.

balding is a new word, formed after the pattern of *graying.* Some people object to this new formation, but I don't see why: there's no better way of saying what is meant. Example: "Every afternoon and evening, Alziro Zarur, 48, a squat, *balding,* onetime actor who now bills himself as Jesus' latter-day apostle, speaks to millions of Brazilians . . . ."

bard. Don't use *the Bard* as a synonym for Shakespeare, as in "In this Rowse biography it can be said that at last we have a worthy life of *the Bard* (Shakespeare)."

barrister. The British have two kinds of lawyers, barristers and solicitors. We don't have that distinction; therefore it's downright silly to use *barrister* as a fancy synonym for *lawyer:* "They both pointed out that they had received quick assurances from their attorneys—including Jack Greenberg of the NAACP legal defense fund and C. D. King, the Georgia *barrister* (lawyer) who visited them regularly—that reports of their impending deaths were highly exaggerated."

basal is now often used instead of *basic*. Don't do it. *Basic* sounds better.

based. Don't use this word as a preposition, as in *"Based on sales,* (Our sales show) this is the best liked pickup in the world."

basis. Like *based on, on the basis of* is much overused as a preposition. It can always be either left out or changed to *on, by, after, for, because of, with:*

His main duties there are to work *with graduate students on an individual basis* (with individual graduate students).

Sen. Hart has steadily refused to comment on the investigation, and most of the Senators wished only to discuss it *on an off-the-record, "for guidance only" basis* (off the record, "for guidance only").

On (*the basis of*) this kind of evidence, dozens of major medical groups have backed fluoridation.

On the basis of (By) observations from the earth, astronomers have established that hydrogen, ammonia and methane, three gases common on the earth, exist in Jupiter's atmosphere.

On the basis of (After) conversation and travel across this diverse nation, talking with a variety of audiences and being questioned by them, I am convinced that the conservative trend in the United States is far stronger than many realize.

On a long-range basis (For the long range) the committee calls for less emphasis on high income tax rates and a new general tax.

The board took its unusual action in the Haupt matter *on the basis of* (because of) the exceptional facts surrounding that particular case.

It opened at Warner's Cinerama *on a reserved seat basis* (with reserved seats).

be. The subjunctive form *be* is part of literary, formal English and gives any sentence it appears in a pompous, stuck-up air. There are two cases. Some writers use *be* where in normal, everyday speech everyone would say *is* or *are:*

The trouble with the argument is that the conclusion does not follow from the premises, even if they *be* (are) granted in full.

Whether it *be* (is) John Lear or John Ciardi, no alert teacher can afford to miss the informative and stimulating materials it contains.

What is more common is the use of *be* instead of the natural American form *should be*. I'll give a dozen examples to drive home the point:

The most notable such result was the adoption of the Assembly resolution recommending that nuclear weapons *be* (should be) kept out of space vehicles.

All Negro leaders demand that the "power structure" *be* (should be) opened to include them at every level, right up to the policy-making summit.

But the people must be vigilant, too, lest the courts, however unconsciously and with whatever lofty intent, annul the original determination that ours *be* (should be) a government of laws, not of men.

As for civil rights, Sen. Clark suggested that supporters of the bill on Sen. Eastland's committee demand it *be* (should be) reported out.

Three Lower East Side reform Democratic clubs said yesterday that they had sent telegrams to the Department of Buildings to demand that the building *be* (should be) placed under city receivership.

It was recommended, therefore, that a recently isolated Asian strain *be* (should be) added to the vaccine mixture. No one suggests that the really depressed areas *be* (should be) ignored.

When you buy the goose, remember that it *be* (should be) a fat bird and be guided accordingly.

The ravishing Miss Remick is being very feminist and insisting that she *be* (should be) admired for her brains rather than beauty.

Robert E. Kintner, president of the National Broadcasting Company, insisted that members of the company recruited by Leland Hayward, the producer, *be* (should be) left alone and allowed to throw their barbed shafts at whomever and whatever they chose.

When pictures about prostitution are reviewed by the Production Code Administration, the directors are concerned primarily that the picture *not be* (should not be) sordid or lustful and that there *be* (should be) compensating moral value.

I've put in all these various caveats because I think it is essential that certain matters *be* (should be) reserved for the future, so to speak.

See also SUBJUNCTIVE.

beauteous is an ugly, barbaric word that doesn't mean anything different from *beautiful:* "Reported carryings-on in official Washington of a *beauteous* (beautiful) West German party girl brought a demand in the House for a Senate look into possible security violations."

because.   Textbook writers and old-fashioned grammarians don't like the phrase *the reason is because.* They say it says the same thing twice and insist we should always write *the reason is that.*

But idiomatic English isn't as logical as all that. People stick in *because* whenever they feel that their reason needs extra emphasis:

These articles are not the less valuable now *because* disproved by events.

Just *because* we have no such method for dealing with political problems doesn't mean that we shouldn't try to solve them.

One reason the U.S.S.R. has arrested the Yale scholar is *because* it is certain, in its own totalitarian mind, that the U.S. will retaliate in no comparable way.

The reason this book is not a best seller is *because* we're giving it away free.

I don't think any of these sentences would be improved if *because* were replaced by *that* or some other supposedly more correct grammatical form.

beckon means to signal an invitation. You can't *beckon for something,* as in "With Wexler *beckoning for help,* (calling for help) many Yale volunteer workers gravitated toward his school."

become.   Some writers are afraid of the word *get* and change it to *become.* The results are often poor:

There were two small children who *became* (got) lost on their way home from school.

Congress abandoned plans to adjourn tonight after *becoming* (getting) bogged down in a partisan dispute over the $3 billion foreign aid appropriation bill.

bedeck doesn't sound right in a 20th-century sentence:

SAN FRANCISCO *BEDECKS* ITSELF FOR HOLIDAY WHILE REMEMBERING A SLAIN LEADER

befall, like other verbs with the old prefix *be-,* is archaic English: "The noncommuting world should have some knowledge of the catastrophe that daily *befalls* (hits, faces) our stalwart suburbanites."

begin. The past tense is *began,* not *begun:* "In Zurich, Switzerland, she *begun* (began) divorce proceedings against Romanian-born André Porumbeanu."

behavior pattern is now so common we forget that *behavior* alone usually means exactly the same thing: "Dr. Perera has found no consistent *behavior* (*pattern*) associated with hypertension."

behest is old-fashioned. Say *request:*

And now, apparently at Stevenson's *behest* (request), President Johnson is coming to New York to speak himself to the representatives of the world community.

It was the first time that the business men's group, formed at the *behest* (request) of Treasury Secretary Douglas Dillon had testified on Capital Hill.

"Boy! To go crazy, you gotta be out of your mind!" exclaims yet another innocent at the *behest* (request) of his author.

behoove is another old-fashioned word that doesn't fit into a modern sentence. Change it to *should:*

I think *it behooves you broadcasters to* (you broadcasters should) clear up these misconceptions.

Meanwhile, *it behooves doctors to* (doctors should) use the existing antibiotics judiciously, and with restraint "to minimize the further emergence and spread of resistant organisms."

Sometimes *behoove* is used unidiomatically:

Yet the spiraling prices *behoove* (force, lead) many of us—even the "wine snobs"—to take a second look into our own backyard of California for something of real value at, say, $1.50 to $2.50 a bottle.

being. *See* ABSOLUTE CONSTRUCTION, -ING.

belittle means to *disparage*. It's a good word *not* to use, since it often sounds wrong:

> Miss Neway's power lies not only in her voice but in her dramatic abilities and the woman she creates, of classic tragic stature, *belittles* (dwarfs) all that surrounds her.

> For example, a woman who has put on weight and feels un-attractive or a man who has done badly in business or suffered a failure feels too *belittled* (discouraged, low) to enjoy the pleasures of sex.

beseech is an old English verb that has two past tenses, *beseeched* and *besought*. If you use this old-fashioned word, at least use the newer form *beseeched* rather than the medieval *besought*: "So was Tennyson when he *besought* (beseeched, called), 'Ring in the valiant man and free, The larger heart, the kindlier hand!' "

bespeak is another of those old-fashioned verbs with *be-* that are better left alone:

> The pickup in attendance last weekend, after published reports of the show's distress, and the occurrence of several personal incidents that *bespoke* (showed, proved) the enthusiasm of people for the film dispelled the anxiety of the producers . . . .

> The pooling of such vast facilities on such short notice *bespoke* (showed) vast preparations.

best (verb) is headline jargon for *defeat*: "In doing so he *bested* (defeated) the segregationist Alabamian in the third round of his campaign to arouse white voters against the civil rights bill."

bestow, instead of *give*, is often used deliberately to add dignity to a sentence, but the effect is just the opposite:

> The current generation of managers seems anxious to *bestow* (give) a mantle of legitimacy *on* (to) both themselves and the companies over which they preside.

> Not all of the kudos *bestowed upon* (given to) her was for physical feats.

> *Bestowing* (Giving) a regal touch to any number of occasions, from cocktails to the grand ball, our majestic mush-

room cape has all the poise, the presence, the posh beauty a woman desires in her furs.

Svelte, bejeweled models are pictured cradling martinis or happily *bestowing* (giving) bottles of whisky *on* (to) their beaming boyfriends.

bête noire is the French word for *bugbear*. It's a prize example of the danger of using French words, since nine times out of ten it's misspelled *bête noir* (without the final *e*):

Repetition, a basic of learning and a television *bête noir* (bugbear), is still a problem and not always painless despite occasional musical revues that review lessons prosaically learned.

The French call the object that causes this kind of persistent botheration a "*bête noir.*"

better. First there was the common idiom *had better*. Then it got shortened to *'d better,* and finally even the almost inaudible *'d* fell by the wayside. Now the established idiom is simply *you better do that* (without the *'d*) and that's the way it more and more appears in print. Here are some samples from my collection:

"Mr. Preller cannot know about the workings of the committee," said Mr. Wagner. "Besides, he *better* get on the ball or the people in his district will throw him out."

With Dream Whip's country-fresh flavor, you *better* cut every piece this big.

But sextuplets *better* not come up too often. That will mean crowding the earth hopelessly.

I *better* marry, because I have the ambition to be a good wife and mother.

Growled an Omaha banker: "Those who take advantage of these court decisions *better* have the cash next time they want to buy something."

Better, in this sense, is an idiom that's clearly on its way in.

betterment is a bookish word for *improvement*: "On what basis does Sir Alec believe that the economic and social *betterment* (improvement) of its own people is the highest objective of the Soviet government?"

between you and I ranks with *ain't* and *like I said* as one of the most common and famous grammatical "mistakes." Why do so

many people say *between you and I*? Some grammarians think
the warning against *it's me* has scared people away from using
me even where it is correct; but I don't believe in that theory.
Rather, there seems to be a feeling that *me* at the end of a sentence or phrase sounds too emphatic and that when you want to
play down the mention of yourself together with someone else
you say *you and I* (or *X and I*) as a fixed combination.

I've heard people say *between you and I* thousands of times,
but have never seen it in print—it's the kind of "mistake" that
always gets caught. But I did find an excellent example in a personal letter: "The trouble he had, the shaking and twitching of
his hands when he concentrated and the fact that he would have
just as hard a time saying a word today as he had had saying the
same word yesterday prompted *Mrs. Greenberger and I* to seek
special help for him in the school system."

Will *between you and I* ever make the grade? I wonder.

beverage should never be used as a synonym for *drink.*
bi- is not a live prefix you can use freely, and the copywriter who
wrote "The *bi-button* jacket is sans breast pocket" should have
stuck to *two-button.*
bid is headline jargon for *ask to:*

> JOHNSON *BIDS* CONGRESS ENACT
> CIVIL RIGHTS BILL WITH SPEED
>
> ACHESON *BIDS* U.S. REMAIN IN EUROPE
>
> CASTRO *BIDS* CUBA INCREASE OUTPUT

blame on. Old-style grammarians and textbook writers call this
a colloquialism that should be marked wrong on papers. However, *blame on* seems blameless to me:

> When Clare Booth Luce *blamed* everything *on* the Ameri-
> can newspapermen, she was repeating the familiar act used
> about China.
>
> Even the Kennedy Administration's economists unanimously
> *blamed* the early cut-off of the second Eisenhower era up-
> swing *on* unduly restrictive economic policies . . . .
>
> Some people lose big chunks of cells with clots or heart
> attacks and *blame* it *on* old age.
>
> SLOW PROGRESS *BLAMED* ON LATINS

blond or **blonde?** Let's get this straight. A *blonde* (with an *e*)
is a woman with fair hair; *blond* (without the *e*) is an adjective

meaning fair-haired. Here are some examples of the current confusion:

> Italian men get very excited over *blonds* (blondes).

> Ford, 46, eldest grandson of the late inventor-industrialist, has been widely linked to a tall, slim, Italian-born *blond* (blonde), Mrs. Maria Cristina Vettore Austin . . . .

> "Something very radioactive is going on," said Gene Barry as he kissed the *blond* (blonde) on Ch. 4 . . . .

> *Blonde* (Blond) and boyish Chuck Percy, 43-year-old *wunderkind* of Chicago business as head of Bell & Howell, camera makers, is failing in his bid for governor.

bona fide is a Latin phrase that shouldn't be used where a simple English word would do as well: "Show the F.C.C. your contacts with your community have been wide and deep; show us you have made a *bona fide* (real) effort to serve."

-born is a favorite of the sentence-stuffers:

> *Paris-born* (Born in Paris), Mr. Sichel came to the United States in 1886 and became a member of the Stock Exchange in 1899.

> *Texas-born Mary Jean Kempner*, now living in Manhattan, travels, she says, "compulsively, to the Far East, Europe, the Near East, and the Arctic." (Mary Jean Kempner was born in Texas and now lives in Manhattan. She says she travels . . . .)

> *Mississippi-born and Illinois-raised,* he went to college in Kentucky where he played basketball for four years. (He was born in Mississippi and raised in Illinois. He went to college in Kentucky . . . .)

> *See also* ADJECTIVES, HYPHENS, SENTENCE STUFFING.

bracket, in such phrases as *high-income bracket,* is usually unnecessary.

brook (verb). This obsolete word doesn't belong in a modern English sentence and should be replaced: "If, therefore, it seems an impertinence for an Englishman, an Anglican priest with a parochial care, to broach a problem which the countrymen and fellow Carmelites of the two saints have thus far hesitated to assault, the venture may perhaps be pardoned on the grounds that the situation *brooks of* (allows) no delay."

buff, meaning *fan* or *devotee,* is a fine example of a colloquial word now firmly established in standard English:

Indian *buffs* and serious archeologists traveling through North Carolina this winter will find two new museums . . . .

We Gernsback *buffs* read his predictions with both awe and respect, since he foresaw radar as early as 1908 . . . .

A Mozart *buff* whose taste in reading matter runs to historical memoirs, Jones is one of 25 members . . . .

burgeon is a fancy word that can easily be replaced:

This interest is reflected *in the spate of paperbacks now burgeoning on urban issues* (in the current spate of paperbacks on urban issues).

In Monteverdi's musical and theatrical masterpiece *burgeon* (sprout) the seeds of the great operas of succeeding centuries—hints of Verdi, Wagner, and Richard Strauss.

With the transition from entrepreneurial to managerial control, however, *burgeoning* (growing) profits are not enough and hence the search for alternative means of imparting a moral justification to corporate power.

burglarize is one of those awkward words ending in *-ize,* but a good substitute is hard to find. *Rob* won't do because there's a legal distinction between a burglar and a robber. *See also* -IZE.

but sometimes slips in where there's no strict logical contrast between what has been said and what follows: "Burt Lancaster's enormous new home, replacing the one burned to the ground in the Bel-Air fire, is hidden from the street by trees—*but* they say it cost $1,000,000 at least."

There used to be a prejudice against using *but* at the beginning of a sentence, but not any more. Sentences like these are common:

It cannot be proved definitely that the L'anse aux Meadows site was the original New World community established by Leif. *But* 12 radiocarbon datings of charcoal from the smithy and fossil bones from the old kitchens indicate the settlement was a going concern about 1000 A.D.

The part the Jewish leaders of Christ's day played in bringing about the crucifixion does not exclude the guilt of all mankind. *But* the personal guilt of these leaders cannot be charged to the whole Jewish people either of His time or today.

Don't spoil the effect of *but* at the beginning of a sentence by putting a comma after it: "It had been stolen in a daring daylight robbery of a fashionable beach resort jeweler in Pompano Beach, Fla. *But, this was recovered.* (But this was recovered.)"

See also AND, COMMAS.

but which is usually wrong; cross out *which*: "Often with American advice, the South Vietnamese government adopted schemes that may have been good in principle but *(which)* worked poorly."

buy. The phrase *a good buy* (or *a bad buy*) is now standard English, as in "To some people, the Brooklyn Bridge is just *a bad buy*; to the late Joseph Stella it was the high altar of the American Dream."

If you use a new idiom like this one, don't try to hide it behind quotation marks but use it straight:

Upper-income women took pride in their ability to choose the "*better buy*" (better buy) and thus reflect their good sense and good educations.

Don't be afraid either of the other new idiom with *buy:*

"I don't *buy* that theory," he said. "It's too pat."

C

callow youth is a stock phrase anyone should be ashamed of using: "The first time I read this book—or, more accurately, a part of it—was as a *callow youth* on my first visit to Paris."

can or may? Traditional grammar says that *can* should be used only for ability and *may* only for permission, but 20th-century Americans don't care. *Can* for permission is used constantly by everybody:

Only the Government *can* sell liquor in Finland, and only holders of special permits *can* buy it.

HIGH COURT HOLDS, 8–0, THAT STATE
CAN *ENJOIN* VIOLATIONS OF ITS
'RIGHT TO WORK' LAWS

These expenses, when paid, *can* be deducted in full on either, or split in any proportion desired among these returns.

The state has prohibited the singing of the fourth stanza of "America" or the "Star Spangled Banner" as a substitute for prayer. They *can* be sung during patriotic ceremonies, however.

Excavations at No. 2 Hoher Markt *can* be visited on Tuesdays, Thursdays, Saturdays and Sundays from 9 A.M. to 1 P.M., and on Wednesdays and Fridays from 3 to 7 P.M.

Ocelots do not enjoy diplomatic immunity, even when owned by embassy personnel, and *cannot* be kept in communities where they are not wanted.

Before the ecumenism schema *can* be introduced, debate must conclude on the schema on bishops and the government of dioceses.

canine. Never use *canine* as a synonym for dog: "He has a choir of singing *canines* (dogs), he says, among which can be found singers, crooners, whistlers of recognizable portions of the national anthem . . . ."

can't help but. Some people have a prejudice against the common idiom *can't help but,* but there is no reason why it shouldn't be used: "The unexpected explosion by Sen. Dodd (D-Conn.) against the leadership *cannot help but* improve the prospects for fundamental reform of Senate procedures."

can't seem to is a popular and idiomatic substitute for the awkward phrase *seems not to be able to:*

The steel industry just *can't seem to* raise its price without some sort of government action.

Pressed by the Spellers for details on her friend Anastasia's death, its time and place, Mrs. Smith *could not seem to* give exact answers.

CAPITALS. Use capitals only when you have to; use lower-case letters whenever you have a choice. This means you should limit your use of capitals to the first letters of proper nouns, the pronoun *I,* the first words of sentences, and a few other long established usages. Don't use capitals as an attention-getting device; when you want to emphasize a word or phrase, underline it so that it will appear in italics in print. Don't use the old-fashioned device of capitalizing important nouns in a sentence, as in "Omar made tents and *Verse,* for people who made big demands on the here and now. Lumin makes *Gas Candles* for the same people."

For the use of capitals after a colon, *see* COLONS.

For the use of capitals in referring to God or the Lord, *see* HE.

case. Watch out for the little word *case* and weed it out whenever you can. Most often it can be replaced by *so:*

To date, this has not been as much *the case* (so) with the less glamorous vintages of Italy, or the variable, though often entirely elegant, wines of Spain, Portugal, and Chile.

Mr. Gilpatric quietly insisted that for a conflict to have existed he would have had to be in a position to gain from the contract award to General Dynamics. This was not *the case* (so), he said, because he left the firm in 1961.

Under our American system everybody is innocent until proved guilty, and even then the verdict is subject to appeal and reappeal. This is not *the case* (so) here.

This year I am unable to do so because I can't find 10 books that seem to me good enough to be raised high above the rest. This is particularly *the case* (so) in fiction.

They always say, "We like this, but our readers won't take it. This I'm sure is not *the case* (so)."

Sometimes *case* can be replaced by other words: "*In that case* (Then) Rockefeller turned out to be right. *In the present case* (Now), as above noted, the New Hampshire-California odds against Rockefeller are substantially heavier than in 1958, and if he loses these primaries he cannot conceivably be nominated."

Sometimes *case* can be left out altogether:

As is usually the case (As usual) these days, a convention or mid-afternoon feast is occupying the space.

Apparently there were some anonymous calls involved in (*the case of*) tracking down Inspector Karl Silberbauer.

catalyst means a substance that causes a chemical reaction of two other substances to each other. It is now a fad word, freely bandied about to mean anybody who brings people together: "His fantastic initiative as a *catalyst* between people and a bridge to events that would otherwise be unlinked . . . ."

Catalyst is a good example of a word that has become a cliché among the intellectuals but is unintelligible to most of the population.

catharsis, just like *catalyst,* is an overused fad word that's apt to puzzle many readers. It means an emotional purge. Here are some random examples:

> At the kill my response was neither outrage nor elation but a kind of *catharsis.*

> So far from being bitter, Oursler is gentle about it, even magnanimous. It is almost as though he wrote the book as act of *catharsis.*

> The boy's awful recollections are hidden away in recordings and photographs, part of his weird search for a sort of *son et lumière catharsis.*

> In one of his first essays at serious drama, a *cathartic* sort of exercise in a 1943 flop called "I'll Hit the High Road," Milton Berle was roundly condemned for his performance . . . .

cease is the formal word; the everyday English word is *stop:*

> There does reach a point at which product differentiation *ceases to promote* (stops promoting) welfare and becomes wasteful.

> To force a thoroughly addicted cigarette smoker to *cease* (stop) would, in the first place, probably not work, and, in the second place, might create, from the increased tension and eating problems, increased fetal hazards.

> Will Shakespeare has *ceased to be* (stopped being) a shadowy figure.

> This is clearly outdated because Col. John A. Powers *ceased last July to be* (stopped last July being) the "voice of the astronauts."

> It was sensible, to begin with, because all the Republicans' reasons for being tempted by Sen. Barry Goldwater *ceased to operate* (stopped operating) when President Kennedy was assassinated.

center around is a good example of a firmly established illogical idiom. Strictly speaking, you ought to say *center on* (a single point); but practically speaking, things have a way of *centering around* a less sharply defined focus of interest or debate:

> Concern about international liquidity *centers around* actual reserves of governments and central banks . . . .

> Discussion *centered around* what kind of action to take to

comply with both the spirit and letter of Executive Orders 10925 and 11114.

Roger Reynolds, executive vice president of Regnery, said that the objections *centered around* the use of the terms "conditional baptism" and "archdiocese" in the text of the novel.

Occasionally you do find *center on* in print, but it gives you the feeling that the writer meant to say *center around* and changed it to the more "grammatical" or "logical" form: "The sex scandal centers *on* (around) the death of the Italian-born beauty who apparently led a double life as a dentist's receptionist by day and an exotic playgirl by night."

certitude means blind faith that goes beyond mere *certainty*, but the current fad is to use *certitude* as a pompous synonym for *certainty* even when there's no difference in degree:

A. Philip Randolph long ago abandoned any belief in one-man miracles and any legislative *certitudes* (certainties).

About all that can be said with *certitude* (certainty) is that India's next prime minister will, like Mohandas K. Gandhi and the remote, unsmiling Nehru, come from the ruling National Congress Party.

character, like CASE or NATURE, is often used as an unnecessary filler word: "A price change *of this character* (like this) can cause difficulty in the normal flow of merchandise from manufacturer to distributor."

characterize is widely abused as a long synonym for *call:*

Campbell has been *characterized as* (called) "aggressive" by one source, because of its diversification into convenience foods other than soups.

Judge Bazelon *characterized retardation as* (called retardation) the "ugly child" of the psychiatric profession neglected for years but that has now suddenly turned into a beauty because the study of retardation has become "prestigeful."

In Canada, too, after the Canadian Medical Association issued a report that *characterized cigarette smoking as* (called cigarette smoking) "a grave and extensive health problem," cigarette commercials have been voluntarily restricted to late-evening hours.

His foes in the Senate, however, insisted upon *characterizing Mr. Nitze as* (calling Mr. Nitze) possibly pacifist or unrealistic regarding the requirements of military power today.

Mrs. Vijaya Lakshmi Pandit of India *characterized President Kennedy yesterday as* (called President Kennedy yesterday) "one of the world's greatest sons," whose death had cast a shadow across the world and "posed a challenge to people everywhere."

Even when *characterize* is used properly, it can usually be changed to a shorter word: "Concern with the clinical details of sex life *characterizes* (shows in, marks) much contemporary writing and certainly all bars are down, as even a cursory reading of the year's fiction demonstrates."

charismatic comes from theology and originally meant someone endowed with extraordinary divine grace. It is now a great fad word among the intellectuals and freely used instead of *popular:*

Actually the dilemma of the Social Democratic Party arose in 1952 with the death of Kurt Schumacher, its *charismatic* chief.

Michigan's *charismatic* Gov. George Romney forged his image as a man who can get things done—and as a dark horse bet for the 1964 Presidential nomination—by getting things done.

Bucky Fuller . . . is a *charismatic* man who attracted a cultic following even in the days when he seemed to the unclouded eye little more than some kind of a nut.

chef-d'oeuvre is the French word for *masterpiece.* The plural *chefs-d'oeuvre* looks odd to the ordinary English reader; so you better stick to English: "His very first production established the company's reputation, but it has taken years to develop a repertory of Felsenstein *chefs-d'oeuvre* (masterpieces)."

chide is an old-fashioned word brought back into the language by the headline writers. It should normally be changed to *reproach, blame* or *criticize:*

STUDENT EDITORS *CHIDE* (BLAME) BARZUN
FOR PESSIMISM ON LIBERAL ARTS

Hughes had to spend half the spring arguing that he would have shown poor faith had he held his fire until the personalities he *chides* (criticizes) were no longer alive to rebut him.

I was slow to realize that she was writing in an old comic tradition, but not so slow as the critics who *chided* (blamed, reproached) her for being a kind of Dos Passos *manqué*.

chief executive is an expression used solely to avoid repetition of *the President*. Change it to *he, the President* or his name, whatever sounds most natural:

> With obvious feeling, the President said that some law-makers apparently did not realize the importance of the aid program—perhaps because they are not charged with carrying out foreign policy. *The Chief Executive* (He) expressed his deepest emotion of the half-hour news section in appealing for passage of his foreign aid program. . . .

> A source close to the royal family said the doctor made the trip despite the distress in the Kennedy family over the assassination of the President because he had been asked by the *Chief Executive* (Mr. Kennedy) himself last week to do so. *Mr. Kennedy's* (His) widow urged Foley to carry out her husband's wishes.

> In the Gallup Poll's initial check on President Johnson's popularity with the American public, the new *Chief Executive* (President) comes up with an extremely high rating.

circumstances. Fowler's *Modern English Usage* says, "The objection to *under the circumstances* and insistence that *in the circumstances* is the only right form, because what is round us is not over us, is puerile." I agree.

clad is obsolete; the modern word is *dressed:*

> *Clad* (Dressed) in open-necked suntans and Army clod-hoppers, with Harkins always at his side, the poker-faced McNamara would begin by hearing from the local Vietnamese commander . . . .

> It is Mr. Leivick's dramatic fancy to take a Jew from Dachau, still *clad* (dressed) in his concentration camp stripes, and move him backward through time to the thirteenth-century German town of Mainz.

> A lady union official has told Congressmen that the scantily *clad* (dressed) waitresses in the bunny clubs should be covered—by the minimum wage law.

There's also *unclad*, which is a prissy euphemism for *nude:* "This is because some prudish resident caused a big ceiling painting of *unclad* (nude) goddesses to be covered with whitewash."

claim. Fussy grammarians insist that *claim* should only be used in the sense of *demand* and not in the sense of *state, assert, maintain;* but common usage doesn't care about this distinction:

> It has sometimes been *claimed* that hereditary factors are responsible for the high risk of prematurity among Negroes.

> Although some supporters of the defeated bill, which was drafted by a Judiciary Subcommittee, *claimed* it could have been passed, others conceded the new proposals will have a better chance.

> Grolier, which *claims* to control 30 percent of the encyclopedia market, looks for sales to reach $130 million in fiscal 1963, versus $106 million the year before.

CLICHÉS are hackneyed expressions like *fly in the ointment, out of the woods,* or *a little bird told me.* There are many thousands of such clichés in daily use by everyone, and it's impossible to draw a line between those you should avoid and those that are indispensable because there's no better way of saying what is meant. You'll have to use your own judgment. For example, I wouldn't know what to say instead of *conspicuously absent* if I wanted to express just that idea; on the other hand, I'd never write *in the arms of Morpheus* instead of *asleep.* But you may feel differently.

If in doubt whether an expression is a cliché or not, assume that it is and avoid it. Most commonly used quotations from the classics or the Bible are now clichés.

client means someone who consults a professional; the word shouldn't be used as a euphemism for the *customer* of a bank or store.

climate is now a fad word referring no longer to the weather but to all kinds of other things. It should usually be changed to *conditions:*

> "A psychologist's role is not to play God," says Miller. "He's not there to advocate human behavior, but to examine it and provide *a climate* (conditions) for improvement."

A working mother, far from creating a stress for her children, seems to give both them and herself *a better psychic climate* (better psychological conditions), particularly if her work is part-time.

cogent, cogency are rare words that can usually be changed to simpler synonyms: "The *cogency* (clarity, force, power) of his explication of the complicated ins and outs of Keat's thought illuminates what has only been dimly understood before."

cogitate, cogitation seem to be used only when a writer is desperate for a synonym for *think* or *thoughtfulness:* "Yet it is impossible to believe Toscanini would not have been pleased to see this selection, which ranges from portraits of the utmost thoughtfulness, of the most intense, inward-turned *cogitation* (musing, pondering), to the most expansive, commanding expressions of a born leader of men, who is possessed by a spirit larger than himself."

cognition, cognitive are fancy words for *knowing* or *"of knowing."* Both are used in a faddish way:

The intellectually relevant aspects of the low-income *cognitive style* (outlook) must not fall by the wayside, limiting education to preparation for manual occupations.

Since the roots of their failure lie in the deprivations of their environment, of their preschool experience, such children come to school with nothing like the tools, the *cognitive background* (knowledge), the self-security that 5-year-old and 6-year-old middle-class children possess.

But most vital of all, Dr. Hirsch's *cognition* (knowledge) that woman must be perceived and enjoyed as a complete person in her own design and sexualness; fully the equal of man.

cognizant is just a long word for *aware:* "President Johnson himself, who has become *cognizant* (aware) of the nation-wide demand for a sound fiscal policy, is beginning to refer frequently in his speeches to the principle of 'frugality.'"

cognoscenti (pronounced *konyo*SHEN*tee*) is a stylish Italian word meaning *insiders* or *those in the know:* "But for *the cognoscenti* (the insiders, those in the know), this year's top country is Guatemala, where the most In resort is Chichicastenango ('Chichi' to the real swingers)."

cohort once meant a company of Roman soldiers; now it's used most often in the plural (. . . *and his cohorts*) to refer contemptuously to someone's followers. It's a poor word to use, whether the insult is intentional or not:

> Under the plan now tentatively visualized by A. Philip Randolph, leader of the Washington March, and his *cohorts* (fellow fighters) in the civil rights battle, the start of the Senate filibuster would be accompanied by mass gatherings in churches, in union halls, in civic centers and other places throughout the nation.

> I don't believe the phrase expresses the feelings of a majority of the whites, but of enough of them to give the Goldwater *cohorts* (followers) their hope.

> Exactly what happens to Brock's *cohorts* (fellow workers) at the welfare service hasn't been resolved.

coincidentally is a long word that can easily be spared:

> Hysteric squeals emanating from developing femininity really went out (*coincidentally*) with the payola scandal and Presley's military service.

> Some of the utilities chose not to reply, but they found a champion in Morris Jacobs, a fellow member of Sonnabend's on the American Jewish Committee—and *coincidentally* (also) chairman of Bozell & Jacobs, New York advertising and public-relations firm which represents 75 gas and electric utilities.

COLLOQUIALISMS. *See* SLANG.

colloquy is a fancy synonym for *discussion* or *debate:* "*A* broader *colloquy* (debate) on funerals as a symptom of a society and its attitude toward death and life could be a useful extension of the healthy controversy generated by Miss Mitford."

COLONS. Poor writers use a period to mark each break between two sentences; good writers use a semicolon to show the connection between two sentences and a colon to show that the first sentence builds up to the second. Here are three examples of nicely used colons:

> Aspiring plumbers, engineers and physicists on signing their first contract of employment don't bargain their liberty away: American baseball players do.

> A broken home is not necessarily an indicator of poor

mental health: a greater proportion of mental patients come from intact homes than the general population.

Honesty, they said, was just not involved: the quizzes were rigged to provide entertainment, which they did.

In each of these examples a period would have been possible but dull; a semicolon would have been better; but only a colon points up exactly what the writer was trying to say.

Sometimes the sentence before the colon contains a word like *question* or *conclusion:*

But the question is going to arise one of these days: just how many bright new pianists is American concert life going to be able to absorb?

The question is: should a Presidential candidate tell a former President of the United States his political views, or should he keep them to himself so he doesn't confuse the issues?

At a recent CORE workshop I reached a disturbing conclusion that has been forced on me many times in the past months: something ugly is happening in the struggle to achieve full equality for all our citizens, something that can destroy the very goals we seek.

Sometimes the verb is left out of the sentence before the colon:

The theory behind the prescription: blood clots form in the arteries that nourish the heart muscles themselves.

A couple of TV advertisers became interested in him. Result: he will star in an NBC-TV special Feb. 20. . . .

Her daughter's report: bunnies would work just for tips.

Sometimes the verb is left out of the sentence *after* the colon:

But now in a corner of Staten Island known as Tottenville these former dope addicts are talking and talking. It's all coming out: the bitterness, the fears, the frustrations, the cravings, the nightmares, the inadequacies of themselves.

For the moment, the spicy froth obscured the most significant developments in the Baker story: a behind-the-scenes struggle in the Senate Rules and Administration Committee over whether to investigate the case or white-wash it.

The all-powerful Securities and Exchange Commission will soon find itself facing the same problem as many of the companies it regulates: too much room at the top.

Note that in all these examples the first word after the colon is *not* capitalized: if you use a capital, you spoil some of the effect of the colon.

See also SEMICOLONS.

come is an affectation in sentences like these:

About midnight the temperature dropped sharply into the deep 30s and *come morning* (in the morning), although the sun was climbing into the same old, monotonous blue sky, it was necessary to defrost a quarter-inch of frost from the windshield.

Came the war. (Then came the war.) Johnson served briefly with the Navy in the Pacific . . . .

come up with is now a well-established idiom: "The Latin American bishops *came up with* pamphlets both for and against a separate schema."

COMMAS. Too many commas make for slow, old-fashioned writing:

The defense disputed the contention that a disclosure of secrets would be inevitable, and, of course, denied evil intent on anyone's part. (The defense disputed the contention that a disclosure of secrets would be inevitable and of course denied evil intentions on anyone's part.)

He would be forgiven for even this by some voters but, unfortunately, he recently said, in effect, that, unless Sen. Goldwater or any other aspirant is willing to run on a platform that suits him, he may not support the national ticket. (He would be forgiven for even this by some voters but unfortunately he recently said in effect that unless Sen. Goldwater or any other aspirant is willing to run on a platform that suits him, he may not support the national ticket.)

Still penniless, Gauguin eventually went to Arles, in the south of France, to live with his friend, Vincent van Gogh. (Still penniless, Gauguin eventually went to Arles in the south of France to live with his friend Vincent van Gogh.)

Sandwiched in between, was the top robbery anywhere, for mode of execution, and for proceeds. (Sandwiched in between was the top robbery anywhere for mode of execution and for proceeds.)

There's also a trend now toward leaving out the comma before the last item in a series:

> It has for some years been common opinion that Hoffmann, now eighty-three, has during the past decade been growing steadily *in vigor, freshness, spontaneity, and depth.* (. . . in vigor, freshness, spontaneity and depth.)

> . . . the cohabitation in one environment of creatures as different *in their political conformation, coloration, feeding habits, and all the rest as Goldwater and Javits.* (. . . in their political conformation, coloration, feeding habits and all the rest as Goldwater and Javits.)

Some writers go beyond these accepted rules and leave out commas where most people would still consider them indispensable. It's up to you whether you wan't to follow these pioneers:

> We got more than twice the anticipated number of replies. Thank you David Ogilvy.

> Was it you who said give me a nice-looking car that really moves but doesn't cost too much?

> The assumption is the readers share the tastes of the editor and it is the only assumption under which you can put out a good magazine. I assume my taste is shared, if not let people read something else.

Some other pioneering writers use a comma where you'd probably use a period: "A tall Indian has magenta challes folded on his shoulder. You go up to him and lift them off for examination as though he were a counter, he takes no notice."

See also AND, BUT, EITHER, HOWEVER, SO, THOUGH, TOO.

commence is the formal word for *begin* or *start:*

> Mr. Cohen *commenced* (started) his career in the theatre as the co-producer of *Angel Street* . . . .

> Just put Barry in the White House and utopia will *commence* (begin).

communicate is a long word much overused instead of *tell, inform, be in touch.*

compare takes the preposition *with* or *to.* The ad headline "COMPARE AGAINST ALL OTHERS" is poor English.

compensation is income-tax English for *pay.*

complain takes the preposition *about,* not *against:* "Big business men complain *against* (about) big government when the Justice Department files an anti-trust suit against them but their smaller competitors and customers frequently cheer on the trustbusters from the sidelines."

complected instead of *complexioned* is a mistake warned against in all the textbooks, but it still appears in print: "This exciting twosome is so fashionable, so glamorizing you'll want to try it even if you aren't delicately *complected* (complexioned)."

complete (verb) should be changed to *fill in* or *out* in the common phrase "*complete* (fill in, out) this form."

comply with is a pompous synonym for *follow.*

comport is not a word that's part of ordinary English. Change it:

Equivocation *ill comports with* (hardly suits) a call for "a declaration of conscience."

Impatience *may poorly comport with* (poorly suits) the profundity of the issues and (*with*) the age and massive bulk of the Roman Catholic Church, but men no longer have generations at their disposal . . . .

This is all prelude to the registering of dissatisfaction—dissatisfaction with the way in which New York *comports* (behaves) itself as the nation's cultural and communications center.

conceit is a fancy word meaning a fancy phrase or expression: "They feel, to use one of Barzun's *conceits* (phrases), as though man were being called upon to become a 'self-programming Univac.' "

conceive is much overused as a synonym for *think* or *imagine:*

He said "it would appear" that those who wrote about the commission's policy "can only *conceive* (think) . . . in theoretical and hypothetical terms, namely, if a Negro and a white man of exactly equal capability applied for a job, which one do we say should be selected?"

In this tranquilizer-pill, traffic-ridden, television-happy, radioactive moment of our own mid-century can we fully *conceive* (imagine) an institution's survival across 2000 years?

concept is now one of the great fad words. People seem to have forgotten such simple words as *idea, rule* or *plan:*

> There is, to be sure, a certain hardheadedness behind the "good citizen" *concept* (idea).

> The *concept* (idea) that a combination of Kerr-Mills and private health insurance will give America's older citizens adequate protection against the economic hazards of ill health is plainly an illusion.

> "These things take time," said one hopeful company executive at Studebaker headquarters in South Bend last week. "We have a marketing *concept* (plan) now, but it will take time to get results."

> In the area of criminal insanity, Texas follows the widely used McNaughten *concept* (rule).

> The first Vatican Council of 1870 proclaimed the *concept* (dogma) of papal infallibility.

> Evidence of this is the fact that the most widely used college textbook in our colleges today is "Economics" by Paul R. Samuelson, whch expounds these *concepts* (ideas).

> As voiced by the National Urban League in its demand for a national "Marshall Plan for Negroes," the *concept* (idea) of equal opportunity must be expanded to include the "*concept* (idea) of indemnification."

concerned with is an awkward phrase that can often be changed to a shorter word: "His work for the company *was largely concerned with* (dealt mostly with) a single corporate acquisition and he also had some dealings with Boeing during the late fifties."

concerning is an unnecessary long preposition. Use *on, about, for:*

> These are the questions still unanswered at the close of two days of open hearings by Attorney General Lefkowitz *concerning* (on) ticket scalping and kickbacks in the theater.

> The Government categorically denies that any government official leaked any information *concerning* (on, about) the investigation of this grand jury to any member of the press.

> Simultaneous visits here today by the Emperor of Ethiopia

and the Queen of Greece had important implications *concerning* (for) Spain's foreign and domestic policies.

L. P. McLendon, special counsel for the Senate investigation of Robert G. Baker, said today he was confident that the Rules Committee would make a full disclosure of any findings *concerning* (on, about) Mr. Baker's alleged use of his Senate influence to further outside business interests.

concomitant is one of the most ponderous words in the language. Try *side, aspect, effect:* "It is essential to realize that the psychological *concomitants* (sides, aspects, effects) of poverty cannot be dealt with so long as the environment remains unchanged."

condign is a rare word. It appears mostly in the set phrase *condign punishment,* but is beginning to crop up elsewhere too:

Her book is tart but tonic. She believes in the *condign* (fitting, deserved) punishment of stinkers . . . .

Caroline passes her "11 plus" as triumphantly as she does her less *condign* (regular?) test as fledgling author.

conduct (verb) is a formal word for *carry on, run, do:*

The Negro coalition has *conducted* (carried on) almost continuous negotiations with various white political and business leaders since Nov. 10, but without notable success.

The voting was *conducted* (carried on, done) under overcast skies with intermittent sunshine.

confidant(e). A *confidant* (without final *e*) is a friend of either sex in whom one confides. A *confidante (with* final *e)* is an intimate girl or woman friend. To be on the safe side, leave out the final *e:*

Discoverer, agent, *confidante* (confidant) and friend to the star, Arthur Landau opened his secret files.

Cardinal Suenens has emerged as the Pope's closest friend and *confidante* (confidant).

congruent is book language for *matching* or *match:* "In this section Sultan abandons his tone of righteous indignation in favor of a sophisticated treatment of the ironies involved in trying to reconcile political with economic principles and rhetoric with reality in a society where ideologies and institutional interests are *less than perfectly congruent* (a less than perfect match)."

connection. The cumbersome preposition *in connection with* can usually be changed to a simpler word:

He went on to say that he was as anxious as anyone else to see a well-reasoned solution to the question that has been raised *in connection with* (on, about) smoking and health . . . .

The adverb *in this connection* can often be left out:

Publishers are interested to learn if anyone close to President Kennedy was designated by him as a literary executor, or at least as his preferred interpreter of the history of his Administration. Arthur M. Schlesinger Jr., Harvard historian and special assistant to the President, is being mentioned *(in this connection)*.

In this connection is also often used to show the transition between two paragraphs. It's usually better to cross out *in this connection* and start the second paragraph without transitional adverb:

"I believe," he said, "that sophisticated members of the labor movement would say that labor has a responsibility for the behavior of the President. The President and Congress don't assume postures unrelated to the political forces and countervailing forces."

(In this connection,) Mr. Reuther said that one of the most serious failures of the merger of the American Federation of Labor and the Congress of Industrial Organizations was that "we frightened the opposition and mobilized them but we did not mobilize the labor movement."

consensus of opinion says the same thing twice: "With or without a tax cut, business will keep gaining through '64. That was the consensus *(of opinion)* among economists from industry and universities at the annual Economic Outlook conference . . . ."

consequently is a four-syllable word meaning *so:*

Consequently, (So) it is up to the salesman to vary his presentation, but all too often he runs through it in the same manner, stressing the same points and without changing a word.

Consequently, (So) it appeared that the House civil rights strategists hoped to give Mr. Smith an avenue for a graceful retreat by getting the petition movement under way.

Consequently, (So) a reorganization of the Alliance is under study in Sao Paolo, Brazil . . . .

conservative estimate is a silly synonym for *low estimate:* Estimates range from an avowedly *conservative* (low) 100,000 by one leading psychiatrist to a probably exaggerated 600,000 by the homosexual president of the Mattachine Society . . . ."

constabulary is an example of what Fowler called "polysyllabic humor." Avoid this kind of writing: "About a third of these horses provide seats from which the *constabulary* (police) may survey and control the populace."

constitute.   If pomposity is wanted, *is* or *are* aren't good enough. So writers use *constitute:*

Bad black and white TV pictures of masters, worse than found in not-moving cheap reproductions, *hardly constitute* (are hardly) a service to the cause of art.

The connection he continually draws between Shakespeare's written lines and the social and political mutations of the era *constitutes* (is) the essential value of his lively, continuously fascinating book.

What all this goes to prove, the institute said, was that the newspaper *constitutes* (is) an important emotional prop for the average New Yorker and that its removal produces "psychotrauma."

The United States and Britain are reported to be ready to vote for such a proposal provided that it *merely constitutes* (is merely) a recommendation . . . .

Out-of-wedlock births now *constitute* (are) about 6 per cent of all births in the United States, as compared with 3 per cent at the end of World War II.

The liberals contended that passage of the two-month provision *constituted* (was) an admission that Congress would not continue the present session long enough to dispose of the regular appropriations and other legislation they regard vital.

This increase in female tippling *already constitutes* (is already) a "social problem of unrecognized seriousness," Dr. Wertham noted.

contact.   There used to be a prejudice against using *contact* as a verb, but it's fading away.

contemporaneously. *Simultaneously* is bad enough as a common synonym for *at the same time,* but *contemporaneously* is worse: "Almost *contemporaneously with* (at the same time as) the duPont announcement came word from Melbourne, Fla., that Homer R. Denius, guiding spirit of the Florida syndicate which hoped to build a Twelve called Eagle from designs by Charles Morgan, gifted young St. Petersburg designer, had notified New York Yacht Club officials that his group had decided to withdraw from the 1964 picture." (Of course you might argue that the 7-syllable word *contemporaneously* fits well into a 57-word sentence.)

contemporary (noun). Don't use *contemporaries* when you mean people of the same age. There's always a simpler word:

His stepdaughter, Fernanda, when she heard the list of her indicted *contemporaries* (friends, guests) and their smart addresses, merely moaned, "Oh, no. . . ."

The plaintiffs have the civil right not to be segregated, not to be compelled to attend a school in which all of the Negro children are educated separate and apart from over 99 per cent of *their white contemporaries* (the white children).

context sounds stiff and academic when used figuratively to mean circumstances rather than words:

In such a *context* (situation), the United States might find it advantageous . . . to begin trading with China, as the first, preliminary step to an eventual accommodation in Asia on the basis of the present status quo.

The psychiatrist would further point out that the imposition of a penalty is a complex interpersonal transaction, and that the interpersonal *"context"* (conditions, situation, set-up) in which the penalty is delivered is at least as critical a factor in determining the outcome as the penalty itself.

CONTRACTIONS. See APOSTROPHES.

contrary. Don't say *on the contrary* or *to the contrary* when you mean *no* or *not so:* ". . . or that socialization of an activity reduces costs because no profit is allowed. *The fact is to the contrary.* (It isn't so.)"

converse (adjective) is the technical logical term for what you and I call *reversed* or *the other way round:* "Against the argu-

ment that the Vice-President is out of the swim because things
have turned sour, there must be weighed an argument that is
exactly *converse* (reversed)—the argument that things have
turned sour because the Vice-President is out of the swim."

However, most writers who use the fancy word *converse* don't
mean *reversed;* they simply put down what they think is an
elegant synonym for *contrary* or *not so:* "There is a general
fallacy that naive country bumpkins are the ones who are taken
in by quacks. *The converse is true.* (Not so.) The educated man
who is skilled in his own field is a much easier mark." (If the
converse were really true, quacks would be taken in by country
bumpkins.)

convince. The traditional idiom is *to convince someone of
something;* but there's a new idiom springing up under our noses
and more and more people say and write *he convinced him to
do it:*

> This strategy was adopted after House Speaker John W.
> McCormack failed to *convince* Rules Chairman Howard W.
> Smith *to call* hearings this month.

> When the President set out to *convince* Northern Democrats
> on the House Judiciary Committee *to support* a compromise
> with the Republicans . . . .

> When Mr. Johnson was Senate majority leader, he *con-
> vinced* a Senator *to vote* against the dividend credit to break
> a tie.

cooperation. *Thank you for your cooperation* is stiff; *thank
you for helping us* is better.

cordially yours, to my ears, has a fake ring of pretend-chum-
miness; but I guess it's here to stay.

corpulent is not as good a word as *fat:* "Naturally, only the in-
credibly clever, *corpulent* (fat) Nero Wolfe knows the answer."

couched can easily be replaced by *phrased:* "The note, the text
of which was broadcast today by the Havana radio, was *couched*
(phrased) in language Cuba normally reserves for her enemies."

course of time means *time;* cut out *course of:* "In an amazingly
short (*course of*) time, the Profumo Affair has become little more
than a footnote to history . . . .

critique is now the fad word for what used to be called *criticism:*

The author of this *critique* (criticism, review) is himself a youthful writer whose works have been published in Soviet literary journals.

But *Mary, Archetype of the Church* will be instructive for Protestants also because of its *critique* (criticism) of the excesses of certain forms of folk piety.

Aside from its considerable value as literature and propaganda, *Uncle Tom's Cabin* is extremely interesting as a woman's book: the unusually complex gallery of female types, the presentation of the slavery issue as an appeal to woman's conscience, the *critique* (criticism) of women that lies behind Mrs. Stowe's denunciation of social evil.

Robert F. Wagner was elected Mayor later that year and, spurred by Miss Ferber's devastating *critique* (criticism), Our Bob did what came naturally: he set up a committee . . . .

cum is the Latin word for *with*, snobbishly used like this:
Four hours before Governor Stevenson spoke, we called on him in his Waldorf suite as he was starting his usual breakfast-*cum*-work (breakfast-with-work), a half grapefruit before him, the *Times* at his plate . . . .

Ogilvy's soft-*cum*-snob (soft-and-snob) sell has won him nineteen prestigious clients . . . .

Apartment burglars as a class can also be subdivided economically-*cum*-geographically (economically and geographically), for one will work in a particular section of the city that another won't go near.

-cy. For some writers, three- and four-syllable words ending in *-ance* or *-ence* aren't long enough; they add an extra syllable by changing the endings to *-ancy* or *-ency:*

If *competency* (competence) in a foreign language helped the high school student communicate more effectively, his curriculum would include that language.

Miss Mdivani flaunts and relishes *flamboyancy* (flamboyance).

They exhaust themselves to gain success, they destroy themselves in acts of impulsive *deviancy* (deviance).

But considering the remarkable *resiliency* (resilience) of

the tobacco industry over the years, snapping back from bad publicity and public disfavor . . . .

~~The high-flown banalities of the script in its constant over-~~ simplification of basic and complex human and social problems, and the cheapness of plot result in a melange of meandering melodrama, mouthed pieties and pretentious *irrelevancy* (irrelevance).

cynosure is a highly literary word meaning *center of attraction*. It's slightly obsolete, and there's no point in digging it up: "In nineteenth-century America, the builder of a better mousetrap was supposed to have been a *cynosure* (center of attraction)—provided, of course, that the mousetrap was properly patented."

D

DANGLING PHRASES.   Here's a classic example of a dangling participle: "Mr. Zapruder, filming the Presidential motorcade, recorded the exact instant the President was shot. *Then, sobbing, his fingers slipped from the camera.*"

Of course the writer meant that Mr. Zapruder was sobbing; but what he wrote was that his fingers were. He'd started his sentence with a participle and when he'd finished it, he'd left the participle dangling.

Sloppy writers are liable to this mistake and dangle not only participles but all kinds of other phrases. In the following examples I'm not going to suggest rewrites; what the writers should have done is construct their sentences differently in the first place:

Writing about 2,000 words in three hours every morning, "Casino Royale" dutifully produced itself.

Crossing the continent, the list of great houses could be lengthy.

What is most remarkable, *talking to Harris,* who is a New York Negro, and a co-defendant, Ralph Allen, a 22-year-old white youth from Melrose, Mass., *is their lack* of posturing and their quietness of tone.

Using various selections from the Bible in German, rather than the traditional Latin text of the Requiem Mass, *the excerpts included* the Psalms, Ecclesiastes, Isaiah and other portions.

Having said all this, however, *there is still something* of François Mauriac's "Thérèse Desqueyroux" which comes through . . . .

Examined from the industry side it is found that those industries of the greatest mobility possess one or more of the following characteristics . . . .

To get a rather good guitar, one that will satisfy you after you learn to play, *the going price will be* about $75, and the going price is what you actually pay.

In addition to Communists, Malaysia is opposed by the conservative Pan-Malayan Islamic Party . . . .

Unlike a course, you do not have to "sign up" for any specific period of time.

But like any compromise plan which shoots down the middle, the reactions from the extremes are at best pretty questionable.

Like many clichés, its exact meaning is puzzling.

Like Bismarck, Dr. Adenauer's historic mission was to lead a fledgling German state . . . .

Like most politicians, but unlike most distinguished lawyers, his view of the world is intensely personal.

Born to luxury and power, her life ended in a bleak Venetian prison after a sensational trial that rocked Europe.

Once known as an "Uncle Tom," his career is over.

As an actor very much in demand in television and films, Falk's availability for "Josef D." was a stumbling block.

A six-footer, Mr. McKay's physique has become slender with the passage of years.

An old-fashioned liberal with an aristocratic flourish in the manner of Franklin Roosevelt or Averell Harriman, *Mr. Ballard's family* has long and celebrated antecedents in New Jersey.

A diplomat as well as a poet for more than 30 years, his eyes filled with tears as he called the award an honor for Greece . . . .

A onetime management consultant who in five years at Westinghouse brought the company from malaise to new health, *Cresap's own health* has been bad ever since a bout with hepatitis last year.

Son of a store proprietor, an altar boy "as long as I can remember," *his bearded presence* in ecumenical gatherings has probably done more to change the traditional American tri-faith Protestant-Catholic-Jewish religious image in recent years than that of any single churchman.

See also LOST THREAD.

daresay sounds bookish in the U.S.: "*I daresay that* (I guess, I think, I suppose) English has suffered more sea changes since the fourteenth century, when it began to assume a character recognizable to us now, than French, Spanish, Italian, German, or Russian."

DASHES. Use dashes where they belong; don't use them for jobs done better by other punctuation marks. Here's an example of the regular use of a dash, to mark a break for contrast:

Why? One big reason: the official IRS explanation of the new system is very technical—and the instructions for the return are practically no help at all.

And here's a bad example of using dashes for dashes' sake:

If your problem is reaching the Public with your product story via publicity—whether it be *any* Product—Personality or whatever—why not call him?" (If your problem is reaching the public with your product story via publicity, whether it be any product, personality or whatever, why not call him?)

dastardly is a piece of old-fashioned rhetoric: "The recent events in Saigon and the murder of the President and his brother while his wife and daughter were enlightening the people of the U.S. on what our tin soldiers of fortune were doing to her country, will certainly be the most *dastardly* (cowardly) act in the history of our nation."

data. There's much to-do in the grammar books about whether the Latin plural *data* should be used with a singular verb, but the people have spoken. The normal sentence now reads: "The available *data* again *seems* to support the thesis."

DECADES. Write *the twenties, the thirties, the forties, the 20s, the 30s, the 40s,* etc., without capitals or apostrophes.

deceased is a legal word that shouldn't be used as a euphemism for *dead* in ordinary writing: "Memories of *the deceased* (the dead, those who died) inspired many contributions received yesterday by the Neediest Cases Fund."

declare. Don't use *declare* as a synonym for *say.*

decrease is too formal a word for most purposes; change it to *cut, fall, drop, shorten, lessen:*

> The teachers visit the houses of their pupils, thus *decreasing* (shortening) the social distance between the awesome school institution and the home.

> Cases of polio reported in the United States *decreased* (dropped) to the lowest number on record.

> There is *decreased* (less) sibling rivalry and *increased* (more) enjoyment of other children.

See also INCREASE.

decry is a pompous word; change it to *condemn* or *blame:*

> MANY IN CONGRESS *DECRY* (CONDEMN)
> ITS RECORD

> In *decrying* (condemning, blaming) the conduct of Halberstam & Co., Time wrote that "they have a strong sense of mission."

deed is a formal word that shouldn't even be used humorously: "The face-lift today is like dyeing one's hair, *a deed* [an act] once committed with the same secrecy (and stigma) as heisting a bank but now as commonplace as a manicure."

deem is a word for pundits; leave it alone even if you *are* a pundit:

> Its actions are more convincing than the words which, as yet, Messrs. Erhard and Schroeder *deem* (find) it expedient to use.

> The doctors argue they have a right to prescribe any drug they wish—as long as it is *deemed* (found, thought) safe enough to market.

> In Colorado such a contract was *deemed* (found) to exist because a football player was given a leaf-raking job on campus . . . .

> It was an adventure to serve with the Time-Life-Fortune

Commission on the Freedom of the Press, even though its report was rightly *deemed* (thought) disappointing.

---

de-emphasize is a long, awkward word. Try instead *play down* or *soft-pedal:* "Producers of CBS-TV shows were put on notice yesterday that the network wants cigarette smoking *de-emphasized* (soft-pedaled, played down)."

DEFINITIONS.   Whenever you use a word that may be unknown to your reader, it's your business to define it. Good writers know how to do this casually and elegantly:

On the operating table, he locates the ileocecal valve, *where the small bowel joins the large,* takes a tape measure and starts measuring upward.

Nor does the wife have time before her husband leaves to cook the rice, curried meat, fried vegetables and chapatties *(thin pancakes of unleavened white bread)* that he expects to eat at midday.

If possible, define a word as something done by you, the reader: "Double jeopardy means *you can't try a man a second time on the same charge after he has been acquitted.*"

Poor definitions are of two types: either they dodge the job of defining altogether or they're harder to understand than the word they define:

What are hives? *Hives usually occur from an allergy to something taken into the body. Foods and medicine are the two most frequent causes.*

Achieving identity means *discovering one's autonomy as a person learning both the strengths and weaknesses of one's personality and the meaning of human consciousness with its consequences in self-initiated action.*

My prize catch of a definition is this one:

Fransen defines this method of existentialism as "the systematic exposition of the necessary *a priori* conditions for the possibility of a given real existence in the wholeness of its human situation."

See also EXPLANATIONS, RARE WORDS.

---

deign is shorter than *condescend,* but it's not the word people use. Stick to *condescend.*

delectable always sounds arch; don't use it:

"Barefoot in the Park" is a *delectable* (delightful) exercise in the art of party-giving, and the sound of popcorn is heard throughout the land.

Following the intermission there was a *delectable* (charming) set of Prokofieff "Visions Fugitives," enchantingly set by Mr. Barshai for strings and played with ravishing fantasy by the ensemble.

delineate, delineation. *Draw* has one syllable; *describe* has two; *delineate* has four. So why use *delineate?*

The Governor's advisers believe that he can successfully *delineate* (draw) two pictures of Mr. Goldwater . . . .

Obviously I had to live through torturous personal self-doubts to question such accepted truths about the nature and role of woman as I did in *delineating* (describing, writing about) the feminine mystique.

An anonymous short novel that *delineates* (shows, describes) in striking detail the strange passions of a young Frenchman whose love affairs went beyond normal bounds.

Spender, in his foreward, emphasizes the fact that modern writers have found the *delineation* (description) of sensual experience a liberating force . . . .

delve is one of those words that have lost serious standing but aren't funny enough for humorous use: "She also *delves into* (writes about) the harried life of pediatricians and the way TV turns children into salesmen pressuring the whole family."

demean is a pompous word for *debase* or *degrade:*

TREATMENTS OF SLICKNESS AND VULGARITY *DEMEAN* (DEBASE) THEMES OF CONSEQUENCE

Sometimes *demean* is wrongly used instead of *disparage:* "It is an office nobody campaigns for, an office the politically knowledgeable traditionally have *demeaned* (disparaged) . . . ."

demeanor is too hefty a word for *manner* or *air:*

Golding's scraggly beard is not as full as Jeremiah's, nor is he as forbidding in *demeanor* (manner).

President Johnson's plea for help, his take-charge *demeanor* (air, manner, attitude) and his conservative appearance seem to have released a whole new outpouring of great expectations for the economy.

His *demeanor* (face, expression) was stolid when Judge Fosseen began reading the indictment.

demise shoudn't be used as a fancy word for *death*. When you mean *death*, write *death*:

Mr. McKnight doubts that Lambaréné will survive its creator's *demise* (death).

Although Mr. Susskind says that "East Side" is healthy, his letter campaign is in a TV tradition of legitimate pressure to convince networks and sponsors that the property is as hot as ever and that its *demise* (death) would be a distinct loss.

The *demise* (death) of Puritanism is the latest phase in a conflict, as old as Christianity itself, between Eros and agape . . . .

demonstrate. Nine times out of ten the long word *demonstrate* can be replaced by *show*: "Krips *demonstrated* (showed) that he had obviously dissected the symphony though he didn't always *demonstrate* (show) the deeper perceptions that make a great performance."

denizen is another one of those would-be humorous words:

Many other *denizens of Madison Avenue* (Madison Avenue people) agree with this observation.

Denizens of (Those who work in) new office buildings have not only grown accustomed to the loneliness of the operatorless elevator, they have also developed a conditioned reflex.

depict, like *portray*, is overused as a synonym for *act* or *play* a part: "Mr. Schildkraut will *depict* (play) the patriarch of a dynasty in the Yiddish theater at the height of its glory . . . ."

Then there's the use of *depict* as a pompous synonym for *describe*:

It *depicts* (describes) Rockefeller as almost single-handedly laboring in 1945 to insure that the UN charter permit mutual security alliances.

deprecate. The dictionary meaning of *deprecate* is "express strong disapproval of; protest against." But the word is rarely used that way; most people use it to mean *disparage*. A few— following the advice of the grammarians—use *depreciate* instead of *deprecate* whenever they're tempted to fall into that trap.

My advice is to use neither *deprecate* nor *depreciate* but use simpler words and avoid the whole confusion.

Here's an example of *deprecate* used in the dictionary sense:

The United States, Britain and Brazil joined France in abstaining on a paragraph that *deprecated* (disapproved, regretted) Portugal's failure to comply with a previous Council resolution that was adopted July 31.

Next, here are a few examples of the common, wrong use of *deprecate:*

No politician has ever spoken more *deprecatingly* (disparagingly) of his own chances for the Presidency . . . .

This is not to *deprecate* (make light of, underrate) the enormity of the Congressional burden . . . .

Shannon, by the way, admires Farrell and *deprecates* (thinks little of, dislikes) O'Hara.

There were also enough subsequent *deprecating* (slighting) comments to indicate that a major controversy is developing . . . .

Finally here's an example of a writer scared into using *depreciate:*

Rabbi Silver, however, tended to *depreciate* (make little of, play down) the importance of the size of his congregation . . . .

depth. The fashionable thing now is to study everything in *depth,* do everything in *depth,* say everything in *depth.* Here are some ideas for getting rid of all this *depth:*

"These promotions," the announcement said, "provide increased *depth* (strength) of management for A & S . . . ."

The first part of the book—an attempt to explore *in depth* (fully, thoroughly) the Chinese and Soviet national personalities and their considerable differences—is undoubtedly the best section.

Literature taught imaginatively and insightfully will help students to understand a Huck Finn, a Billy Budd, a Holden Caulfield, provide the *depth in* (full, thorough, meaningful) communication that can be found in great literature.

derive is overused (and often misused) as a synonym for *get* or *find:* "Those kind-hearted but misguided souls who *derive pleasure in* (find pleasure in, get pleasure from) feeding pigeons can find an ample supply of subjects on which to indulge their fancy in the several excellent zoos provided by the city."

descend shouldn't be used as a pompous synonym for *go down*.

descry is an over-literary word. Replace it by *detect* or *make out*: "I seem to *descry* (detect) the hooves and horns of the deliberately contrived best-seller."

desideratum. An unnecessary Latin word for *need*: "But for all its peripheral merits, 'Rugantino' hardly seems the musical *desideratum for* (need of) Broadway at the moment."

designate, designation are long words for *name, call* or *tag*:

William Needles is noteworthy as the actor *designated* (named, called upon) to play the Hermit . . . .

The authors *designate* (call) this phenomenon *(as)* being "weller than well."

Collectors were able to obtain "first day of use" cancels then. No such *designations* (tags) will be applied to current mail emanating from Dayton in the tagged-stamp tests.

desire, which means a passionate longing, is commonly used as a decorative synonym for *wish* or *want*:

However, collectors *desiring* (who wish, want) covers bearing the tagged stamps may request this service from the Postmaster, Dayton, Ohio.

A strong *desire* (wish) to take a leading role in the continuing growth of an expanding organization is a first-order requirement.

Mayor Wagner said today that Costikyan has expressed a *desire* (wish) to leave the post · . . . .

How does Lyndon Johnson go about getting the *desired results* (results he wants)?

desirous. Those who're not satisfied with the effect of *desire*, go one step further and use *desirous*:

Now we quite agree that everybody *desirous of going on* (who wants to go on) to college . . . should most certainly be encouraged to go ahead.

According to associates, Dr. Wiesner has been informed by M.I.T. that it will probably be impossible to hold open jobs that he *is desirous of assuming* (wants to assume) unless he returns shortly to the institute.

destined to is a pompous phrase. Cut it out: "After reversal of the excise tax reductions, which *were destined to meet* (later met) strong Administration opposition . . . ."

deteriorate, deterioration are unnecessarily long words:

The House of Commons had been told that with mutinous soldiers rioting in the republic, on Africa's east coast, the situation was *deteriorating* (getting worse).

Therefore, since most observers of the U.N. believe that the admission will be a certain event of the autumn of 1964, the United States will be confronted with an inescapable choice between the further *deterioration* (decline) of the U.N. and setting out new and uncompromisable terms for its reform.

determine, determination.   These heavy words are very common in legal, academic and journalistic prose. Make it a practice to change them to *fix, set, test, find, figure out, decide,* and you'll have gone a long way toward improving your writing:

It would also *determine* (study, find out) the potential impact in regional planning and what the bridge would mean to industrial and population growth in Suffolk and on the New England side of the sound.

The commission demanded that the two companies along with four others take action within 60 days to cancel existing price-fixing agreements and *redetermine* (reset) prices.

Using these tables, any reader can, with the help of his physician, *determine* (figure out, find out) his own susceptibility to coronary heart attack.

While it was the number of stresses that determined the risk of impairment, the combinations of the types of stresses determined psychiatric diagnoses. (It's the piling up of stresses that makes people mentally ill, but what kind of illness they get depends on what kinds of stresses they're under.)

The major responsibility of the chiropractic board is the composition of examination questions to *determine* (test) candidates' fitness to receive a license.

The constitutional provisions *regarding the determination of a President's inability* (on how to decide whether a President is unable) to carry on his duties after he is disabled are obscure.

This is the procedure on which Senator Byrd and his committee have been insisting as the only method by which the amounts, the spacing and the allocation of the tax cuts could be responsibly *determined* (fixed) by Congress in the line of its constitutional duty.

The choice of extracts for this anthology has been *determined* (decided) first of all by the quality of the writing.

The obstetrician-gynecologists' offices were flooded by engaged couples anxious to have their Rh type *determined* (tested).

The final terms bar the bank from guaranteeing payment "except when the President *determines* (finds) that such guaranties would be in the national interest."

detriment, detrimental are formal words for *damage, harm, harmful:* "Such policies, he warned, would be highly *detrimental* (harmful) to the economy."

develop shouldn't be used in its police-blotter sense: *"It developed, according to Inspector Kronbar,* (Inspector Kronbar said) that Mary Lee was last seen on Aug. 28 . . . ."

devoid of is a fancy way of saying *without:*

Largely *devoid* of (without) any sophistication in foreign affairs, the Vice President accepted intensive coaching from the experts . . . .

We can never forget that her distinctive services were utterly *devoid of* (without) any segment of prejudice or selfishness, disregarding race, color, creed or the person's station in life.

This is a film *devoid of* (without) sentimentality, *of* (without) the mawkish reverence too often brought to bear upon the travelers to the promised land.

Mr. Walpin contended that the "accusation is *devoid of* (without) the slightest merit."

dialogue has had a tremendous career as a fad word in the last few years. What it means in its fashionable sense is often hard to say—*debate? discussion? understanding?* or just *talks?*

The fact that the country's first serious *dialogue* on civil rights in a century began around graduation time seems to us instructive.

Sen. Goldwater delivers such extravagant retort that *dialogue* is rarely possible . . . .

VATICAN MOVE IS CALLED BOON TO JEWISH-CATHOLIC *DIALOGUE*

The Negro community has needs as urgent as hunger, as hard as rock—yet the rhetoric of today's *dialogue* hides the reality.

"Militancy" thus makes the public confrontation between the races chiefly a *dialogue of black demand on white guilt.*

dichotomy is just a long word for *division* or *split:*

The *dichotomy* (split) between the King and his play is fatal to "Richard III."

Among many *dichotomies* (divisions), all inexact, by which one patient, you, can divide all other patients, is the too-quiet versus the too-noisy.

different than is now an established idiom and examples are easy to find:

The need, no *different* now *than* it was a decade ago, is generally conceded to be desperate.

The Conservative Party is in a tizzy, but for *different* reasons *than* were anticipated.

"I don't feel any *different than* I felt before," Sir Alec said after becoming a commoner.

Unruffled by the news was Radcliffe's president, Mrs. Mary Bunting, who said: "I have no indication that there has been any serious trouble and the situation does not seem any *different than* in previous years."

Some writers seem to share the grammarians' prejudice against *different than* and go out of their way to avoid the phrase; but I think *different than* in the following examples would have been an improvement:

The world today is indeed *a very different one to that which* (very different than the world) Trotsky must have visualized.

With an Asian Secretary General and with Asians and Africans playing a much greater role in the Secretariat than before, the United Nations is a far different institution *from what it was* (than) when it began operating nearly 18 years ago.

difficult to overestimate is a pompous phrase meaning *great* or *much*. Sometimes a writer gets confused and says *difficult to underestimate* instead: "*It would be difficult to underestimate the harm done* (Much harm has been done) to the Goldwater cause within the party by his foreign policy statements."

dilemma means the problem of choosing between two things; but the fad is now to use *dilemma* as a synonym for any kind of *problem* or *trouble*:

> The historians may decide that the division of powers is a *dilemma* (problem) beyond the power of a President to *(re)*solve.

> The result is a Who-am-I? *dilemma* (problem) known as "the identity crisis."

dimensions is a pompous word often used to mean *size:*

> The *dimensions* (size) of the initial assault on this encrusted poverty will be small.

> Last night be reinforced the impression he made when he performed at Philharmonic Hall—that here is a *mature talent of major dimensions* (mature, major talent).

dire is a word that doesn't belong in the 20th century: "What will happen to Kenya's big game now that the colony has gained its independence? There have been some *dire* (terrible) predictions . . . .

directive is just a long word for *order.*

dis- shouldn't be prefixed slaphappily to any word that comes to hand: "We have *disenjoyed* (gone through, suffered from) a lot of ridiculous restrictions on the foibles of mankind in this country, including Prohibition . . . ."

disallow is not as good as the shorter word *reject:* "Unfortunately, he does his own argument considerable disservice when he castigates the defensive position of union leaders as a posture and simply *disallows* (rejects) their arguments without answering them."

disassociate, disassociation. These long, cumbersome words can be shortened by one syllable to *dissociate* and *dissociation.* However, people don't seem to go for this idea:

Sen. Goldwater has tried to let the John Birch society down gently by *disassociating* himself from its leader, but not its members.

Rabbi Eisendrath said the "mind is staggered and the heart is enkindled" simply by the prospect of the possible implications of the Catholic church's official *disassociation* from the age-old charge of deicide leveled against the Jewish people.

Perhaps we need the long forms *disassociate* and *disassociation* to express fully the opposite of *associate* and *association*.

disclose, like *reveal,* means to bring something hidden into view or make a secret known. Both words are now used mostly as pompous synonyms for *show:*

BRAZIL *DISCLOSES* (SHOWS) WARMTH FOR U.S.

A study of major party nominations since the convention system began in 1832 *discloses* (shows) that only four broad categories of men have been chosen.

A comparison of these international precepts with the U.N. Charter *discloses* (shows) that every one of them was set forth in that document in 1945.

discrepancy. Don't use *discrepancy* when all you mean is *difference:*

One is soon aware of a certain *discrepancy* (difference) between the table of contents and what is in the book.

There is considerable *discrepancy* (difference) in standards among the suppliers of the fabrics.

disinterest, disinterested. All the textbooks warn against using *disinterested* (which means *impartial*) when you mean *un*interested. But people keep on doing it:

The bystanders—all upright citizens—are *disinterested* spectators but once back in their respective vehicles each yields to avarice and the wild race is on.

At the Strollers Club, this night, Billy Rose seemed *disinterested* in those jigsaw-pieces suddenly settling into place.

In the soggy and bleak countryside he seeks the diversion of writing his memoirs, she takes refuge in drinking and petty gambling and they share an ineptitude and basic *disinterest* in hunting and gentleman-farming.

Would it surprise you to know that Alston has been the

manager of the Dodgers for the past ten years only because DiMaggio expressed a *disinterest* in the job?

~~I think the battle against~~ *disinterest* and *disinterested* is already lost.

distaff is an archaic word now solely used for fancy-synonym purposes:

> Scranton grew up in a household dominated by its *distaff* (female) population—the Duchess, his three older sisters, his nurse, his nurse's aunt, his tiny, tough Grandma Scranton, and a menagerie including two bitches and a mare.

> The liquor industry, which until a few years ago followed an unwritten rule not to portray women at all in advertising, this year is making a blatant pitch for the *distaff* (women's) trade.

divulge. Why not say *give* or *give out*? "According to Mr. Stolow, the youth, whose name he would not *divulge* (give) 'didn't know what to do.'"

doff. It's time to forget this old-fashioned word:

> I *doff* (take off) my hat to Mr. Harris while crying "Hurrah!"

> Still, the private Berle *doffs* (takes off) his fedora, walks on his soles and lets the teeth shine through.

-dom is not a live suffix and doesn't look right when attached to modern words:

> The latest chapter in *filmdom's* (the movies') most celebrated romance comes nearly three months after violet-eyed Liz Taylor affirmed: "I'll be Mrs. Burton in three months."

> After listening to speeches from most of Yale's *officialdom* (officials), Prof. Hendrickson stepped to the dais . . . .

> *Moviedom's* (The movies') newest comedy team, Jackie Gleason and Steve McQueen, gets off to a faltering start . . . .

> The first indication Kelso gave of becoming *horsedom's most distinguished fluke* (the most distinguished fluke in horseracing) was on June 22, 1960.

> *Movie stardom* (To be a movie star) has been Bobby's goal ever since an agent saw him impersonating Maurice Chevalier . . . .

domicile shouldn't be used as a pompous synonym for *home:*

"The town house figures prominently in the Baker case as the one-time *domicile* (home) of his secretary, Nancy Carole Tyler, and her cousin, Mary Alice Martin."

don, like *doff,* should be taken out of circulation: "Keith Michell, co-star of "The Rehearsal," *donned* (put on) his costume—brocaded coat, silk hose and buckled shoes—when he remembered that he'd left his gold cigaret lighter at the Manhattan Hotel pharmacy next door."

donate, donation. Don't use these words as synonyms for *give* and *gift:* "I can see no reason in the world for asking taxpayers who earn less over their lifetime to *donate* (give) the cost of education to alumni who earn more."

don't. Most people seem to think that saying *he don't* instead of *he doesn't* is a mistake made by the uneducated. It isn't. *He don't* is a natural English idiomatic contraction on the pattern of *he won't* used commonly by millions of people. Because of the prejudice against it, it rarely appears in print. Here are two good examples I came across:

"Somebody bought it for him in Miami Beach in 1928," a guy at the table said. "He wears that and a 10-year-old pair of Thom McAn shoes. *He don't* buy anything for himself . . . ."

"The root of the problem," says Ferrell, "is despair. A man says to himself, 'I've been down so long till down *don't* bother me.' "

doomed literally means *condemned to a terrible fate.* The word shouldn't be flung around lightly like this: "Those who had hoped that something encouraging concerning the proposed merger of the National Association of Engine and Boat Manufacturers and the Outboard Industries Association would come out of the recent OIA directors' meeting *are doomed to disappointment* (will be disappointed)."

DOTS are beloved by the mail order copywriters:

There's color, excitement, adventure in every issue . . . menus, food and wine lore, restaurant reviews . . . and RECIPES—an average of over 75 each month (more than 900 a year)!

But the fact remains that those who DO prepare for the

boom times ahead will reap big dividends for their fore-
sight . . . and avoid the blunders other will make.

Our photographers were allowed to take thousands of color
photographs of grounds . . . homes . . . landscape features
. . . lawns . . . terraces . . . fountains . . . gazebos . . . walks
. . . trees . . . flowers . . . hedges.

My advice on using dots like this is, don't. If you *must* mark
a breathless pause in your sentence, use a dash.

DOUBLE NEGATIVE. Schoolchildren are taught they must
never use a double negative. This hasn't stamped out the double
negative as a natural English idiom, but it has driven it out of
print except in quotes from supposedly illiterate people:

The child returned the script to her teacher and said: "No,
ma'm, *we don't talk like that no more*."

"*There never was no complaint made to me*—except one
. . . and that time by a competitor."

Another novel had been sent in earlier with a note saying,
"I *would not let no one* handle my manuscripts but Doubleday."

However, the double negative is very much alive and perhaps
the iron rule against using it in writing will someday relax. Even
now educated people are quoted as using such mildly double
negatives as this:

"A state frontier is a state frontier," Khrushchev replied.
"And every state, whenever its borders are violated, shoots
the violators." "*Not to keep people in, we don't*," snapped
Cook.

Wasn't it unusual for a girl to decide to be a doctor? "Oh
no, *not today it isn't*," said Miss Gwon.

Senator Milward L. Simpson of Wyoming said: "They've
just warmed it over like hash to make it more palatable."
Asked if it were now palatable, he said, "*Not to me it
isn't*."

As these examples show, double negatives in idiomatic English
are understood to reinforce each other rather than canceling each
other out. But the textbooks insist that two negatives make a
positive. This unidiomatic rule leads to sentences that have to be
solved like algebraic equations:

Many, and probably most, of the Italians *refuse to concede*
that the basic principle of freedom of conscience, as enunci-

ated by Pope John XXIII in his last encyclical, "Pacem in Terris" ("Peace on Earth") *does not constitute an invitation* to Italians, or at least "permission" for them, to become Communists.

Start a conversation some midnight about the Death of the Novel, and someone is sure to mention our modern *refusal to suspend disbelief.*

DOUBLE PREPOSITION is what I call this sort of thing: "It is probably safe, though unpopular, to say that the chance of a Negro being admitted *to* and aided *by* most of our institutions is much greater if he lives in Africa than in Alabama."

In this example the phrase *and aided by* reads like an afterthought stuck in later by the writer. The sentence would have been easier to read if he'd put *and aided by* between dashes: "It is probably safe, though unpopular, to say that the chance of a Negro being admitted to—and aided by—most of our institutions is much greater if he lives in Africa than in Alabama."

Here are some more examples where dashes would have improved a double-preposition sentence:

The House committee method is by legislation, some sections of which pose issues of constitutionality *submitted to, but as yet unresolved by, the Supreme Court* (submitted to—but as yet unresolved by—the Supreme Court).

Intimations have lately been reaching us of a rapidly developing craze among young people in England for *the music of, and public appearances by, a group of pop singers called the Beatles* (the music of—and public appearances by—a group of pop singers called the Beatles).

The career of Hofmann has consisted of a continuous *meditation on and enactment of the creative way revealed by our time* (meditation on—and enactment of—the creative way revealed by our time).

Of course the best solution is to avoid double prepositions altogether and construct your sentences in a less bookish way.

due to is being used regularly as a preposition, in spite of the grammarians' objections. I see no reason why it shouldn't:

Three months ago, "The Memoirs of a Lady of Pleasure" ("Fanny Hill") was, *due to* legal difficulties, on the tip of every tongue.

"Despite a firm 40-week commitment, ABC granted Lewis'

request to withdraw *due to* differences regarding the format," the network said.

Belly Dancer Lesia "Little Athens" challenges Yvonne De Carlo to prove she can strip as well as she can belly dance, *due to* remarks made by Yvonne on TV.

Frederick Carder, 100, founder of the Steuben Glass Works in Corning . . . was forced to sell his plant *due to* war shortages to Corning Glass Works . . . .

dwell, in the sense of *live*, is obsolete: "Why must there still be debate as to whether the federal government shall give assistance and help to those who *dwell* (live) in the slums?"

dwelling shouldn't be used as a synonym for *house*. When you mean *house*, say *house*:

It is not unusual to see an individual scrubbing a sidewalk or the exterior of his *dwelling* (house).

Mrs. Bartlett then moved to another *dwelling* (house) in the vicinity.

The *dwelling* (house) is handsome, but the property itself, especially its trees, shrubs and flowers, is worth a visit.

dynamics, used outside of physics or music, is a pompous fad word meaning *workings, movements* or *actions*:

He said that Father Weigel had displayed a "great understanding of the *dynamics* (workings) of American democracy."

Some day we may very well compensate for our emotional and motivational *dynamics* (activities? ups and downs?) by drowning in paper.

E

early. Don't use *at an early date* as a fancy synonym for *soon*: "It seems unlikely that the favored project of the past—entry of Britain to the Common Market—can be revived *at an early date* (soon)."

Another poor substitute for *soon* is *at your earliest convenience*.

echelon is the current fad word for *rank*:

John Steinbeck said today that the arrest of Prof. Frederick

C. Baarghorn on a charge of espionage had resulted from a *lower-echelon* (lower-rank) mistake in the Soviet Union.

I am inclined to believe it will leave out in the cold little boys with bows and arrows, weary sophisticates (*of the forward echelon*), and fanciers of true-life crime.

edifice is a ridiculously pompous word:

Also in this vicinity stand three important *manorial edifices* (mansions).

St. Paul's Cathedral is being cleaned of grime, at the expense of an anonymous donor. The *edifice* (cathedral) was completed in 1710.

EDITORIAL WE. *See* OURSELVES, WE.

-edly. In theory there's nothing wrong in adding *-ly* to make an adverb out of a past participle ending in *-ed*; but in practice most words ending in *-edly* sound stilted and unnatural:

She *assertedly* (They say she) invented the Scavenger Hunt, a big favorite at parties for a while.

In fact, they have helped to change *markedly* (greatly, sharply) the character of these institutions.

My friend reached *tiredly* (sleepily?) into his pocket, hauled out a small vial and took a pep pill.

Katherine Anne Porter's "Ship of Fools" *was unmeritedly* (didn't deserve to be) fawned over as a novel of profound statement and cosmic scope.

Words in *-edly* sound particularly bad when the *e* is silent in the participle but sounded in the adverb:

The first Southern President now sits in the White House—to smile *amusedly* (in amusement) upon such presumption.

As an ant he could not bear grasshoppers—*mistimedly drunk* (drunk at odd times), ungainly, ill-smelling, bad-spelling people.

What ought to be our most august lawmaking body, the Senate, has felt *unembarrassedly free to provide* (no embarrassment in providing) a national platform so that the cheapest of cheap crooks could broadcast accusations against men not yet tried and found guilty.

She looked down at Mr. Utamaro sitting *relaxedly* (relaxed) in his hard chair.

See also -LY.

educationist makes a poor substitute for the noble word *teacher:* "She gave up *an educationist's* (a teaching) career to help her husband."

educator is slightly better than *educationist,* but that's about all that can be said for it.

effect. Don't use *to the effect that* as a conjunction: "They cannot bear their work to go to waste in some yellowing file, and so from time to time they reprint it with a brief introduction *to the effect that* (that says) allowances must be made . . . ."

effectuate should be changed to *put into effect* or *carry out:* "This movement has abandoned the kind of policies that can be *effectuated* (put into effect, carried out) only by leaders willing to sacrifice their 'middle-class respectability.' "

effort. Don't use *in an effort to* as a preposition: "A number of measures are being tried *in an effort to* (to) protect schools already built without installing conventional protective screens and guards . . . ."

egregious is a literary word meaning *remarkably* or *extraordinarily flagrant.* Many people don't know its exact meaning, and so it's better to avoid it: "A bureaucrat spends approximately one-twelfth of a century with tax amnesia, and his *egregious* (outrageous) lapse goes unpunished."

egress. You'd think that no modern writer would seriously use this rare old-fashioned word, but you'd be wrong: "The tweter provides for *egress* (an opening) for both hands."

either, at the end of a sentence, should be used without a comma:

This is *no idle chatter, either* (no idle chatter either).

There is precious little alliance in the Alliance for Progress. And *not much progress, either* (not much progress either).

ejaculate is sometimes used as a synonym for *say.* Don't do it.

elapse is a pompous synonym for *pass* or *go by:*

In the days which will *elapse* (pass) before Jan. 18, 1964, when the Executive budget is submitted to Congress . . . .

This reasoning was plausible, in Moscow no less than in Western capitals. The years that have since *elapsed* (gone by), however, have proved that it was wrong.

elect, election. These words should be reserved for voting; when you mean *choose* or *choice*, say so:

> VINSON *ELECTS* (CHOOSES) TO QUIT HOUSE
> AFTER 50 YEARS

> The decision of which plan to *elect* (choose) must be made a month before a person turns 65 and irrevocable thereafter.

> Professor Richard Hofstadter, of Pulitzer Prize celebrity and Columbia University employment, has *elected* (chosen) to delve for such roots in the national past.

> It was "penetration of the life she had *elected* (chosen) to discover and explore."

> The recent court decision refused to permit the executors of an estate to change their original *election* (choice) to deduct administration expenses on the income tax return.

electronic has to do with electronics and shouldn't be used as a dressier word when you mean *electrical*. Here's a suspicious example: "The beep line comes and goes among teen-agers all over the U.S.—a kind of *electronic* (electrical) equivalent of the old-fashioned tree trunk on which people used to hang messages."

ELEGANT VARIATION. *See* SYNONYMS.

elicit is an overformal word for *get* or *bring:*

> A campaign to *elicit* (get) favorable notices from prominent Americans has been started by "East Side/West Side."

> Just as the British Broadcasting Corporation's original program kicked up a to-do in London, the N.B.C. variation *elicited* (brought) the predictable quota of viewer protests . . . .

eliminate, elimination are long words used much too often. Try instead *get rid of, do away with, cut out, wipe out, take out, leave out, drop, stop, end,* etc.:

> The proposal looks to an ultimate goal of *eliminating* (dropping, ending, cutting out) most of the countless special deductions and allowances, through which taxpayers are able to reduce the amount of income subject to taxation.

> In our education, religious elements have gradually been *eliminated* (dropped, left out) by judicial interpretation.

> The reliance on automatics also threatens to *eliminate* [do away with] those elevator men who have long served as a

combination tout, retriever of stray children (and dogs), critic of delivery boys, and professional eavesdropper.

The Government and the securities industry have given top priority to an 11-point program for *eliminating* (stopping, ending) the worst of the "grave abuses" of investor trust recently uncovered in the securities markets.

The amendment would have *eliminated* (dropped) the requirement that deductible entertainment expenses be "directly related" to the business of the taxpayer.

Mikhail A. Suslov, who has opposed some of Premier Khrushchev's internal policies, appears to have *eliminated himself from* (taken himself out of) consideration.

It destroys the myth of the "slick press agent" and *eliminates* (ends, does away with) much of the obscurity and confusion surrounding the molding of "public opinion."

Representative Edwin W. Willis of Louisiana declared today that the civil rights bill should be sent back to the House. Judiciary Committee to *eliminate* (take out, cut out) its "unconstitutional" provisions.

Many tax authorities have been impressed with the idea as a means of eventually *eliminating* (plugging) many loopholes *from* (in) the tax system.

The lure was the *elimination* (saving) of a week or more of tedious, time-consuming library work.

Dr. Galbraith declared that those who argued that a steady expansion in economic output was a necessary condition for *the elimination of* (wiping out, stamping out) poverty had a valid case.

Such a development would have extremely important consequences when the Council takes up the decisive stage of the African-Asian campaign to bring about the independence of Portugal's African territories and the *elimination* (end) of South Africa's white-supremacy policy.

June Shagaloff, NAACP education specialist, while admitting "the critical need for higher standards," contends that they "cannot substitute for the *elimination* (end) of segregation, which is inherently discriminatory and unequal."

else's. While grammarians still argue about such expressions as *someone else's* or *nobody else's*, the idiom is becoming so firmly established that even *who else's* is beginning to appear in print:

"You get nervous. What if something happens—would it be your fault? You are driving, so *who else's* fault could it be . . . ."

elucidate is just a pompous long word for *explain.*

'em, instead of *them,* has two uses in current writing. The first, of course, is putting on paper the way people pronounce *them.* The second is more interesting: more and more writers seem to be using *'em* whenever they mean the general public or an unspecified group of people:

"Anybody can knock *'em* dead without a script," a network official told me, "but only a true artist can do it with seven writers."

CRITICIZE *'EM,* THEN SELL *'EM*

There's a literary bank robber in San Francisco who held *'em* up at pen-point, so to speak, and all in the best possible cause.

MONOLOGUE BY CUSHING WOWS *'EM* IN JERSEY CITY

On contact, a mechanism is triggered inside the casing, releasing a tranquilizer which is injected into the target. The effect is immediate, police said—"it knocks *'em* unconscious without harming them."

emanate is a pompous word that can either be left out or changed to *come:*

They further claim that despite the sound and fury *emanating* (coming) from some Senators . . . Mr. Baker's influence has been exaggerated.

High up in the emotion-stirring, traffic-building category are the ads *that emanate from* (by) Compton.

The wry misanthropy *which emanates from* (of) almost everyone is too generalized an emotion to make for necessary nuances of personality.

There have also been whisperings lately that Miss Sutherland is a "cold" singer—whisperings such as usually *emanate* (come) from Latin rivals, who assume that any singer of Anglo-Saxon or Celtic origin is "cold" by nature.

The purpose of the permanent setup is to make news (*emanating*) from the White House immediately available to television.

Chief problem for architect Karl H. Porter of San Jose, who designed the $822,000 school was to muffle the noise *that emanates from* (made by) 110 children.

embrace is a stuffy word for *hold, contain, take in, take up:* "A Rockefeller holds convictions on national and world affairs often more explicit and more progressive than those *embraced* (held) at the Democratic center."

eminently is a pompous word; say *highly:* "If Salinger wins a striking victory in California—which is regarded as *eminently* (highly) possible—the lesson will not be lost on Democratic leaders outside California."

empathy is a fad word. Strictly speaking, it means what the Germans mean by *Einfühlung* (in-feeling), which is the ability to put yourself in the other fellow's shoes. Example:

Few can explain the extraordinary King mystique. Yet he has an indescribable capacity for *empathy* (understanding people) that is the touchstone of leadership.

However, the current use of *empathy* goes way beyond that:

Malamud's collection of warm and funny short stories, "Idiots First," evoked *empathy* (sympathy) for his hounded characters . . . .

The emphasis is on funny people and funny happenings . . . . The *empathy* (human touch? feeling for people?) is there, but . . . .

Nobody in Washington today believes the Mayor has a chance. It's more than balance. Personal *empathy* (magnetism?) is important too.

Her soliloquy about sex is a gem; her bewilderment at the evening's goings-on is indeed *empathetic* (pathetic? moving?) . . . .

emphasize is a long word. *Stress* says exactly the same:

A recent court decision has *emphasized* (stressed) the importance of properly making the executor's election to deduct administration expenses either on the estate tax or the fiduciary income tax.

Republicans avoided *emphasizing* (stressing) their disagreement with the President's policies.

He *emphasized* (stressed) his disappointment that more than a year after the signing in Geneva of an agreement guaranteeing the independence of Laos, the country had achieved neither the peace nor the stability he said was her right.

Mr. Lowell *emphasized* (stressed) that the commission was not in favor of violating laws, instituting quotas, removing from a job anyone to make way for a Negro . . . .

Unlike the annual statements of this group in other years, it doesn't *emphasize* (stress) its own sectarian beliefs . . . .

employ shouldn't be used as a fancy synonym for *use:* "The off-camera narration by Trevor Howard was excellent, and off-camera voices were artfully *employed* (used) for welcome sound track change of pace."

See also GAINFULLY EMPLOYED.

emporium hasn't been funny for a hundred years: "It is just above a row of neighborhood stores—a newsstand, a fish market, a fried chicken *emporium* (place), a pizzeria and Vincente's fresh vegetable stand."

encomium is a long, old-fashioned word for *praise:*

For Uppman's Masetto, deserved *encomiums have* (praise has) already been penned in vast quantity.

For once, however, the *encomiums are* (praise is) deserved, if a trifle exaggerated. This is indeed a first-rate thriller. . . .

Gross's personnel record at the L.A. board of education glows with such *encomiums* (praises) as "Outstanding" and "Don't let this man go."

Although all the participants in "Any Wednesday" deserve commendation, I don't think it would be amiss to single out Sandy Dennis, the heroine, for *a special encomium* (special praise).

encompass means *contain* or *take in.* It doesn't mean whatever it's supposed to mean in this sentence: "There is a blazing sense of the furious minutiae to be *encompassed* (done? gone through? observed?) by the cadets—the standing at attention, the marching, the handling of rifles, the housekeeping in the barrack, the bayonet drills."

encounter is often misused as a longer and more decorative word than *meet.*

end product. Cut out *end:* "Do our educators want the (*end*) product of their effort to be a scholar or a person?"

end result. Ditto: cut out *end.*

endeavor. Don't use *endeavor* as a formal synonym for *try:*
Mr. Lundborg cautioned the group that the pursuit of per-
fectionism by many corporations in *endeavoring* (trying)
to find absolutely correct answers to all business problems is
a complete fallacy and is injuring these concerns.

We normally possess built-in stabilizers which *endeavor*
(try) to sustain a constant outer and inner environment. . . .

endemic shouldn't be used unnecessarily outside of medicine:
"*The Way We Live Now*, the third division, explores such *en-
demic* (native?) phenomena of our American time as Billy
Graham."

engage in is often used as a fancy word for *do, be busy with:* "The
U.S., while keeping its present six divisions in West Germany,
might still reduce the total number of troops stationed here, particularly those *engaged in* (working on) support activities."

enhance, which means *heighten* or *increase,* is sometimes used
loosely as in "Such schooling does not *enhance* (advance), but
rather retards, its low-income pupils."

ENGLISH TITLES. *See* SIR.

enormity (which means *outrage*) is now used commonly to mean
enormousness (vast size):

Indeed, the very *enormity* of his success, and its extent, have
seemed to rule him out of the consideration of highbrow
critics.

By coincidence I had read this letter just after going through
a book of reproductions of Rodin's sculpture, and the stag-
gering *enormity* of his lifetime production made Rilke's advice seem all the more pertinent.

ensue seems to be gaining ground as a fancy synonym for *follow:*

A charade then *ensues* (follows) whereby "militant" Negro
leaders gather at various city halls; sympathetic white
leaders listen to their demands . . . .

On the night I saw the play, this was the climactic scene,
followed only by fragmentary references to *ensuing* (later)
events.

His first assignment was to traffic duty, but in the *ensuing*
(following) years his duties took him into every activity of
the department.

Then *ensued* (followed) four more intense days that produced seven stiff U.S. protest notes . . . .

In the (*ensuing*) years since "Exodus," she has appeared in three French movies . . . .

A friendship *ensued* (grew, developed) between top officials of Braniff and of the Appleton agency that resulted in yesterday's account switch.

Its basic preoccupation is with a couple who married almost as their passion cooled and who have devoted *the ensuing 10 years* (the following 10 years, the 10 years since) to stimulating—and simulating—their love . . . .

entail is a very formal word that can often be changed to *mean* or *result:* "It is therefore problematic how long such a program should be continued without better scientific evidence to justify the major costs to the general public *that are entailed* (it will mean, that will result)."

enthuse is a verb formed fairly recently by cutting off the tail end of *enthusiasm.* To me it seems unnatural and ugly: " 'This WEU arrangement,' *enthused* Belgium's Paul-Henri Spaak (Belgium's Paul-Henri Spaak said enthusiastically), 'removes the cork from the bottleneck.' "

entity is sometimes unnecessary and can be left out: "Many seem to regard the men and their work as separate (*entities*); they like the former and are reserved about the latter."

envisage, envision are running neck and neck as fad words for *see, foresee, imagine, have in mind, consider, contemplate:*

The Administration *envisioned* (had in mind) a carefully controlled program of construction, even taking care to avoid bull-dozing away trees in residential areas.

We cannot accept economic policies which *envision* (look to, foresee) 4½ per cent chronic unemployment by 1980, when current trends indicate that most of that 4½ per cent may be black.

By this, I mean they can *envisage* (see) possibilities, conceive of the future.

For central London and other big-city areas, the plan *envisions* (foresees) underground highways routing traffic, unimpeded, through the city.

The death of millions by nuclear war has been *envisioned as* (considered) feasible with today's weapons.

"A multiplicity of suits may be *envisaged* (foreseen, imagined) involving actions against a great number of next-of-kin and legatees innocent of any participation in the matter, other than having received their share of the estate."

"But I'd like to make it very clear—I do not *envision* (see) myself as others do, shaking out there in the wings, wringing my hands, waiting to be called by the party, as a compromise candidate," he said.

Some eminent lawyers and political scientists long have argued that the Constitution *envisages* (contemplates) that the Vice President, when there is one, shall make the determination of Presidential "inability" when the President is in this state and cannot or will not so declare.

The dream of a 50% across-the-board slash—*envisioned* (foreseen) by the U.S. Trade Expansion Act—is no more.

There's also this prize example of *vision* used as a verb:

HOUSE VOTE IN '63 ON RIGHTS IS SEEN
KATZENBACH *VISIONS* (SEES) PASSAGE
BY CHRISTMAS RECESS

See also VISUALIZE.

equally as says the same thing twice:

At least some officials and politicians here are now talking about trying to make the Negro schools *equally as good as* (equal to, as good as) the white while at the same time continuing the fight for public school integration.

Equally as (Just as) hollow, however, are the councils in hospital corridors of surgeon, internist, chaplain, intern and resident.

equine shouldn't be used as a synonym for horse: "Despite the acute *equine* (horse) shortage, we sharply reduced the price of our finest styles."

-er. Yes, you can form a noun by adding *-er* to a verb, but there's a limit to how far you can go. Here are two examples of poorly made *-er* words:

But a police spokesman said the department hasn't tested the *quieter* (tranquilizer gun) on humans or animals—and doesn't intend to. (The writer made up the word *quieter* to avoid the repetition of *tranquilizer gun*; he would have been better off repeating it.)

The fastidiousness of the effort to scrub the bathroom clean to some extent supports the portrait of the killer as a homosexual. It also has led some detectives to speculate the *knifer* (killer) was a woman. (This writer used *knifer* in desperation because he was afraid of repeating *killer* and couldn't use *he*. He should have repeated *killer*.)

eradicate is a long word; *wipe out* is shorter and better: "He supports a tax cut to *eradicate* (wipe out) unemployment and calls for 75 million jobs."

erstwhile goes back to 1569. After 400 years it's too musty for everyday use:

Richard H. Paul, who lately returned to private law practice after a 19-month stint as chief counsel of the now disbanded Securities and Exchange Commission special study group, gave his *erstwhile* (former) employers a bit of working over yesterday.

In Chicago, *erstwhile* (once, formerly) "Hog Butcher for the World," the packing houses once employed 20,000 workers, heavily Negro.

But the *erstwhile* (former) Sadie Thompson still has the gams to make shorts worth wearing.

eschew is a formal, legal-sounding word. Change it to *avoid, keep away from, stay away from, drop, leave;* don't use *shun*, which is a word mainly used in headlines:

The nineteenth-century poet von Platen had tried to *eschew* (avoid, drop) romanticism in favor of classicism . . . .

Yet again he is interested in so much else, and again he *eschews* (avoids) the abstract.

When his 85th birthday rolled around on New Year's Day, the author of "A Passage to India" *eschewed* (avoided) any public remembrances or large party . . . .

Dr. Jonathan Miller, the 29-year-old British pathologist who, as a member of the successful "Beyond the Fringe" troupe, *eschewed* (left, dropped) the dissection of cadavers to tickle American funny bones, is planning to make his movie debut.

Another contender, who has so far *eschewed* (stayed off, kept away from) TV, is Jovito Villalba . . . .

In this age of anxiety, the question of giving the dying patient a painless and untroubled passage must not be obscured by a society which seems uneasy and denying of death, and inclined to *eschew* (avoid) mature responsibility.

For the most part unaware of what nationalism really means, these lands, torn by regionalism and ancient ethnic quarrels, *eschew* (avoid, keep away from) both democracy and Communism.

especially. It's a superstition to think that *especially* is a more elegant word than *specially:*

Twelve *especially* (specially) fine stories, long out of print . . . .

There are two aspects of this proposal, however, that are not spelled out completely in the big Anouncement, and it seems advisable—very much in your interest, as well as in ours—to call them *especially* (specially) to your attention.

espouse, espousal are bookish words that should be replaced by *hold, support, take up.* (*Embrace* is just as bad as *espouse.*)

The theory of *personality, espoused here,* (personality held here) is consistent with the concept which holds that mental disease is not a fixed, everlasting entity . . . .

To begin with, American parties are not democratic organizations of citizens *espousing* (holding) generally uniform views . . . .

From the beginning, he has *espoused* (supported, taken up) contemporary music. He was an early exponent of Aaron Copland.

The elements of coincidence and over-simplification were very marked in the premiere; on the other hand, its *espousal* (support) of the value of education was in contrast to the essentially anti-intellectual attitude of so many video shows.

-ess. It's a good rule to use only the long-established *-ess* words like *actress* or *waitress* and leave other words as they are:

If the seer *(or seeress)* turns out to have supernatural powers in that line, we plan to set up a brokerage called Witchcraft, Inc. (The word *seer* alone would have been better.)

Raskolnikov fights out with himself the decision to murder an old *pawnbrokeress* (pawnbroker, woman pawnbroker) just to prove his independence of conventional morality.

There is much about the Shaws' relationship that will never be known, though English *Authoress* (author) Janet Dunbar's sympathetic biography tells a great deal about the little-appreciated Mrs. G. B. S. (The ending-*ess* here sounds snide.)

essay (verb) is a pompous word. Most often nowadays it means little more than *do:*

Earlier this season Perry Wolff of CBS News *essayed* (did, produced) two programs—on the theater and the Parthenon —with an artistic result that was Greek to me.

Now 49, the red-haired daughter of one of the world's foremost families was in Chicago to *essay* (play) the role of a woman reunited with an old flame.

establish is sometimes used as a long word for *find:* "Dr. Guerra pointed also to the difficulty of devising a written test to *establish* (find, measure), a pupil's ability to speak a language."

et al. is an ugly Latin abbreviation meaning *and others*. There's always a better way of saying it: "They were fine satires to go along with the running 'T.W. 3' serial on *Robert Baker, et al.* (Robert Baker and his friends)."

et cetera should never be spelled out. The normal written form is *etc.*

-eth, the obsolete form of *-s,* shouldn't be used as a style device. It's neither solemn nor funny—just phony:

The answer *maketh* (makes) the heart glad and the spirit rejoice.

DAVIS CUP *RETURNETH* (RETURNS)

EROEFFNUNGSFEIER: THE SNOWMEN *ENTERETH* (ENTER)

(Here the writer added the phony -*eth* to the plural verb form, which didn't end in -*eth* even a thousand years ago.)

eupeptic means having good digestion. It's a word few people are familiar with and shouldn't be used casually in the general sense of *cheerful:* "He is alarmingly *eupeptic* (cheerful), full of cracks, up early, boyishly imprudent . . . ."

EUPHEMISMS. There's nothing wrong with using euphemisms to spare other people's feelings or sensibilities, but still, the real word is always better than a substitute. So, as a rule, avoid euphemisms whenever you can. For examples, *see* PASSING, SENIOR CITIZEN, UNDERPRIVILEGED.

euphoria is a psychiatric term meaning an abnormal state of well-being and happiness. It is now a fad word, widely overused to mean *cheerfulness, optimism* or just general *high spirits:*

> Despite the *euphoria* (optimism) created by the treaty, the Soviet Union's behavior regarding Germany has raised questions in the United Nations about the possibility of another Berlin crisis.

> Today Marvin is back on the streets, as they say, but at the time he was heading off to prison and enjoying the curious *euphoria* (happiness) that comes over New York's professional burglars once they have been caught.

> There are few works in the repertory, even among the great masterpieces, that exude the kind of *euphoria* (happiness, bliss) that this one does.

> In his *euphoria* (happiness), Erhard proudly showed off the 10-gallon hat Johnson gave him . . . .

event. Don't write *in the event that* when you mean *if:*

> There may be a clause holding the seller liable for damage *in the event that* (if) an encroachment or a property restriction comes up years later.

> *In such an event* (If so), would it necessarily follow that the top rung of the evolutionary ladder had been attained by creatures resembling humans?

> Mr. Tonahill dismissed the possibility of $100,000 bail for Ruby, *in the event he is* (if he should be) released, as "ridiculous."

And don't use the word *event* in this fashion:

> S. KLEIN'S GREATEST
> MINK *EVENT* (SALE) OF THE YEAR

eventuate is a long word for *happen, result, come about, turn up:* "Maybe the most charming aspect of racing yet will *eventuate* (result, turn up) if we can conquer the stupid idea that betting a horse inside the walls constitutes the sport of kings, while betting the same gluepot by telephone is a crime."

every so often is a common idiom; but *every so seldom* is just plain impossible: "*Every so seldom,* (Every once in a long while), a book comes along which does nice things to your funnybone."

everybody, everyone. *See* THEY.

everybody knows. Don't be a snob; don't blithely assume that "everybody knows" whatever you happen to be familiar with. Beware of this kind of thing:

> *Bruckner was, as everyone knows, Mahler's musical mentor,* and it is easy to trace similarities between the two composers in the technical realm.

> *Anybody who is older than an Eagle Scout can remember the scandal.* There was a grown man, a dreamer in denims named Jackson Pollock, tacking canvas to the floor and dribbling paint on it.

> As *almost everyone knows, the Durham rule,* first announced in 1954 by the United States Court of Appeals for the District of Columbia Circuit, is an attempt to bring some reality to the consideration of criminal responsibility.

> *With the work of Dr. E. M. Butler as widely known as it is,* it is absurd to ask "how many schoolboys and schoolmasters today have ever heard of Winckelmann?" and then proceed to put Winckelmann on the *map as though he had been forgotten since the death of Pater.*

> *See also* OF COURSE.

everyplace is commonly used instead of *everywhere:*

> Things like this were going on *everyplace* in New York where Nelson Rockefeller has business.

> "*Every place* I go is a public appearance."

everytime (one word) is often used: "*Everytime* we try to really show you how the Talon Zephyr zipper looks, someone pipes up and says: you made the picture too big."

evidence (verb) is not as good a word as *show:*

> That Langner stood in awe of G.B.S. is *evidenced through* (shown on) every page of the book.

> That these advantages have not escaped the attention of economy-minded taxpayers is *evidenced* (shown) by the many thousands of plans which have been put into effect during recent years.

Interest outside Akron was *evidenced* (shown) by a small flood of letters of inquiry about the case . . . .

---

evidently is very common, both in speech and in writing, but it's simpler and shorter to say *it seems, clearly* or *of course:*

Evidently (It seems that) the Hansons also have a gift, that of knowing what Cézanne confessed unwillingly only to himself.

The Prime Minister evidently (It seems that the Prime Minister, The Prime Minister of course) hoped to use this support for a "hard line" foreign policy to rally Australians behind his Government . . . .

Evidently, (Clearly,) paperwork has become a national addiction, most of its victims incurably hooked.

The committee *evidently* (of course) is interested in Mr. and Mrs. Novak's business relations with Mr. Baker.

evince is one syllable shorter than *evidence*, but still not as good as *show:*

No other Republican has yet *evinced* (shown) interest in running.

It is widely believed today that it is a solemn part of one's duty as a responsible member of a democratic society (and the Kennedys have obviously given this belief a new chic) to *evince* (show) some concern for those things which used to be more or less the province of the aristocracy.

evolve is an unpleasantly formal word. Usually a simpler word will do: "In recent years various companies have *evolved* (drawn up) formal guidelines to help employes decide whether to accept or refuse Christmas gifts."

exacerbate is annoyingly long. Change it to *sharpen, make worse, aggravate, irritate, madden:*

Localism is built into Congress and is only *exacerbated* (sharpened, made worse, aggravated) by the rapid growth of the giant of national power.

In many towns it is no longer possible to ride in a taxicab without the *exacerbating* (irritating, maddening) accompaniment of the radio-transmitted directions of the central dispatcher.

The messy oil situation is more a matter of politics than

profits . . . . It was *exacerbated* (aggravated, made worse) by a Senate amendment to the 1962 foreign aid bill . . . .

Bad timing of tax reduction can nullify its impact, or even *exacerbate existing conditions* (make existing conditions worse).

This nightmare takes place in broad daylight, with us as its helpless, wide-awake victims, and the power it exercises over us derives in large part from our constant *exacerbated* (sharpened) awareness of the oddity of being able to laugh at horrors that, though outrageous, ring absolutely true and ought to be making us howl with dismay.

exact (verb) is a stiff word that can be replaced in various ways:

The role of the hero in history is not one to be *exacted of* (required from, called for from) every leader.

He *exacted* (forced) every ounce of musical juice from the Tschaikovsky, but didn't squeeze it out, or let it overflow like an open water main in the beginning.

The Washington Irving house *exacts charges of* (charges) $1 for adults and 60 cents for children.

examine. Don't use *examine* when all you mean is *look at, look over* or *check:* "*Examining* (Looking over, Checking) the faulty motor, the flyer-mechanic decided the trouble was a loose nut and bolt."

except. Don't use *with the exception of* instead of *except.*

excess. The legal phrase *in excess of* translates into normal English as *over:* "Many company officials, when questioned about their policies toward hiring Negroes referred to President Kennedy's Executive Order 10925 prohibiting discrimination against any employe or job applicant by Government contractors with contracts *in excess of* (over) $50,000."

EXCLAMATION MARKS. Once upon a time exclamation points were respectable punctuation marks, but not any more. Thanks to the advertising copywriters, they're now almost useless for emphasis and often look ridiculous:

Each month the WORKSHOP's amazing Speed Reading Course teaches you how to cut through your daily business reading in half the time—with greater comprehension and retention of facts and figures than ever before!

If, after 30 days, you do not like the hair piece we make for you . . . if you are not completely satisfied . . . you will get your money back!

Play the records on your own 33⅓ record player—and be thrilled by the exciting result! Take ten days to enjoy every record, every one of the more than 130 selections. Then, if you wish, send them back without cost or obligation!

You're trying—not buying. And you have everything to gain, nothing to lose! Mail the card today! No stamp, signature, or addressing needed.

In short, you will discover how to master the secrets that make for success in ANY field—and put them to work in your own life!

In ordinary editorial prose, exclamation marks often look quaint:

Ah, there is the fly in the ointment of this paradise!

How many misconceptions, exaggerations, and historical absurdities might be finally laid to rest!

He can write rings round anyone else in his business, but, oh, how murky, how impractical, how visionary his thinking!

"I have not abandoned hope. Period!" Sen. Mansfield said yesterday in an interview with United Press International.

execute. Don't say *execute* when you mean *sign* (a document).

exercise care. It's short and better to say *take* care: "Special care should be *exercised* (taken) to protect youth from literature and shows that may be harmful to their age."

exhibit shouldn't be used as a pompous synonym for *show:*

Her opening Bach "Toccata in E Minor" *exhibited* (showed) insight, imagination and emotional power.

The "Clorox case," in short, *exhibits* (shows) signs of becoming a cause célèbre.

existential is often used haphazardly as a fad word, vaguely hinting at the philosophy of existentialism:

Martha Lear doesn't ask any deeply embarrassing political or *existential* (ethical? metaphysical?) questions—to judge from her style, she probably doesn't have any.

The practice of politics is *an existential* (a practical?) art; it can deal only with the immediate.

"If you're an actor, you are what you are *when* you are."

Thus *existentially oriented, perhaps* (?) . . . .

expectorate is an old-fashioned euphemism for *spit*, going back to 1827. It's out of place in modern writing: "Thoreau has handed down an account of a breakfast with the Old Oysterman of Wellfleet, who in the course of the entertainment *expectorated* (spat) repeatedly into the fire, across the food which was there preparing."

expedite is an overformal word. *Speed up* is better.

expenditure is a long word for *expense* or *cost:* "Although public relations budgets may be small compared with advertising *expenditures* (expenses, costs), public relations men feel that they nonetheless can play an important role in the 'communications mix.' "

experience (verb) is a fancy long word for *feel, live through, go through, have:*

"What am I doing wrong?" parents ask when they begin to *experience* (have) trouble with their children.

During the past two weeks commercial banks in New York have *experienced* (had, felt) an exceedingly strong demand from business men for credit . . . .

Notice the kind of person who enjoys it. Then *experience* (handle, drive) the Continental yourself.

Unless a wholly unforeseen slump lies just ahead, the country is now *experiencing* (going through) the longest peace-time economic upswing on record . . . .

Belgium is another country which has been *experiencing* (having, going through) a rapid advance in the cost of living while output is soaring.

Long-term confinement with a few people is *experienced* (felt) as intensely stressful.

The deep psychological shock that we all *experienced* (felt, lived through) as a result of John F. Kennedy's murder will take long to overcome.

But for any insight into the young lady's feelings about the ordeal she *experienced* (went through), the program has nothing to say.

Then h quickly *experienced* (went through) the varying
and exaggerated emotions of a regular quarterback in the
National Football League.

Much trouble was experienced (There was much trouble)
in drafting the declaration.

You will *experience* (feel, have) greater leg room and knee
room.

expertise.   It's now a fad to say *expertise* instead of *knowledge:*
"Obviously, he says, a lot of his *expertise* (knowledge) is drawn
from experience in the inner workings of government departments."

EXPLANATIONS.   When you have to use a phrase or technical term that may be unfamiliar to your readers, it's your business to explain it. Do it simply, briefly and effectively. Use
words and ideas your readers are familiar with, but don't talk
down to them. Here are two fine examples of how it's done:

He charged that U.S. companies were "ganging up" to prevent his company from selling drugs under their generic
names in Latin America. *The generic name is the chemical
shorthand way of describing a drug. Such drugs differ in no
way from their trade name counterparts.*

To win more than $8,291, Mr. Belli had to prove that the
airline carrying the renowned pianist at the time of his
death was guilty of "willful misconduct." *Why? Because of
a 1929 treaty called the Warsaw Convention, which fixed
that sum as a limit of liability of the infant, international
airlines so that their growth would not be stunted by damage
suits.*

Don't explain more than is necessary for the purpose in hand.
In the following example the reader didn't need to be told about
the musical meaning of the word *fugue:*

He called it a "fugue state" at a bail hearing in Dallas,
where Ruby is awaiting trial as the killer of Lee Harvey
Oswald, Kennedy's accused assassin. *"Fugue" is a music
term that describes an interweaving of melodies.* Dr. Brom-
berg said that in medical parlance it is a condition when
"consciousness is suspended, people act automatically, but
are not aware of what they do or say."

Don't explain things your reader is apt to be thoroughly
familiar with:

South Vietnamese officials indicated privately that they could hardly be expected to honor such obligations, even if Mrs. Ngo Dinh Nhu's visit had been official, since in their view they were bound only by acts of the new Government that took over in Saigon two weeks ago. *In the coup in Saigon, Mrs. Ngo Dinh Nhu's husband and her brother-in-law, President Ngo Dinh Diem, died.* (This had been headline news for months.)

The actress, *who reportedly plans to marry Richard Burton, the actor,* indicated through her lawyer that she was unwilling to pay money for her divorce. (This had been headline news for years.)

See also DEFINITIONS.

explore every avenue is one of the most tired clichés. *Explore every opportunity* is no improvement: "Both were part of the same basic purpose; that is, a determination to resist encroachment and a determination to *explore* (look into, search for, take) *every opportunity* to build a durable peace."

expostulate is an old-fashioned pompous synonym for *say*. See SAID.

expound is a pompous synonym for *explain, show, spell out:* "As for his own amendment on Title VII, Mr. Cotton said that, when he presented it in the conference, Mr. Dirksen 'listened patiently while I *expounded* (explained, showed) the merits.' "

extant shouldn't be used as a highfalutin substitute for *is* or *are,* as in *"Still extant are* (There are still) people for whom reading is no more extraordinary than breathing—and just as necessary—but they are becoming rare."

extend is needlessly formal when you mean *give:*

Less than two years after formal recognition was *extended* (given) . . . .

At the same time, however, we should gradually *extend* (give) options to the Chinese for the purpose of inducing them to moderate their policies.

extended. Don't say *extended* when you mean *long,* as in "an *extended* (long) visit."

extensive. It's fashionable to say *extensive* instead of *large, wide, broad:*

In 1962, the Royal College of Physicians, in Britain, issued *an extensive* (a broad) review of the subject.

Of the fourteen new brands that the tobacco companies have introduced with *extensive* (wide) advertising and on a national scale in the last five years, very few have been taken up by the smoking public in a way that their manufacturers have considered satisfactory.

extent.   *To the extent that* is not as good as *as far as* or *so much that:*

Today was Vinson's 80th birthday. *To the extent that* (As far as) fellow lawmakers would let him, he planned to observe it routinely.

"We don't believe half a loaf is better than none. Half a loaf may spoil our appetites *to the extent that* (so much that) we won't want the other half."

extinguish.   The simple word is *put out.*

extrovert.   When the words *introvert* and *extrovert* became fashionable, people found it easier to say and write *extrovert* rather than the more correct *extravert.* By now *extrovert* (with an *o*) is the established form and the use of *extravert* (with an *a*) seems pedantic:

No actor could duplicate the exuberant frenzy of Fred Flintstone, the Stone Age *extrovert* . . . .

Novel-writing requires an extensive and *extrovert* observation.

Two *extraverted* corporate types are rivals for his ballpoint-pen scepter . . . . (The *a* in *extraverted* seems like a last-minute correction.)

eye (verb) seems a necessary evil in headlines, but shouldn't be transplanted into text matter:

"Mr. Queen?" asked a voice like temple bells, *eyeing* (looking at, considering) the Queen dishevelment doubtfully.

(For a *voice* that is *eyeing, see also* MIXED METAPHORS.)

Harold Bache, who will turn 70 in June, *eyes* (looks at, considers) the prospect for Wall Street's next 50 years with zest.

F

facilitate is a four-syllable word. Try instead *ease* or *help:* "He took up the matter of underground nuclear experiments, saying he believed that such improvements might *facilitate* (ease, help) agreement on a complete nuclear-test-ban treaty."

facilities is a long, ugly word. It crops up frequently because it can be used as a sort of all-purpose synonym for *building, plant, room, space, setup, center,* etc. The best way to avoid *facilities* is to use the specific word for whatever you're talking about:

> The Department of Public Works closed a comfort station serving Tappen Park, a neighborhood haven frequented by old folks. It cited reasons of economy. Mr. Maniscalco was outraged. He said the absence of *toilet facilities* (a comfort station) would keep the old folks away.

> The mountainous heart of Basutoland is now being opened by providing *facilities* (camps) for trips far into the Malutis. The first of the permanent camps planned . . . .

> Leaders of the industry plead for a $36 million expansion program for the City's Fashion Institute of Technology. They want to enlarge *that facility* (the institute) . . . .

> The Tottenville, S.I., project known as Daytop House had been started without sufficient education of the community and, specifically, the surrounding residential area. Despite a $390,000 grant from the National Institute of Mental Health, the future of *the facility* (Daytop House) looks bleak.

> There has been concern in New York and Washington about unemployed workers and unused *productive facilities* (plants) . . . .

> A spokesman for Columbia University said that "among the *facilities* (buildings)" for which applications are likely to be made are the Center for International Studies, the School of Social Work, a library at the Lamont Geological Observatory in Palisades, N.Y., a science auditorium, and an engineering laboratory.

> The United Nations headquarters was designd for a maximum membership of 70. Officials have had a difficult time providing additional *facilities* (room, space) in the present structures.

Furthermore, he said, only 167 care and treatment *facilities* (centers) exist in the whole country, with 105 of them small units caring for five to 50 children in residential treatment and 62 operating as day centers for 15 to 25 children each.

"I doubt it," Rogers said. "There will always be cliques, young people who don't accept the help of *structured facilities* (organizations)."

factor is the right word when you mean one of the causes contributing to a result, as in "The Mayor said three *factors* were involved in his decision." But don't use *factor* in sentences where it is unnecessary:

What about *the personal safety factor* (personal safety)? In the past, none of the exchange scholars has been arrested . . . .

The further circumstances of its being Thanksgiving Eve contributed *yet another factor of* (to the) consternation.

facts.   Some people have a prejudice against the phrase *the true facts* (or *the real facts*); facts, they say, are true by definition, so the adjective *true* is unnecessary.

I don't share that prejudice; it seems natural to me to speak of *true* or *real* facts in contrast to false facts or lies:

So what is new in my present study are *the real facts* about James's temperament and work, which in 15 years of sheer adulation have not been revealed.

The American role in the bloodstained but purgative coup d'etat in Viet Nam is a subject demanding serious inquiry, if only because so much bosh is sure to be talked about it unless *the real facts* are understood.

FAD WORDS.   A few years ago the word *charismatic* was unknown to everyone except a handful of theologians; now it appears in print every day. How come? Because of a mysterious process by which a word becomes a fad and is taken up by speakers and writers.

A few fad words become almost indispensable after a few years—*image* and *status symbol*, for instance. But most of them never reach that stage, and it's a poor idea to use them as long as they may be unfamiliar to many readers. There's always a better word to express what you mean. For examples of fad words, *see* ANXIETY, CATALYST, CHARISMATIC, DIALOGUE, EMPATHY, EUPHORIA, MYSTIQUE, POSTURE, RATIONALE, VIABLE.

fail to. "Despite eight red lights and heavy traffic on 96th St., the President's car *failed to* cause a stir." This is correct but not very idiomatic English; the normal way of saying it is "the President's car *didn't* cause a stir."

Most sentences with *fail to* can be improved by using *don't* or *didn't* instead. Some examples:

At least one profound weakness exists in two-thirds of all our institutions of higher learning. They *fail to* (don't) require students to study American history.

It is significant that Republican efforts to drag civil rights into the arena of partisan politics *failed to* (didn't) bring them victories . . . .

In releasing brief, company-furnished descriptions of the three competing designs, the FAA *failed to* (didn't) answer as many questions as it posed.

What determines the election is the number of voters who pull the lever, not the good wishes of the large number who *fail to* (don't) vote in an off-year.

America's only entry in the 67th annual race, a 1901 De-Dion owned by J. B. Nethercott, of Los Angeles, *failed to* (didn't) get started.

This *failed to* (didn't) satisfy Sen. McClellan and three other Senators who said explicitly that Mr. Gilpatric was wrong to advise Defense Secretary Robert S. McNamara on a contractor to develop TFX.

But the unbridled Lewis who cavorted so happily on "Tonight" *failed to* (didn't) emerge on ABC.

Sometimes *fail to* is canceled by another negative word and the sentence should be recast as a positive statement: *"Not a* (Every) single one of these papers that I heard or read *failed to mention* (mentioned) international suspicion."

failure. As I just showed, the phrase *fail to* should usually be replaced by *don't* or *didn't*. When the noun *failure* is used, the rewrite job gets a little more difficult; but since almost any sentence with *failure* sounds stiff and pompous, you shouldn't shirk the job:

Despite these concrete achievements, participants and outside observers at the second session have criticized *the Vatican Council's failure to move* (the Vatican Council for not having moved) decisively on measures to enhance

Christian unity and to take away a historic prop to anti-Semitism.

But (*where*) impatient Latin Americans are disappointed with the Alliance *is in its failure to* (because it didn't) provoke the social reforms it desires.

A failure by the House to act this year is possible (It is possible that the House won't act this year) even though the Administration and GOP minority leader Charles A. Halleck, Ind., have come to terms on a bipartisan civil rights bill.

Mr. Eshkol reportedly expressed bewilderment *at the U.S. failure to* (that the U.S. didn't) back an Israeli-favored resolution calling for direct Arab-Israeli talks on the issue.

The complaint raises the basic issue whether the owners of a newspaper were confronted by a situation which legally justified *their failure to consult* (them in not consulting) the union as generally required by Section 8(a)(5) of the Taft-Hartley Act.

famed is journalistic jargon; the normal word is *famous:* "Mr. Baker has hired Edward Bennett Williams, *famed* (famous) criminal attorney, as his counsel."

far be it from me is stilted and old-fashioned:

Far be it from me to (I won't) impede a public mandate (though I'm not sure this is one), but . . . .

Far be it from me to (I won't) cavil at what ladies will, or better yet, will not wear.

feel badly. Some fusspots have the notion that *feel badly* is incorrect and that the only correct form is *feel bad.* They're wrong: *feel badly* is right when you mean you're sorry and *feel bad* is right when you mean you don't fell well. Here are a couple of examples of the idiomatic use of *feel badly:*

In a final word. Mr. Dionne said, "We *feel badly* about this article . . . ."

Joseph McD. Mitchell has been expelled from the International City Managers Association—and he *feels rather badly* about it.

feline, like *canine,* should be taboo. When you mean *cats,* say *cats:*

OLDER *FELINES* (CATS)
RATED FASCINATING PETS

female (noun) is right when used for animals, but wrong when used for people:

> Our favorite character is created by Estelle Parsons, the lone *female* (woman) on hand who epitomizes the non-logical and thoroughly clinched mind.

> Book-club rolls are, to use an ungallant verb, weighted with *females* (women).

feminine shouldn't be used as a substitute word for *woman:* "The problems of being Jewish and being *feminine* (a woman) were the principal topics of two religious conventions in Chicago."

fete shouldn't be used as substitute word for *dance* or *ball:* "Just before the most recent 'April in Paris' ball, which attracted many cafe society figures, papers were served in an $88,000 lawsuit against Claudius C. Phillipe, the American French Foundation, Inc., and others connected with *the fete* (it, the ball)."

field is often unnecessary and can be left out: "During his college years at Amherst, he experimented in *(the field of)* electronics as it related to high-fidelity music systems."

FIGURES. There are few words that look as pompous as spelled-out numbers:

> At *sixty-four,* Hutchins, who was dean of the Yale Law School at *twenty-nine* and president of the University of Chicago at *thirty,* is a strikingly handsome man.

> Several people in California who were friendly to the Center wanted us to move out this way, and had to put up *ninety-five thousand dollars* in pledges to underwrite the purchase of this property. We bought it in July, 1959, for *two hundred and fifty thousand dollars.* What with fees of one kind and another, the cost of remodeling, new furniture and fixtures, and so forth, the total came to *two hundred and ninety-four thousand dollars,* which made our net cost just about *two hundred thousand.*

> The estimated value of all the property stolen by burglars in the United States last year was *a hundred and seventy-one million dollars,* of which, again going by the 1961 study, *thirty-eight* per cent was cash, *thirty* per cent was

personal property, *twenty-five* per cent was merchandise, and *seven* per cent was jewelry.

Spray pin of round and marquise diamonds, *forty nine hundred seventy five dollars*, including federal tax.

Of course these examples are exceptions. The common printers' rule is to spell out only numbers under 10 (some stylebooks say under 11) and use figures for everything beyond. This is more sensible, but often has an odd effect when numbers under 10 and over 10 are used in the same sentence:

In New York, *nine out of 10* murders are solved quickly, almost easily.

He was catapulted into his ambassadorship after *13 years as a newsman and two* as a State Department custodian of press relations . . . .

The same odd effect happens when numbers are spelled out at the beginning of a sentence that has figures in it:

Eleven laughing and joking miners trapped nearly *200* feet underground took part in their own rescue yesterday.

Twenty-five persons were feared to have died today in a fire that swept a *60-room, four-story* hotel.

Twenty-six of the last *39* kidney transplants attempted at the University of Colorado Medical Center and Denver Veterans Administration Hospital appear successful, a member of the surgical team reports.

One hundred and forty-three years after his death in Rome at the age of *25*, John Keats is more alive than ever.

Seventy-five paintings—including *34* Picassos and other works from pioneers of modern art—have been donated to the Guggenheim Museum.

The rule of spelling out numbers at the beginning of a sentence is almost universal, but I've found a few exceptions:

All the flavor, all the fragrance of top young leaves is brewed right in. *100%* pure tea!

He asked Dr. James what harm would be done with a year's delay. The reply: "*75,000* additional children with neglected teeth and another four million cavities that could have been eliminated."

The 1963 version of hell on wheels was the most fantastic in history. *84* cars began. Exactly *7* finished. *3* of the seven were Peugeots.

In the third sentence of this last example the writer used the word *exactly* to move the figure 7 away from the start of the sentence. Sometimes the phrase *a total of* is used in the same way:

> *A total of 129* miners were underground on the night of Oct. 24 when a dam burst . . . .

> *A total of 258* persons, including juveniles, adults and some students from nearby Swarthmore and Bryn Mawr College, have been arrested in demonstrations Wednesday and yesterday.

I think these artificial devices—and the whole business of spelling out figures at the beginning of a sentence and up to 10 or 11—are silly. The simplest thing to do would be to use figures for all numbers except where there's some special reason for spelling them out.

See also ROMAN NUMERALS.

finalize is jargon for *make final* or *put in final form* or *shape:* "He didn't say how, but he was 'quite sure' the appropriate program would be 'firmed up and *finalized* (put in final shape)' at the convention in the resolutions the delegates will pass."

financial is sometimes used as a coy euphemism for *money:* "Indeed, *the necessary financial arrangements for them are often lacking* (there often isn't enough money)."

fine. *In fine* is an old-fashioned, formal phrase: *"In fine* (In short), Mr. Kahn stands out as a man of illimitable action."

first . . . second. These two words are sometimes used in the same way as *former* and *latter*. Both style devices are awkward and force the reader to look back to see which noun was first and which was second. Instead of using *first* and *second*, repeat the two nouns: "Beyond non-violence lies only a choice of surrender or violence, and there is no reason to believe that the Negro resistance would accept *the first* (surrender) without having a fling at *the second* (violence)."

flame shouldn't be used coyly to mean *lover*, as in "She's just been cast as the heroine of a movie in which one of her leading men is her former lover, and another is her current *flame* (one)."

flay is a headline word that shouldn't be dragged into ordinary prose: "At a press conference, Rockefeller *flayed* (criticized, attacked) Goldwater . . . .

fled. The past participle *fled* is now too quaint for conversational use; people usually say *ran* or *escaped*. Do the same in writing:

> When the train pulled into a station they bolted for the side doors and *fled* (ran) onto the platform.

> The ballet star *fled* (escaped) to the West two years ago.

foe is obsolete; use *enemy:*

> ### HIGH COURT PLEA IS LOST BY *FOES* (ENEMIES) OF TRADE CENTER

> Mohammed Boudiaf, one of President Ahmed Ben Bella's chief *foes* (enemies), was released from prison last night.

> Stress is usually defined as man's *foe* (enemy), but in many ways stress is essential if an individual is to lead a rich, full and productive life.

following. Don't use *following* as a preposition; say *after:*

> The United States and Argentina appear to be on an economic collision course *following* (after) the failure of U.S. Under Secretary of State W. Averell Harriman's mission to save American oil contracts.

> The Federal Housing Administration has held off enactment of a new regulation on home improvement work for a second time, *following* (after) protests by financial institutions . . . .

> As the members of the executive council left the pseudo-French Regency room of the Americana *following* (after) a two-hour meeting . . . .

> Fulton Lewis Jr. and George Hamilton Combs, commentators for the Mutual Broadcasting System, were back on New York's WOR last night *following* (after) a one-day blackout.

for is one of the most common prepositions in the English language, but when it's used as a conjunction, it sounds stiff and formal. The best thing is to leave it out (and perhaps replace the period by a colon):

> The result is a staggering blow for Britain's new Prime Minister Sir Alec Douglas-Home. *For as* (As) the influential Guardian pointed out the following morning, if the Tories cannot hold such seats as Luton, their prospects of winning a general election are slim indeed.

Watson's tight timetable varied little from his normal workaday schedule or, for that matter, the normal schedules maintained by many another top executive. *For as* (As) masters of vast corporate empires which transcend political and social boundaries to reach into all facets of American society, their spheres of influence stretch beyond the board room into everything from government to the arts, from education to charities.

There's also a use of the preposition *for* with an infinitive verb form that sometimes makes a long sentence puzzling and hard to read:

The truth is that *for* either the Administration Democrats or the Republicans *to seek* to undermine the other by putting new civil rights legislation on the chopping block of partisanship-for-its-own-sake was so riskful and reckless that both had to turn from it. (The only way to improve this sentence would be by rewriting it from scratch.)

For a painting *to be seen* as emerging from a web of imagination brought into being by many minds, including those of non-painters (one recalls the influence of Mallarmé on Cézanne and of Éluard on Miró), apparently compromises its status as an evidence of creative uniqueness. (This sentence too can be improved only by a complete rewrite job.)

foregoing is a word that smells of musty legal documents. Say *this* or *these:*

Bearing *the foregoing* (these) general propositions in mind, in our policy toward China . . . .

The foregoing (This) line of thought may have been influential in Mr. Coolidge's announcement not long afterwards that he didn't "choose to run" for re-election in 1928.

It should not be concluded from *the foregoing* (this) that the theater in our time is an unrewarding or an unnecessary experience.

FOREIGN WORDS. It's a good style rule to avoid foreign words—they cause nothing but trouble with their spelling, pronunciation, case endings, gender endings, plurals and all kinds of other exotic fine points. There's almost always an English word that'll do the job just as well or better. Even if there doesn't seem to be an English word for what you want to say, think twice before you use a foreign word—your reader may never have heard of it and be puzzled without a definition.

See also FRENCH WORDS, GERMAN WORDS, ITALIAN WORDS, LATIN PHRASES, LATIN PLURALS.

forgather shouldn't be used archly or humorously: "The restaurant is the only place we know of in town that today serves this great dish, which could once be ordered wherever serious epicures *forgathered* (met, got together)."

former . . . latter. Avoid this awkward style device; it's easier on the reader if you simply repeat the nouns:

Assuming that public funds are given to both the public schools and the parochial schools, is it fair that all— Catholic and non-Catholic alike—can have a say in the running of *the former* (the public schools), but that no non-Catholic at all can have a say in the running of *the latter* (the parochial schools)?

We do not expect professional football to replace baseball as the national pastime at an early date. But we do insist *the former* (football) will not really come of age, so to speak, or hit the peak of its potential as a mature addition to the American athletic scene until the two leagues get together for one giant playoff. (This example is particularly bad because the reader keeps waiting for *the latter* and it never comes.)

See also LATTER.

forth is obsolete and has no place in a modern sentence (except for *back and forth*): "But the alarum went *forth* (out), and preservation groups got into action."

forthcoming. It's always simpler to say *coming*: "Mr. Johnson told of Mr. Heller's *forthcoming* (coming) departure in urging passage of legislation increasing salaries of top-level government officials."

forthwith is also obsolete; use *immediately* or *right away*.

fortuitous is a long, awkward word meaning *by chance;* but most people nowadays use it with the mistaken notion that it means *fortunate:*

But to get back to that *fortuitous* (fortunate) location: in no other place on earth could a lively promoter find so many suckers . . . .

His movements were pure 18th-Century, and his *fortuitous* (fortunate) good looks, straight out of the period.

forward (verb) is not as good a word as *send*.

fourthly, like *secondly* and *thirdly*, doesn't need the *-ly:* "Fourthly (Fourth), the European nations, collectively, would have a greater share in the system of deterrence by means of the mixed naval force than through present arrangements."

fraught with is now unfit for serious use:

A Harvard psychiatrist described student sexual behavior as *fraught with* (full of, beset by) "neutrality, avoidance, pretense, anxiety, and an enormous complexity of ignorance."

On February 20th, having studied the briefs and deliberated on them, Judge Harvey delivered his decision, in the form of a nine-page essay *fraught with* (filled with) suspense.

FRENCH WORDS. Don't be a snob; don't infuriate your readers by casually using French words and phrases. It's always better to say it in English; if you use French, you're apt to misuse the French word, put the wrong ending on it, misspell it—or just annoy your reader. (Even those of them who understand French will resent your snobbishness.)

Here are some choice examples from my collection:

Whereas the Stevenson story moves with a kind of Victorian *ampleur*, Thomas' adaptation is crisp, swift and tensile. (Why not *amplitude?*)

Mr. Liebling was born Abbott Joseph Liebling in 1904 into a well-to-do *haute bourgeois* household at 93rd St. and Lexington Ave. (It isn't *haute bourgeois*, it's *haut bourgeois;* anyway, *upper-middle-class* would have been better.)

The tax cut will surely stimulate the economy; and hence the sooner it became a legislative *fait accompli*, the earlier this effect would occur. (What's wrong with *the sooner it became law?*)

Gide in his own way explores in his works the morality of self-realization and *disponibilité.* (Meaning what?)

Though cricket, school and war years seem somehow *déjà vu*, the story suddenly comes to vivid life when Mr. Waugh gets to his writing . . . . (The psychological term *déjà vu* doesn't belong here; what the writer meant was that *cricket, school and war years have been done before.*)

Whether the lady is a Bovary or, as she puts it, "a bitch," or the man a *nouveau-vague* Casanova or the last of the romantics is neither suggested nor defined . . . . (It isn't *nouveau vague,* it's *nouvelle vague;* in English, it's *new wave.*)

He is what the French call a *"mauvais coucheur,"* as many poets are, simply from excess of sensibility. (*Mauvais coucheur* means *poor sleeper.* Does that mean someone who lies awake nights worrying about the state of the world? The writer doesn't say.)

To take the chill off *après*-swim, there is always the all-encompassing shift. (Is *après*-swim supposed to be more elegant than *after swimming?*)

In most instances, the author is either the person who functioned as *éminence gris* in the formation of the collection —or is a local museum specialist in the field of the collection. (It isn't *éminence gris,* it's *éminence grise;* in English, it's *gray eminence.*)

In adapting Carson McCullers' short novel to the stage, Edward Albee has resorted to a narrator, a *conferencier* who is frequently and somewhat loftily present . . . . (Why call him a *conferencier?* Why not *master of ceremonies* or *emcee?*)

Naturally, he would have to go about choosing the writer as carefully as he would any other investment, and if he picked a lemon—*tant pis.* (Or, as we say in English, *that's just too bad.*)

Let the West recover its civilized and humane impulses; let it eschew ideology and violence; . . . let it draw back, above all, *pas trop de zêle.* (Sure, Talleyrand said this in French; but why not tell American readers that he meant *not too much zeal?*)

I'd like Miss MacInnes even better if she had more concision; as a vintage, she's a bit too *moëlleux* for me, fruity rather than dry. A question of taste, I suppose. (*Moëlleux* has something to do with bone marrow and seems to be a wine connoisseur's term. How snobbish can you get?)

See also BÊTE NOIRE.

frequency is a heavy word that's often unnecessary: "The question being heard *with increasing frequency* (more and more often) here is: why?"

fret sounds old-fashioned in sentences like this: "Man-on-the-sidewalk interviews have shown that the people's serenity in Westchester is not easily *fretted* (disturbed)."

fruition is a pompous word that's almost always misused. People think it means *harvesting* or *bearing fruit,* but actually it means *enjoyment.* Better stay away from it: "Mr. Kennedy tried to *bring to fruition* (harvest the fruits of) seeds planted both by Lincoln and Roosevelt."

fulsome is another pompous word continually misused. It means *disgustingly overdone,* but most people use it as a more impressive synonym for *full* or *big:* "Here in the United States, where we tend to do everything rather more *fulsomely* (fully, thoroughly) than in other countries, we indulge our children correspondingly more."

function (verb) is abused as a scientific-sounding synonym for *work:* "If an individual *functions* (works, lives, acts) below his stress end-point, he does not realize his true potentials and enjoy the great therapeutic satisfaction of accomplishment."

fundamental is a long word; *real* or *basic* is shorter: "There is no *fundamental* (real, basic) opposition in committee or in the House itself to the legislation."

furthermore is a heavy conjunction used mostly to staple the last sentence in a paragraph to the preceding one. It's better and makes for easier reading if you use *also* or join the sentences together without any conjunction at all. Two examples:

> . . . Much of the radiation emitted by the stars and planets is absorbed in the earth's atmosphere. *Furthermore, the* (Also, the; The) turbulence and dust in the atmosphere distorts the picture that is finally received on earth.

> The blunt truth is that some of the Democratic Left is displeased and unhappy. But they have no place to go in the Presidential election except to Johnson's side. Thus, the President is taking little political risk by moving fiscally to the political center. *Furthermore, he* (Also, he; He) is so ardently championing anti-poverty welfare programs and civil rights that much of the sting is removed from his economies.

See also MOREOVER.

FUSED PARTICIPLES. *See* -ING.

future date is jargon. Avoid it: "There is talk of bringing it in *at some future date* (sometime), but there is always such talk."

G

gainfully employed is a pompous cliché. Say *working:*

Ballantine traveled all over the country in search of horses still *gainfully employed* (working).

She understudied Barbara Bel Geddes in *Mary, Mary.* While *gainfully employed* (working) in the latter, she rose from a sickbed to audition . . . .

gainsay is old-fashioned English for *deny: "There is no gain-saying* (No one can deny) that the American edition of the British satirical show represented an important turning point for network TV."

galore is decoratively Irish, but the normal English word is *lots of:*

There are *issues galore* (lots of issues) between Rockefeller and Sen. Goldwater.

Amendments galore (Lots of amendments) will be offered to each bill.

There are *footnotes galore* (lots of footnotes) in Herbert Weinstock's biography of Gaetano Donizetti . . . .

garb is one of those fake-humorous words that should be taboo:

Western *garb* (dress, getup) predominates at the rodeo . . . .

His new comrades marvel at his strange *garb* (dress, getup) and his horrible stories . . . .

GENERAL WORDS. It's a basic rule of writing to use always the most specific word for whatever you're talking about. But in their frantic search for synonyms, writers often switch from the specific word to the general. They should have the courage to repeat the specific word:

"Espionage" opened last night on the network of the National Broadcasting Company and its producer is Herbert Brodkin, who also *prepares* (produces) "The Defenders."

Half a dozen young men and women distributed leaflets before the doors of the Museum on Hofmann's opening night. Signed The Center, these *communications* (leaflets) saluted Hofmann . . . .

In the years between two world wars, Veterans' Day was

known as Armistice Day . . . . The name of the day was subsequently changed so that the tribute would embrace those who perished in the second *conflict* (war).

The Krebiozen controversy would have been settled years ago except for Sen. Douglas' vociferous backing of the *compound* (drug).

On the theory that viewers may not have read everything in their papers and that the *publications* (papers) themselves may have missed a few salient points . . . N.B.C. has put together a pastiche of news . . . .

See also SYNONYMS.

generic is overused in the sense of *typical* or *characteristic*. Sometimes this leads to the mistake of saying *generic to* instead of *generic of:* "The inevitable too-much-of-a-good-thing is in large part *generic to* (typical of) Cinerama, which apparently has to give both audience and producers a long run for their money."

genesis is much too Biblical a word to use casually when you mean *source* or *beginning:*

Granted that the *genesis* (source) of all this is Thornton Wilder . . . .

This is an open manifestation of extremism on both sides that is the *genesis* (source, beginning) of our own self-destruction if we are ever going to be destroyed.

GERMAN WORDS. Like FOREIGN WORDS in general and FRENCH WORDS in particular, German words shouldn't be used snobbishly to show off your knowledge. There's always a way of saying it in English:

His account of 25 years of friendship deserves to be put beside Eckermann, with the advantage on its side that, if Santayana was not quite Goethe, Mr. Cory is a more interesting, and a much more amusing, disciple than the author of the *"Gespräche"* ("Conversations").

He is not one of those doormen who seize upon you with their low-floating eyeballs and make you listen to some sort of prole *Weltanschauung* (philosophy) about what a big operator you have to be to get by in New York.

In these two examples the German words are at least used properly and spelled right. But most often the German that appears in the midst of English is miserably wrong:

WHITHER *BURGOMEISTER* (BÜRGERMEISTER) BRANDT?

(The word *burgomeister* is neither German nor English.)

His several lectures on the U.S. moon program were in such German-accented English that even Argentines who *hablan inglés* could hardly a word *begreifen* (verstehen). (The German word *begreifen* means *conceive* rather than *understand*.)

German also has the baffling feature that its articles are different for different cases and genders. So when you translate *the* as *der*, chances are you're quite wrong:

When *"Der* (Die) Olympischen Winterspiele" was awarded to the happy burghers of Innsbruck . . . .

Through pressure in their Christian Democratic Union he forced *"Der Alte"* ("Den Alten") to keep mum.

Of course you can't be expected to know these fine points of German. But what you *can* do is stay off it.

germane is a formal, academic word meaning *relevant*. It is sometimes used snobbishly: "Miss Tureck knows how to make Bach *germane to* (right for) the piano and the piano *germane to* (right for) Bach."

GERUND. *See* -ING.

gestalt is a German word meaning *shape*. It is used in psychology as a technical term for *general configuration*, and shouldn't be loosely bandied about like this: "Fielding Dawson's poetry can give a nice feeling of (*the Gestalt of*) disassociation."

get. *See* BECOME.

gimmick is listed in the dictionaries as slang. As far as I can see, it has long since graduated into standard English:

When is a *gimmick* a sound merchandising idea?

Except for a few *gimmicks*, the Javits committee program proposed nothing new.

given sounds annoyingly pompous when used as a preposition instead of *in, with, under, what with*:

He was able to get every Democrat to vote against McCarthy, and that was no easy job *given* (in) the climate of the times.

Given (In) the framework of understatement and refinement, Miss Kraus quite naturally avoided angularity of phrase and brittleness of tone . . . .

Given (With) sound psychological health, a start towards moral maturity and valid self-respect, one simply doesn't feel personally insulted by another's bad manners.

Given (With) their special power, the chairmen of Ways and Means and Finance are clearly the most advantageous Hill contacts—both for the lobbyist and his client.

Consequently, while he and his associates go on talking publicly about the progress they have made, privately they are beginning to fear that, *given* (under) the existing form of American society and the existing balance of political power, the evils they complain about simply cannot be remedied.

A debate has started in France on the merits of the new French Constitution, and, *given* (what with) de Gaulle's waspish remarks about the American Constitution, I don't see why an American can't join it.

goes without saying is a silly idiom. It's better to say *naturally* or *of course,* or simply to leave it out:

Pointing the finger at Mansfield, or Celler, is apparently intended to absolve the White House, especially the President and his young untrained associates, from any responsibility for the present stalemate. *That they are frustrated and worried by the 1964 implications of the voters' rebellion in Texas and other parts of the country goes without saying.* (Naturally they are . . . . ; Of course they are . . . .)

It goes without saying that one must (One must) check and double-check flights when they are made as far in advance as mine were. *It also goes without saying that one should* (One should) have plenty of travelers' checks, letters of credit or actual currency.

As goes without saying, writers who worry (Writers who worry) about getting the facts straight usually choose subjects other than Life or the Modern World.

good is sometimes wrongly used instead of *well:* "Or it is for other reasons, such as unavailability of the stage performer, or the fact that the stage performer doesn't photograph *good* (well) enough."

gotten is good American English:

> 20th Century-Fox will bring "Cleopatra" to cities that ordinarily would not have *gotten* the film . . . .

> "We could have *gotten* a lot more if we had had time," said one of the organizers.

graduate. It's old-fashioned to say *he was graduated;* leave out *was:*

> Born in Sedalia, Mo., he (*was*) graduated from Franklin College in Indiana.

> She (*was*) graduated third in the class, with a 94 average, and went on to the University of Texas.

> He had (*been*) graduated from the Christian Brothers' La Salle School in Panama City.

gratefully is sometimes misused to refer to the writer himself rather than the subject of the sentence: "Since the program is intended for the television audience only, there is no studio audience and, *gratefully* (I'm glad, thank God), no canned laughter or applause."

See also HOPEFULLY, REGRETFULLY, THANKFULLY.

gravamen is a pompous Latin word. Say *burden* or *gist:* "The *gravamen* (gist) of the play is that the Pope was wanting as God's vicar on earth when he failed to denounce the Nazi extermination of the Jews in the hideous death factories."

grounds. *Because* is simpler than *on the grounds that.*

guts is listed in the dictionaries as slang. But there's nothing slangy about its current wide use:

> Powers has, in his recent past, put together a 114-day newspaper strike which made him a national figure of unlimited *guts.*

> A good woman is one who loves passionately, has *guts,* seriousness and passionate convictions, takes responsibility and shapes society.

H

habituate (verb) is a long awkward word for *frequent* or *go to:*

" 'I'm involved and I get a kick out of it,' says George N. Gee, a tape watcher who *habituates* (frequents, goes to) Walston & Co.'s 74 Wall St. office."

had better. *See* BETTER.

halcyon days is an ancient cliché; *happy* or *serene days* sounds better.

hapless is an antique sometimes revived in sports writing: "Pittsburgh's Paul Martha and Fred Mazurek, running inside, running outside, but always running handsomely, collaborated to maul Army, 28-0, at Pitt Stadium yesterday, racking up more points, more yards and more humiliation than the *hapless* (unlucky) Cadets have endured this season."

harbinger is a bookish word; use *sign* or *omen:*

Former Gov. Wesley Powell, a proved *harbinger* (sign, omen) of coming trouble, announced he would run as a favorite-son candidate for the Republican nomination for President.

To me anyhow, Ormsby Gore seems less a sport than a *harbinger* (sign, omen) of the future, less an aberration than the prime example of the new model diplomat.

harken (also spelled **hearken**) is obsolete; say *listen:*

Hearken (Listen) to the sound of great world literature . . . read in the mother languages.

When she finally did scale her bonnet into the Presidential ring, after giving all the reasons for refusing to run, it came with such stunning feminine illogic that the audience sat silent for a moment and *harkened* (listened), in befuddlement, to the words . . . .

have. Don't use the perfect tense of a verb (the one with *have*) to refer to something that happened—or didn't happen—at a specific moment or period in the past:

Hasn't he missed (Didn't he miss) her basic point stated in her first paragraph?

The war in Vietnam is not going as well as our officials pretend (it never *has* [did]), but the truce in the cold war is
holding in Korea . . . .

The other way round, don't use the past tense (without
have) when you refer to something that has been going on for
some time and is still going on:

Nobody who *knew him* [has known him] (in the odd way he
lets anyone get to know him) for some years, especially his
advisers, was at all surprised last week when Carmine De
Sapio marched into court in the hope that when his case
comes up he would be granted a re-run of the election for
Greenwich Village district leader.

The perfect infinitive with *have* is also often used where the
simple present infinitive would be enough:

Had Mr. Brown taken the time to make so much as a telephone call to my office or even to *have conferred* (confer)
with Assemblyman Thomas R. Jones of Brooklyn, he would
not have made a statement that . . . .

Hamlet is played by Richard Burton as Hamlet would have
liked to *have been* (be)—masterly, heroic, and never self-
doubting.

He. It's traditional to capitalize a pronoun referring to God,
the Lord, etc., but it's not traditional to overdo this. There's no
point in capitalizing *he* when the reference to *God* in the same
sentence is perfectly clear; nor should *who* or *whose* ever be
capitalized:

He is a man who has obeyed God's commands as though
there were a bargain between them, God's part of the bargain being that *He* (he) would thereafter put no obstacles
between Lot and saintliness.

Does God need a memorial to be built to *Him* (him) in
Washington?

The historic Jewish reaction to Jesus ranges from complete
disregard to a belief that *He* (he) was one of the great
moral teachers of mankind.

First, to brace ourselves for the problem of the relationship
strained by indifference, take a look at it when God's in
His (his) heaven, the stars rejoice and the cash register
whistles while it works.

The perfect gift is one that you give to Him *Whose* (whose)
birthday it is.

hegira, a word few people know or can pronounce properly (it's heJIra or HEJra), refers to Mohammed's flight from Mecca to Medina in 622. Don't use it casually when you mean *flight:* "For most of the century that followed this wholesale *hegira* (flight), the people of Tristan became more and more cut off from the outside world."

hence is shorter than *therefore,* but more bookish:

> Nathan Glazer and Daniel Moynihan, authors of "Beyond the Melting Pot," are writers of this kind, *hence* (therefore, and) embarrassed by the size of their subject . . . .

> Like most successful Wall Streeters, he relies mainly on blue chips. *Hence* (Therefore, And) a periodic visit to Barney's when he's in the market for clothing.

> The results, he believed, clearly showed that air pollution was far less of a factor in producing bronchitis than smoking. *Hence* (Therefore, From that) he argued that it was "inefficient" to embark on a bronchitis control plan "which does not attack the practice of cigarette smoking first."

Hence should also be replaced when it means *from now:*

> The time is several centuries *hence* (from now) and such things are possible.

> Nor is there any mystery as to why Paris and Peking are resuming relations now, rather than a year ago or a year *hence* (from now).

henceforth is stilted; say *from now on:*

> The pirates aren't being put out of business, I gathered, but their activities will *henceforth* (from now on) be confined to the island.

> Now that the part is finished, Huston has vowed that *henceforth* (from now on) he will stick to directing.

her. *See* HIM, ME, THAN, US.

herald (verb) is a medieval word meaning *announce.* It doesn't mean *foresee,* as in the headline "AMA *HERALDS* LEUKEMIA VACCINE," which was followed by this lead sentence: "A vaccine to prevent leukemia was foreseen today by the Journal of the American Medical Association." Moral: when you're tempted to say *herald,* say *announce.*

hereabouts shouldn't be used coyly like this:

> "110 in the Shade" is a musical adaptation of the play called

"The Rainmaker," which was produced *hereabouts* (here) a few years ago.

In case you have forgotten, "Dialogues des Carmélites" is Poulenc's last opera, and was first heard *hereabouts* (here) several years ago . . . .

hereafter is legal-sounding English for *from now on:* "He proposed that *hereafter* (from now on) the committee be instructed to study the qualifications of regions seeking independence."

hereby is extremely formal. Say *now.*

herein means exactly the same as the shorter word *here:*

A partial answer to this query is afforded by the monograph reviewed *herein* (here), dealing with German law on the subject.

Another professional, *herein* (here) identified as Miss B, mused over her curious acquaintance with a key executive of a defense contractor . . . .

hereinafter, even in legal documents, should be changed to *after this:* " 'It's a Mad, Mad, Mad, Mad World' (to be referred to *hereinafter* (after this) as 'Mad') is a comedy spectacular . . . .''

heretofore is stilted; say *up to now* or *until now:* "The whole educational system *heretofore* (up to now, until now) has been operated on a local basis."

herewith has no place in ordinary writing. Say *with this, now,* or leave out. *Enclosed herewith* means *enclosed.*

hiatus is a fad word. Use *interval, gap* or *pause:*

During the recent *hiatus* (interval) Mr. Baker returned to work in his downtown office.

This is currently best being demonstrated in the case of Franco-British relations, which, after a nine-and-a-half-month *hiatus* (interval) since the French barred British entry into the Common Market, have suddenly turned from sour to sweet . . . .

Suddenly, this week, after the fortnight of frenetic activity in the galleries of New York that followed the holiday *hiatus* (interval), everybody paused, as if to catch his breath.

Three ideas have come before the Senate subcommittee on Presidential succession as to how the country can get around the power *hiatus* (gap) that exists when a Vice-President moves up to President.

hid, the past tense of *hide,* sounds archaic. Change it to *concealed:* "One cook, for example, had memorized the first letter of each item on the menu, and thus *hid* (concealed) his illiteracy."

hierarchy shouldn't be used snobbishly like this: "We're the client (one of the real excitement-makers in the business) and we're taking all the bull by the horns and creating our own *top echelon creative hierarchy* [advertising department], where salaries range from stimulating to distinguished to dazzling."

him. In idiomatic English, *he* is changed to *him* when the pronoun is stressed at the end of a sentence:

I daresay it was only natural people should think it was *him.*

Sammy Cahn's song-writing inspiration now is shapely Marlyn Chase, lucky *him!*

I earn a good deal more than *him.*

See also HER, ME, THAN, US.

historic or **historical?** *Historic* means *memorable* or *important; historical* simply means *of history.* The two words are often confused:

TEST BAN TREATY 'YES' IN *HISTORICAL* (HISTORIC) SETTING

In general "Leopard" is too vague and pointless in its story —based on *historic* (historical) fact—of the social upheaval a century ago when Garibaldi was on the march against the enemies of Italy . . . .

hitherto is old-fashioned English for *until now, up to now* or *until then:*

Where controversies have *hitherto* (until now) not existed, he whistles them up.

It is all very frightening to a girl who has *hitherto* (until now) led a sheltered life.

Though it is human to cling to a superior place, we must recognize Europe has recovered and enjoys a freedom of action *hitherto denied it* (denied it until now).

There is hardly a chapter which does not throw some light,

often of very small candle power, on some *hitherto* (up to now) shadowy recess of Shakespeare's life and mind.

The furious Tar Derby reached its climax in 1960, when the Federal Trade Commission, which *hitherto* (until then) had had little success in trying to get the tobacco manufacturers to moderate their claims for filter cigarettes, put its foot down . . . .

homemaker is a silly euphemism for *housewife*.

hopefully is misused in this type of sentence: "The NIMH already has granted $15,000 for planning of the full program, which *hopefully* will start next September." Literally this means that the program will start next September full of hope; but what the writer meant was that the *planners* of the program were hoping *now* it would start next September.

Instead of saying *hopefully* in this kind of sentence, spell out who is doing the hoping—*I hope, we hope, they hope:*

The Metropolitan Opera will present its New York première in the grand manner that the composer intended—*hopefully* (I hope) with a well-doctored libretto and score.

U.S. surgeons had a hot time over a cool, cool question: Is it a good thing to freeze the human stomach to suppress the nagging pain of a duodenal ulcer and—*hopefully* (they hope)—to heal the ulcer?

For the breadwinner who wants to save tax money now on what—*hopefully* (he hopes)—will happen next year, the strategy is . . . .

How can we help young people get an education which will certainly prepare them for life and, *hopefully* (we hope), might also prepare them for college or some form of advanced study?

See also GRATEFULLY, REGRETFULLY, THANKFULLY.

hospitalize is now used far more often than *take to a hospital* or *put into a hospital,* but these older phrases sound better: "He was *hospitalized* (taken to a hospital) in a state of severe shock . . . ."

host shouldn't be used as a pompous synonym for *many:*

Meantime, *a host of* (many) second-echelon Kennedy measures remain unpassed, stalled mostly in the House.

This book will be opened with keen and sympathetic interest by *a host of* (many) former students of Arthur M. Schlesinger at Ohio State University, the University of Iowa and Harvard, and by *an equal host* (just as many) of those who count him among their friends and advisers.

In another sense, a *host* means someone entertaining guests at his home; but more often than not nowadays, a *host* is a professional entertainer emceeing a TV show. This has led to the paradox of the *guest host:* "Bob Cummings will be *guest host* of ABC's new "Hollywood Palace" variety show on Jan. 11."

host (verb) is journalese for *be the host of:*

President Kennedy will *host* (be the host at) a White House luncheon for 45 members of Hollywood's hierarchy . . . .

Cyanamid has *hosted* (been the host at) over 200 visits by local school and college groups to its Central Research Laboratories . . . .

hostelry shouldn't be used as an arch synonym for *hotel:*

On a subsequent evening at a dinner in another celebrated *hostelry* (hotel), watercress and tomato appeared with the first course.

Janet Blair is really lighting up the Empire Room at the Waldorf these nights with some of the brightest and most lilting singing I've heard in that old *hostelry* (hotel) in many a year.

how come is frowned upon by some dictionaries, but it's an almost indispensable idiom in sentences like this: "Well, then, SCI counsel Carl A. Vergari inquired, *how come* Internal Revenue Service agents flushed three bookies out of the joint, which kept its door 'closed' even for regular customers, and booked them for not having the required $50 Federal gambling stamps last December?"

howbeit. *See* ALBEIT.

however is usually put between commas, but there's a growing trend to dispense with those commas and speed up reading. Some examples of comma-less *however* sentences:

TIME *however* is a weekly report of the news.

That does not mean *however* that he is unwilling to give reason and diplomacy their full scope in trying to reduce the burden of fear in world affairs . . . .

She documents her cases, too. *However* it is not the factual history that makes the book a delight to connoisseurs of polemics; it is the barbed phrase with which she harpoons victims.

hubris is a literary fad word, meaning the kind of arrogant pride that's apt to bring on tragedy. Better stick to *arrogance:* "No visitor can talk long to him about government without hearing him say, 'There is no problem that cannot be solved.' That, of course, is the particular *hubris* (arrogance) of our American century."

hue shouldn't be used to mean *color:* "Creamy Orlon cardigan newly *hued* (colored) in soft winter pastels."

humans. English has no single word for *human being*. Since such a word is obviously needed, people made one up by changing the adjective *human* into a noun. This usage is now fully established:

> What tracks need is not a better grade of horses, but a better grade of *humans*.

> It was a case of noblesse oblige on the part of the eagle, for one swipe of its stone wings could have knocked over a score of puny *humans*.

> Dr. Jacob declined to say to what extent the compound had been tried in *humans*.

> They taught that Jew and pagan were equal *humans*.

> Arguing that accidents are bred by the nature of the automobile in a mechanized society run by *humans* liable to err, Justice Hofstadter believes it unjust that an injured party should be denied compensation because some slight fault of his own may have helped cause the accident.

HYPHENS give you a chance to play around with the language and invent some nice combinations of words. Like these examples, for instance:

> An ace trial lawyer fights through to victory after the customary initial *aw-shucks-not-another-case* gambit.

> This is *pipe-and-slippers* history.

> The style throughout is what may be described as *early-business-letter* English.

> Among Indian politicians, few offer better examples of what Americans know as the *barefoot-boy-born-in-a-log-cabin* credentials . . . .

The "*it-must-have-cost-a-fortune* look" . . . .

The campaign has boiled down to "*we-can-do-a-better-job-than-you*" contentions.

No one can be surprised if Nixon lacks active, *from-the-word-go* support in Gov. Rockefeller's state.

But despite the awkward ambidexterity—the sustained *on-the-one-hand-and-on-the-other-handedness*—a few vague themes do appear.

She dreamed up treasure hunts, *come-as-somebody-else* parties, *come-as-the-person-you-like-best-or-least* parties—anything to keep things moving.

But these imaginative uses of hyphens are rare. What's far more common is the ugly abuse of hyphens to stuff extra information into the nooks and crannies of a sentence:

In the *Chinese-dominated* town of Sibu, the *Red-infiltrated* Sarawak United People's Party (SUPP) staged a demonstration that turned into a *90-minute, stone-throwing* riot.

RED-LEANING CAMBODIA
RENOUNCES ALL U.S. AID

Mrs. Kennedy came out of her *health-enforced* retirement last week at the White House . . . .

He said he assured Mr. Johnson the *Kennedy-sought* (and now *Johnson-sought*) $11 billion tax-cut would be approved by the *conservative-led* committee early in 1964.

And then there are hyphenated words that are just plain ugly and should never have been formed:

Is *cash-rich,* blue-chip Campbell Soup Co. . . . looking for a major acquisition or a merger?

His chapters on adolescents are the most stunningly perceptive analyses of the *much-scapegoated* group that I have yet seen.

I

I. Paradoxically, any word used instead of the personal pronoun *I* sounds more pompous than *I* itself:

If there has ever been a more joyous performance of Mahler's "Ich atmet' einen Lindenduft," or a more hackleraising one of the Brahms "Mainacht," the news has escaped *this writer* (me) completely.

In a Herald Tribune preview Sept. 16, *this writer* (I) called the program a "milestone in film journalism" and "an extraordinary personal experience."

Only a few weeks ago, when *this reporter* (I) was in Hong Kong, the China-watchers there still believed that 1963 would again see another slow rise in farm output on the Communist mainland.

Responding to an elusive compulsion, *this correspondent* (I) found *himself* (myself) shortly after 6 last evening in a hotel room where Sen. Barry Goldwater was holding a news conference . . . .

A more impressive performance of any Beethoven symphony has seldom, if ever, come *your correspondent's* (my) way.

This observer, admittedly (Though admittedly) an old Amblerian and Buchanite, *finds himself* (I find myself) obliged to turn in a minority report on "the Ipcress File" . . . .

To *this department* (me) one of the mysteries in the process of Congressional supply of funds and fund authorizations to the Executive concerns the appropriations that lie unexpended at the end of a fiscal year.

For *this corner* (me), the consistently high expectations led only to a series of let-downs, except for the magnificence of the performance of Doro Merande . . . .

To *the chronically comparative eye* (me), once *it gets* (I get) off onto this tack, the upward curl of the dune can even suggest Hokusai's "Great Wave."

What impresses *this column* (me) are the extraordinary and almost abject concessions the Administration makes to scornful business . . . .

A viewer in particular could have (I had) hoped that "T.W. T.W.T.W." would have instituted a moratorium on jokes about President Kennedy and his daughter Caroline.

In this last of his reviews for this page, a reviewer is (In this last review for this page, I am) happy to concur in that opinion of "Vanity Fair" and thus to ring down the curtain . . . .

See also IT, ONE, WE, YOU.

I don't think. Some people object to the idiom *I don't think* as used for instance in this sentence: "*I don't think* any white man knows what it's like, the life of a Negro." It's true that this is illogical and really means "*I think no* white man knows . . . ." But the English language doesn't care about logic and people use the handy idiom *I don't think* constantly:

> *I don't think* the sins of Diem and Nhu form adequate justification.

> *We don't think* outside lawyers can do anything we can't do.

> He said *he didn't think* it was "physically possible" to reach the window by firing from the train.

> Hearings have been held every day and *I don't think* there has been any connection whatever with respect to the civil rights.

This idiom also appears in other forms: " '*I have never been abroad* when American prestige was lower than it is now,' Mr. Nixon said at Idlewild Airport."

-ial. It's tempting to form an adjective in *-ial* or *-ical* rather than use a noun phrase, but it makes for heavy writing. Here's an example where the writer used the rare word *oratorial* rather than the more common form *oratorical.* He should have used the noun *orator:* "He has demonstrated his *oratorial* ability (ability as an orator) with zest in UN session."

-ian shouldn't be used to form rare or new long words—like *obituarian,* which can't be found in Webster's Unabridged:

"After all, I don't want to become an *obituarian* spending my days writing about my dead friends who wrote so much better than I do." (Webster's has *obituarist,* but *obit writer* sounds better than either *obituarist* or *obituarian.*)

-ic seems to have a fascination for poor writers; they stick it in whenever they can and form long, ugly, misshapen words:

> Among political books, by far the most commotion centered around Victor Lasky's *acidic* (acid) diatribe against the late John F. Kennedy.

> Before last Tuesday, the most extensive *telephonic checking* (telephone check) all over the country failed to reveal a single Republican professional of any standing who was even muttering in his beard about drafting Nixon.

Franklin Edgerton . . . one of the foremost *Sanskritic* (Sanskrit) scholars in the United States, died Saturday . . . .

Edna Ferber is an *acerbic* (acerb, sharp), perceptive, witty, opinionated, and thoroughly delightful woman . . . .

His personality was a mixture of *quixoticism* (quixotism), naivete, exuberance, self-indulgence, and emotional imbalance.

His central thesis is that the conventional notions about the free enterprise nature of our economy are made *nonsensical* (nonsense) by the realities of a society dominated by large corporations intertwined with government . . . .

The dramatic, *anecdotic* (anecdotal) and often ludicrous incidents of her life are stressed.

All babies should not be condemned to continuing to *calendrical* (calendar) term before delivery.

In contrast to this near-frenetic display of *virtuosic* (virtuoso) action was the stately "Quetzal Birds of Puebla" . . . .

It is labeled "Business, Society and the Individual" and is known as BSI in the *acronymic* (acronym-filled) world of the embryo corporate executive.

Enough survey work has been done to show that Negro parents, like white parents, are more interested in the quality of education than in the *chromatic* (racial, color) proportions of the classroom.

identical shouldn't be used as a long word for *same.*

identify is often unnecessary:

The inmates were (*identified as*) Robert Philips . . . Albert Gainer . . . Joseph Oppenheimer . . . and Rene Hernandez . . . .

Another bar had a sign in its window *identifying it as a* (that said) "raided premises."

The demonstrators *identified themselves as* (said they were) members of various groups . . . .

identity is now the fashionable word for what used to be called *personality* or the *self:*

Today a girl evades her *identity crisis* (self-doubts) by getting married to a boy who doesn't know who or what he is either.

Swados strips the facades from each character to get at the warm kernel of *identity* (personality, the self).

ideology is a great fad word now, but most often it means nothing more than *idea* or *ideas:*

>If a corporation decides to go along with the dominant *ideology* (ideas) of a region, that does not mean it must defend *that ideology* (those ideas).

>He does not believe in the *ideology* (idea) of the Common Market.

>Therein we find occasional expressions of *the Eisenhower political ideology* (Eisenhower's political ideas).

Ides of March shouldn't be dragged up whenever you're looking for a synonym for *March 15:* "Senate action on a tax cut was pushed back to March 15 by Senate Republican leader Everett M. Dirksen who told a news conference yesterday that the floor action would take place around *the Ides of March* (that time). . . .

i.e. is an abbreviation for the Latin phrase *id est,* which means *that is.* Don't confuse *i.e.* with *e.g.,* which stands for *exempli gratia* and means *for example:*

>In an extensive mangement guide issued last July with military-style pagination (*i.e.,* [e.g.] 1.1-3) and terminology . . . .

>The doctrine of constructive receipt effectively blocks off any attempt to put off receipt of income that has become completely yours—*i.e.,* (e.g.) salary—even if you don't cash the checks until next year.

if sounds bookish and pompous when used instead of *though:*

>Mr. Liebl's Siegfried was lusty and noble, *if* (though) not heroic.

>In her first run for the Senate, she conducted a shrewd, *if* (though) financially pinched, campaign.

>Besides, he thinks that Sen. Goldwater's friends would greatly, *if* (though) inadvertently, assist the Kennedy cause.

>*If* (Though) it looks more like a brilliant analysis than a revolutionary manifesto, it is surely a distinguished public service.

>*If* (Though) it has little to do with creative drama, it is expert in its special field . . . .

>The work becomes an indispensable *if* (though) not al-

together trustworthy reference to anyone who would study the peculiar logic of political success . . . .

If (Though) Miss Graham has simplified the choreography for the role of Jocasta in recent seasons, she has balanced this with an increase in acting colors and dynamics.

Similar to the last example, *if* is also sometimes used to make a complex long sentence out of what should be two shorter ones:

If the (The) Soviet Union has now authorized the Russian Orthodox Church to participate in the effort at reconciliation with the Roman Catholic *Church, it* (Church. This) is undoubtedly because the Soviet authorities believe they will derive an advantage therefrom . . . .

If Tex (Tex) Thornton's business philosophy often confuses his *critics, it is perhaps* (critics—perhaps) because it is so breathtakingly broad and ambitious.

There used to be a prejudice against using *if* to mean *whether,* but this idiom is now universal: "Instead of being horrified, the people I told about it calmly asked *if* I was insured."

In certain sentences where the subjunctive after *if* was once used, it has now been replaced by the indicative: "I would not be surprised if there is no session this fall." *See also* AS IF, SUBJUNCTIVE, WERE or WAS?

if and when is a legal-sounding phrase that can and should always be shortened to either *if* or *when*—depending on whether you refer to possibility (*if*) or time (*when*):

They wanted to be in on the overthrow of Castro *if and when* (if) it happens.

"My husband is a Swiss citizen and doesn't have to bring any money into the country," she said. "*If and when* (If) he does get his divorce, I'd either have to leave the country or marry again . . . ."

If levies were reduced during a period of prosperity, what would be left *when and if* (if) the statistical measures do begin to tip downward?

If and when (When) Lyndon Johnson was mentioned in connection with the Vice Presidency, there was speculation . . . .

If and when (When) a tourist in Lima hears that a coffeepot is bubbling down the street, it will do him no good to go looking for it with a cup in hand.

That will no doubt change quickly enough *if and when* (when) the tax bill becomes law and the United States attains the impressive status of a $600 billion country.

ilk is a silly insulting cliché: "To people of Goodman's *ilk* (sort), the words 'business,' 'corporation,' 'profit' and others in the same vein are indeed obscenities . . . ."

ill-advised is a stale euphemism for *stupid,* etc.: "While holding it 'quite proper' for the association to invite the lawmakers to the cruising convention and to pick up their tab, Earl B. Schwulst, chairman of the board of the Bowery Savings Bank, said the cruise was *ill-advised* (a poor idea)."

illume is shorter than *illuminate,* but no longer part of ordinary English:

"WALK IN DARKNESS" DOESN'T *ILLUME* (ILLUMINATE)

image is a fad word that seems to fill a need. It's hard to see what word could be used instead of *image* in these sentences:

These men had been largely instrumental in producing, after the Labor landslide of 1945, a new Tory *image.*

The State Department is trying to wipe out an *image* of the American diplomat as a three-button, Ivy League snob who lives in a palace overseas, has a staff of servants and can't speak the language.

But in many other sentences *image* doesn't say anything much and should be left out:

The journeymen function of literary criticism, and not the least important one, is (*to give the age its own image*) to say in plain terms what is being achieved.

"I gathered he had his father as a very strong image, and it seems he was interested in becoming like him." ("I gathered he was interested in becoming like his father.")

impair is a pompous synonym for *weaken, damage* or *hurt:*

The friendly and official relations between the two countries cannot but be seriously *impaired* (hurt, damaged, weakened).

The Dixie bloc will have to crack the Celler-McCulloch axis if it wants to *impair* (weaken) the bill.

impart is a bookish word for *tell* or *give:*

Never are there any qualifying adjectives, since obviously they believe they have discovered the truth, which they *impart* (tell, give) directly to their readers.

This *imparts* (gives) a grand Gaullic simplicity to his conception of the tangled complexities that constitute the daily political fare.

impecunious is an unnecessarily long word for *poor* or *short of cash:*

The wealthy dressed and behaved in a way similar to their *more impecunious* (poorer) neighbors.

The investigation disclosed that *the often impecunious Oswald* (Oswald, who was often short of cash,) could have financed the entire seven-day trip to Mexico with less than $30."

impede is a pompous synonym for *hamper, hinder, stop:*

A theory that lack of cash should not *impede* (hinder, stop) spending was set forth in the committee report . . . .

There is more than baggage *to impede* (hamper) far-flung touring.

In recent times the attitude of retributive justice has acquired many ugly connotations that have tended to *impede* (hinder, prevent) thoughtful analysis of its real aims, premises and methods.

There seems at the moment nothing to *impede* (stop) Sen. Dirksen from reaching his own decision about the morality and validity of the old strategy in the Presidential year of 1964.

He has intensified an adversary atmosphere that can only *impede* (hamper) the efforts of all reasonable men to promote intelligent, harmonious solutions.

It is particularly noteworthy, from the viewpoint of public policy, that the nonsustainable investment binges have all along been sustained by more than ample profits, retained earnings and other sources of investment funds, and that they are entirely *unimpeded* (unhampered) by any excessiveness in the tax burden on corporations or on individuals who save a large part of their income for investment purposes. (*Unimpeded* is the kind of word that fits well into a 62-word sentence.)

impend is a rare, bookish word. Say *threaten* or *come up:* "The dentist's techniques have improved so much since the bad old days that—a majority still go to him only when serious trouble *impends* (threatens, comes up)."

imperative. The phrase *it is imperative that* is pompous rhetoric. So are most other uses of the word *imperative:*

> If you are over 40, have a family history of heart attack and are the body type considered prone to coronary heart disease, *it is imperative that you* (you must, be sure to) find out whether you are actually prone to such attack.

> He knew that the emergency that called a Vice President to the Presidency would make it *imperative* (necessary, vital) to obtain the cooperation of Congress.

> I refer to the *imperative* (urgent, vital) necessity of repairing at the earliest possible moment the gaping hole in the Constitution . . . .

> The *imperativeness of* (urgent need for) action has been underscored by Secretary of Labor Wirtz's year-end warning . . . .

impetus is a Latin word meaning *push.* Why say it in Latin?

> The great *impetus* (push) for the program was the enthusiasm expressed by church leaders.

> Your proposed exclusion of tipped employees will give [a] legalized *impetus* (push) to a most dangerous trend in our industry.

implement, implementation are words beloved by bureaucrats. Try instead *carry out, set up,* etc.:

> As far as is known, neither the French nor the Chinese have yet started any diplomatic staff on the way around the world to *implement* (carry out) Monday's recognition agreement.

> It is clear that any attempt to *implement* (carry out) these ideas would result in a gigantic program of urban reconstruction.

> If the board fails to adopt the Allen Report and to *implement* (take) the first substantial beginning steps recommended by the Commissioner, we will have no alternative but to consider the extreme step of an extended school boycott in the fall to meet an extreme problem.

> The actual *implementation* (carrying out) of the proposed

merger involves the usual considerable amount of legal and accounting work.

import, in the sense of *importance,* is archaic: "This possibility, if it is valid, is of such serious *import* (importance) that we do well to ask some hard questions."

importune is a longish, Latinate word for what's usually called *pester* or *urge:* "Tommy Gifford, the charter boat captain . . . has been *importuning* (pestering, urging) me for some time to try to catch a giant squid on a line."

impugn is a bookish word. Try instead *question* or *challenge:* "Thus, today's decision impugns (challenges) the validity of the election of 398 Representatives from 37 states . . . ."

in is sometimes wrongly used instead of *into:* "To have the Philippines now reach back to the year 1878 as justification for jumping *in* (into) bed with Sukarno is as appalling as it is tragic."

in depth. *See* DEPTH.

in length, in size are often unnecessary: "Published simultaneously is a companion volume on the United States by André Maurois, somewhat shorter *(in length)* but covering approximately the same period of time."

in that sounds prissy and academic. *Since* is better:

The novel is useful *in that* (since) it explains how Rodin's familiar masterpieces came into being . . . .

The third non-conformist at Salzburg, Trans-Canada Airlines, was a real maverick *in that* (since) it called for even lower rates.

Opponents say that the substance is harmful to human health in certain instances, and that its addition to the water supply is an invasion of individual rights *in that* (since) it forces all persons, regardless of their wishes, to ingest the substance.

It is rewarding *in that* (since) it lends light to the heat of our passions.

inamorata is old-fashioned: "Her current performance as Charles Boyer's legalized *inamorata* (mistress) . . . ."

inasmuch as sounds formal and stilted. Say *since:*

Network officials said they were aware of the funeral directors' complaint but would have no comment on it *in as much as* (since) it is a matter before the FCC.

He tells the world that at any moment a war could break out between the United States and the Soviet Union, *inasmuch as* (since) the Russian military commanders on the Berlin highway can decide for themselves to open fire on allied troops and vehicles.

NBC's judgment based on a fallacious rating system is horrendous *inasmuch as* (since) it professes to make or break a program by its popularity . . . .

inaugurate is a long word. *Start* and *begin* are shorter and better.

inchoate (pronounced *inKOate*) means *just beginning* or *unformed*; but writers constantly mix it up with *chaotic* and use it to mean *formless* or *shapeless*. Better stay away from it: "Arthur Miller's 'After the Fall' seems to me a thoroughly bad play: structurally *inchoate* (formless, shapeless), verbally vague, psychologically imperceptive."

incidence is a statistical term; the ordinary word for its is *chance:*

The *incidence* (chance) of obesity was higher in mothers . . . .

The *incidence* (chance) of the guilty going scot-free is very great.

incident means a minor episode; the word shouldn't be used when you're writing about a major historic event: "The assassination of President Kennedy came as an incredible shock. . . . The *incident* (event) once more raises the question whether the constitutional and statutory arrangements for the succession to the Presidency are adequate."

incidental to is an awkward compound preposition that should be avoided: *"In addition to this advantage, there would be others incidental to Europe's assuming full responsibility for its own defense."* (Europe's assuming full responsibility for its own defense would have other advantages too.)

inclement weather is a stale cliché.

include refers to some parts of a whole; it shouldn't be used when you give a complete list:

Remaining members of the council *include* (are): State comptroller Arthur Levitt; Senate Minority Leader Joseph Zaretzki . . . . (complete list of council members).

She speaks five languages, *including* (—) Italian, French, German, English, Swedish.

increase, like *decrease,* is a formal word. It's simpler to say *rise* or *go up:* "The nation's projected birth rate this year *decreased* (dropped) moderately, and for the second year in a row there was *an increase* (a rise) in the mortality rate . . . ."

indebtedness is just a long word for *debt:* "Total corporate debt was growing by nearly 200 per cent and the total *indebtedness* (debt) of private individuals rose by 300 per cent."

indeed always sounds pompous. There are various ways of avoiding it. Sometimes *indeed* can be changed to *really, truly,* or *in fact;* sometimes the job can be done by *yes;* sometimes *indeed* should simply be crossed out; and sometimes it's best to underline or italicize the verb.

If the companies are *indeed* (really, in fact) expropriated, there would be no way to reimburse the companies with anywhere near the amount to which they are legally entitled.

I came to realize that human institutions seldom lend themselves to a categorical treatment; that the analysis of a historical problem may well yield multiple answers; *indeed* (in fact), that this is the normal characteristic of the historical process.

There is indeed (Yes, there is) a nightmare quality to this latest off-Broadway revival of the play . . . .

Miss Harris is indeed (Yes, Miss Harris is) the major delight of "Open Season at Second City" . . . .

His had (*indeed*) been a rare and rewarding life.

The CONCISE DICTIONARY provides the essential facts of each biography in the larger work for ready reference by students, research workers, journalists, and (*indeed*) anyone who wishes to inform himself quickly . . . .

Times, indeed, are (Times *are*) changing in Dallas—and thoughout Texas.

Underlying these programs is the growing conviction that low income *youngsters can indeed* (youngsters *can*) be educated . . . .

The odds are indeed (The odds *are*) formidable, but the case of those who stand for Constitutional government is just.

indicate properly means *suggest* or *hint;* but the word is now universally misused as a long, important-sounding synonym for *say* or *show:*

Sources close to the new President *indicated* (said) that a major overhaul of the overseas aid program would be forthcoming next year.

There are no police figures *indicating* (showing) an increase in crime since automatic elevators became popular.

Research studies *indicate* (show) that films about prostitution are popular with women as well as with men.

As the table *indicates* (shows), there were in fact large-scale failures on the Regents tests this year, compared to previous years.

Sen. Jordan, chairman of the committee, *indicated* (said) it would take some time before the committee staff has completed its field work.

His point of view is supported by the evidence of the recovery rates for mental illness, which *indicates* (shows) that the vast majority of stricken persons recover.

In the rare case when you use *indicate* correctly to mean *hint*, why not say *hint*?

The House Ways and Means Committee has *indicated* (hinted) it may not resume hearings until next year on President Kennedy's proposal for health care for the aged through social security. In a form letter, the committee informed some 60 witnesses scheduled to testify that they will be heard later.

indication shouldn't be used as a long synonym for *sign*:

Indications (Signs) mounted today that Prime Minister Nehru is sicker than official statements have led the Indian public to believe.

There were *indications* (signs) from the start that the revolt was meeting resistance.

indicated is sometimes used instead of the simpler *called for*: "A time switch away from the strong Bonanza competitions seems *indicated* (called for)."

indifferent success is a snobbish cliché.

individual is a cumbersome 5-syllable word much overused as a synonym for *person*. Usually it can and should be changed to a simpler word like *people, someone, you*:

Individuals (People) working on different and not obviously related projects are in adjacent labs . . . .

Most *individuals* (people) are today freer than they have ever been to make the decisions that count in life.

Why are some *individuals* (people) capable of self-renewal while others are not?

Just why should such a comparatively small group—composed to no small extent of *individuals* (people) from outside the state and Canada—issue a monthly newspaper in Birmingham?

Individuals (People) may incur debt by borrowing to buy their homes, but they earn enough money to make regular payments . . . .

Every individual (Everybody) has his own stress end-point.

One of the peculiarities of the television medium is that an audience identifies itself with *an individual* (someone) whose appearance affords a thread of continuity from program to program.

Under his proposal, *an individual* (you) would prepay premiums for total health insurance throughout *his* (your) working lifetime and be entitled to health benefits. The premiums would be deducted from *an individual's* (your) Federal income tax bill.

induce takes the preposition *to:* "I shall initiate a campaign to induce the Mayor *into appointing* (to appoint) someone to head a drive against these censors."

indulge in is old-fashioned: "Like most heart patients, he is permitted by his doctors to *indulge in* (drink) Scotch, which happens to be his favorite alcoholic beverage."

ineffable literally means *unutterable;* the dictionary gives the example "the ineffable name of Jehovah." The common use—and misuse—of the word is in the sense of *indescribable* or *indefinable:*

He defined the *ineffable* (indefinable) "style" that made the President and his Jacqueline the most graceful ornaments of the early 60s.

Berlin has now achieved in this post-Cuban year of peace a sort of built-in economic and social momentum of its own, the *ineffable* (indefinable) feel at last of a normal rather than an abnormal big, vital, important, virile city.

The President's bill has been under bitter, persistent partisan attack by Democratic Senators, with a group of "liberal"

Democrats headed by the *ineffable* (indescribable) Sen. Wayne Morse, of Oregon, leading the attackers.

That's where Colonel Whitforth, played by Robert Morley in his *ineffable* (indescribable) style, comes in.

infamous. You can't be infamous *for* something: "Coming from the representative of a family *infamous* (notorious) for being hard against democracy, Mme. Ngo Dinh Nhu's slanderous remark that Ambassador Stevenson is 'soft on Communism' is indeed peculiar."

INFINITIVE. *See* SPLIT INFINITIVE.

influence (verb) sounds awkward with *to:* "The President next must decide whether he can and should *influence* (persuade, move) his old protege, Democratic leader Sen. Mansfield, *to* break the filibuster."

inform sounds bookish in the sense of *fill, underlie, pervade, guide:*

The pace is relentless, the tone is dark and moody, the intelligence that *informs* (fills, guides) it is sharp, cynical, and bitterly authoritative, and the writing is first-rate.

He discusses Joyce, Gide and Thomas Mann in relation to the intellectual ideas which *inform* (fill, guide) their work.

-ing words (participles and gerunds) shouldn't be abused to make clumsy sentences like these:

Stressing that Van Der Beek was not a suspect but was believed to have information that could lead to the killer, police held him as a material witness. (Police stressed . . . and held him . . . .)

Saying the 38-year-old wife of Ngo Dinh Nhu, the brother and powerful adviser of President Diem, had been guilty of "vicious and poisonous anti-American utterances," Sen Young asked the State Department to withdraw her visa and send her back to South Viet Nam. (Sen. Young said . . . . He asked . . . .)

Agreeing that modern youth might not be as obedient or respectful as was expected of the young in the past, Rabbi Silver expressed the belief that this tendency might be a good one. (Rabbi Silver agreed . . . . But he said this might be a good thing.)

Discussing the relationship yesterday at the Greek Archdiocese of North and South America, 10 E. 79th Street, Primate Iakovos, exarch in America of Ecumenical Patriarch Athenagoras, announced a pan-Orthodox gathering of the leaders of 13 Eastern bodies Sept. 19 in Rhodes to decide the question of sending observers to the Second Vatican Council. (Primate Iakovos discussed . . . . He announced . . . .)

Supporting his wife who divorced him two months ago, and four children "on higher standards than he could afford"—plus any outside interest he might have had apparently led to Bradley's difficulties, an official of the Association told The New York Post today. (An official of the association said Bradley supported . . . . This plus . . . .)

There's an argument among grammarians over such sentences as "I believe in young men now taking over." Conservatives say it should be "I believe in young *men's* now taking over," liberals say it's all right as it stands.

As far as I can see, the issue has been decided in favor of the liberals. The possessive case is now the exception, used only with personal pronouns:

Dr. Holt was questioned closely about *his stopping* construction last spring on Public School 90 in Brooklyn.

In tracing Oswald's recent movements, neither Dallas nor federal authorities have made mention of *his having* spent time in the company of any acquaintances in New York.

Police Headquarters stressed that *his having* been a witness at the Martinis trial had "absolutely nothing" to do with Sgt. Reiter's new status.

Otherwise, the possessive case with *-ing* now usually sounds stilted and old-fashioned:

There is nothing at all to prevent a *store's* (store) *being* located directly around the corner from an existing store.

It will be a partitioned country, but there won't be any more talk at the United Nations about *South Africa's* (South Africa) *having* a white minority government.

At times during this century, eighteen months have elapsed without a single *vessel's* (vessel) *casting* anchor off the island's coast.

The stop-gap spending resolution removes the absolute necessity of *Congress's* (Congress) *staying* in session until the regular appropriations are voted.

It is difficult to imagine such an *item's* (item) *receiving* the slightest notice in the preamble of "The Budget in Brief."

A far worse problem for the city gardener than that of *plants'* (plants) *dying* is that of *plants'* (plants) *almost dying*.

See also ABSOLUTE CONSTRUCTION.

-ings. Words in *-ings* are a specially unpleasant feature of educational and psychological jargon: "The critical question at this juncture is not whether present psychiatrically based methods (*and understandings*) are good enough to be 100 per cent successful in the treatment of all offenders."

inherent (pronounced *inHEARent*) is now a fad word, often used instead of the simpler word *basic:*

There is *an inherent* (a basic) incompatibility in this new state of affairs between sovereignty, if that sovereignty involves possession and control of nuclear weapons, and alliance.

Gifts of securities, especially to children, naturally are urged by stockbrokers, who generally note "their potential growth in value" and the "*inherently* (basically) American economic lesson" offered to the child.

The phrase *inherent in* often stands for nothing more than *of:*

Galbraith acknowledged there would be "*misfortunes*" that are "*inherent in personality*" ("misfortunes of personality") but that they would be beyond the control of any rule book.

Truman was in favor of this procedure even though he saw the risk *inherent in* (of) a situation in which the new President might belong to one party and the Speaker of the House to another party.

Mr. Horszowski illuminated all of the lyrical aspects *inherent in* (of) the music of these classicists . . . .

inimical and the even longer **inimicable** are both fancy words for *hostile:* "Their pathetic inventions continue to propagate a heresy *inimicable* (hostile) to marriage, social stability, and international peace."

initial is just a long word for *first* or *early:*

After the *initial* (first) shock of yesterday's ruling had worn off, Mr. Faulk said . . . .

Advances in science may result in people spending the *initial* (first) two to three decades of their lives preparing for participation in the economy and two or three decades in retirement from it.

The New York Governor failed in *initial* (first) efforts to enlist the support of New Hampshire's most powerful newspaper publisher . . . .

The *initial* (early) drop in cigarette sales has long since been recovered.

His *initial* (first) reaction was unenthusiastic.

But that is hard to explain to customers sitting in board rooms in all the *initial* (first, early) confusion.

Not once did this remarkable American mezzo depart from her *initial* (earlier) standard.

The critical support we received the following day, and the continuing lines at the Royale box office, further emphasized the *initial* (first) audience response.

initially should always be changed to *first* or *at first:*

"*Initially* (At first) I had doubts about the wisdom of permitting off-track betting . . . ."

General de Gaulle *initially* (at first) insisted that President Johnson come to Paris.

After *initially* (first) heralding the White House rights package in June, the Negro organizations decided to make a stand behind the subcommittee's language.

Marcie Hubert, *initially* (first) beset by a nervous smirk as she thrusts herself upon the young man . . . .

The other girl, more realistic and *initially* (at first) more unhappy, makes a success of her life in spite of many misadventures.

initiate is a pompous word for *start* or *begin:*

President Johnson *initiated* (started, began) the effort to end the violence by telephoning President Chiari.

The United States should *initiate* (start, begin) steps looking to the construction of a new, sea-level canal through Central America . . . .

The only comparable incident of buying back a road built with Federal funds took place in New York in 1947, long before the Federal System of Interstate and Defense Highways was *initiated* (started, begun).

innate, like *inherent,* is often overused in the sense of *basic:* "The *innate* (basic) cynicism of approach is not even diluted by a suggestion of cinematic or dramatic quality."

insofar as . . . is concerned is an awkward phrase; *as to* is quicker and better: "*Insofar as the attacks on Celler are concerned* (As to the attacks on Celler), there may be many grounds for criticizing him."

instance, like CASE, is sometimes used as an empty filler word: "This is healthy; it happens *in every instance in which* (whenever) someone tries to change the established order of things."

instantaneously should always be shortened to *instantly:*

On each TV show everyone from star to supernumerary gets the word almost *instantaneously* (instantly).

She buys a floppy, wide-brimmed Borsalino because it does something for her and does it *instantaneously* (instantly).

instinct with is a pompous literary phrase: "Some will find it, as I do, *instinct* (filled) with a power approaching that of true tragedy."

institute (verb) is a pompous synonym for *set up* or *start:*

The Conservative Government *instituted* (set up) checks on their health and character.

Southern committee chairmen and their allies in Congress *instituted* (started) a legislative slowdown that blocked his tax-reduction bill and other economic and welfare measures.

institutionalize has been formed after the pattern of *hospitalize* to mean *put* or *keep* (a mental patient) *in an institution.* There's no excuse for using this 6-syllable word: "I am concerned not with the odds but with the stakes—in this case the possibility of a deficient offspring who must be *institutionalized* (kept in an institution) for life."

institutionalization is the logical 8-syllable next step: "Dr. Schoenfeld told the court that *institutionalization would be 'tantamount to signing Klein's death warrant'* (that putting Klein into an institution would be 'tantamount to signing his death warrant')."

instrumental.   Avoid the awkward phrase *he was instrumental in:*

> When William O'Dwyer became Mayor, Lehman *was in-strumental in revamping* (helped revamp) the city's civil service system.

> Some will claim that the press *was instrumental in preparing* (helped prepare) the ground for President Diem's pathetic death.

insufficient shouldn't be used as a pompous synonym for *not enough:* "A list of titles cannot be sent for there are limited quantities of each, *insufficient* (not enough) to catalog."

insure means *cover by insurance;* the word for making sure in general is *ensure:* "The bill will help *insure* (ensure) that no child need be born retarded for such reasons, which are wholly in our control."

intensive is overused as a long synonym for *steady, hard, strong, thorough:*

> In the third day of *intensive* (thorough) interrogation of Mr. Gilpatric, Sen. McClellan brought out . . . .

> Enthralled by "Die Tarnowska" since 1930, Mr. Habe has devoted the past four years to *intensive* (deep, thorough) research on the subject.

> The propaganda was so *intensive* (strong) that it startled many of the bishops.

> The project involves *intensive* (steady) guidance services and extra help in remedial reading.

> The Wylle-Hoffert case is the most *intensively* (thoroughly) investigated murder in the past five years.

> The Ingstads have been searching *intensively* (hard) for Norse settlements since 1960.

> The extraordinary increase in the lung-cancer death rate first became the subject of *intensive* (thorough) investigation among medical people in the late forties . . . .

> *Intensive* (Hard) propaganda warfare, both within and without the area, among the several states of the Middle East, adds to confusion and tension.

interlocutor is a 5-syllable word meaning *one who takes part in a conversation.* Try to get along without that clumsy word: "As long as he was able to do so, B.B. relished good talk—not with *intellectual interlocutors* (intellectuals) who tended to intimidate him, but with young people, students, experts in other fields, and, most of all, women."

intervene takes the preposition *in*, not *into:* "*Into* (In) this dilemma Attorney General Robert Kennedy has usefully intervened."

intimate (verb) is a pompous word. Say *hint:*

> As already *intimated* (hinted), it was a recital totally without flaws.

> Not surprising that the English lawyer of *intimated* (hinted) critical acclaim uses the Michael Brett pseudonym . . . .

> President Johnson *intimated* (hinted) recently that he intends to make full use of television.

intimidate from is unidiomatic: "Let's not by association *intimidate* (stop) anyone from saying what he thinks."

into, instead of *in*, is now used commonly with such words as *research, investigate, examine:*

> An investigation *into* his World War II activities is under way.

> The Tobacco Industry Research Committee is continuing and extending its support of research *into* some of the many clinical and experimental factors . . . .

> President Johnson may be forgiven if his special commission to examine *into* the murder of John F. Kennedy seems on sober second thoughts to be a curiously ill-assorted group.

> "Next Time I'll Sing to You," James Saunders' enigmatic investigation *into* the life and meaning of an actual English hermit, opened Wednesday night.

intrigue (verb). The prejudice against the use of this word to mean *interest* or *fascinate* seems to be a thing of the past.

intrinsic, like *inherent* and *innate,* is overused. Try *basic.*

inundate. It's shorter to say *flood.*

inured to is bookish. Say *used to:* "Emily's murder included grotesque touches that leave veteran homicide detectives, long *inured* (used to) the macabre, puzzled and disturbed."

INVERSION. The normal English sentence begins with the subject and ends with the predicate. If you turn it upside down and start with the predicate, it'll sound artificial:

Chimed in Sen. Abraham Ribicoff . . . . (Sen. Abraham Ribicoff chimed in . . . .)

Ahead lay the prickliest thorns of all: civil rights and a tax cut. (The prickliest thorns of all lay ahead: civil rights and a tax cut.)

Adds a member of the surgical team at Pittsburgh: . . . . (A member of the surgical team at Pittsburgh adds: . . . .)

This artificial type of inversion is different from the natural, idiomatic kind:

The letters asked if the persons had seen the series and *would they comment on it.*

Dr. Betcher asks youngsters *what is their favorite TV show.*

Some day I'd really like to have a round-table discussion about *what is a critic, what does a critic seek to accomplish, what is his point of view.*

Many years ago a wise teacher told me that the really important question about telepathy is not *is it true* but why some people believe it is. (To be consistent, this should have read *but why do some people believe it is.*)

In his nervous, Gothic manner, he abruptly and brilliantly launched a lecture on *what is the culture* of which he is the keeper.

invest with is a pompous literary synonym for *give:*

It is greatly to the credit of the author, as a stylist and thinker, that he provides this voice when the need arises, and *invests it with* (gives it) his own eloquence.

Miss Sarton has *invested her story with* (given her story) considerable elegance.

invite sounds stilted in this kind of sentence: "Indeed, the potential substance of the discussion, which could only be briefly realized in the technical experiment, *invites* (calls for) consideration whether further use of the satellite is really necessary to the larger educational goal of 'Town Meeting.'"

involve is perhaps now the most overused word in English. Whenever a writer can't think of the exact word, he reaches for the all-purpose verb *involve.*

There's no single specific word to take the place of *involve.* Look at the particular sentence and decide whether to use *mean, have to do with, deal with, be mixed up with,* or some other verb that seems natural in the context. Sometimes it's best to leave out *involve* altogether and use a preposition instead. Examples:

There is not the slightest shred of evidence that Gauguin *was in any way involved in* (had anything to do with) Cézanne's resolve to avoid Paris for a time . . . .

Officials who have been *involved in* (working on) the aid operation feel that as long as Arab-Israeli relations remain as they are . . . .

Politics *involves* (means) a continuing conflict of interests and philosophies.

Johnson proteges have been *involved* (mixed up) in the three major scandals that have touched the Kennedy Administration.

The financial agreement *involved the establishment of* (set up) separate trust funds, each in six figures, for Sybil Burton, Richard Burton and for each child.

Forgetting *involves* (means) the blocking of pathways leading to stored information.

The police said that Hasidic Jews here have rarely been *involved* (mixed up) in brushes with the law.

In each case, the incidents took place off the conveyance *and involved* (in) a waiting room or rest room.

The Federal complaint also *involved* (named) one of the corporation's subsidiaries . . . .

Most of his career in Washington *has involved* (had to do with) the passage of legislation through Congress rather than the difficult task of preparing it in the executive branch.

Judge Gassman occasionally attends the opera, but most of the time he is *involved* (busy) only with the law or with his Orthodox congregation . . . .

This group is recording the electrical patterns of brain activity of men in jobs *that involve* (done under) stress.

John F. Kennedy as President was confronted with issues *involving* (of) human destiny.

The proposals *involve* (deal with) such matters as the pay of the Governor, sewer debt limits and the transfer of certain lands in the forest preserve.

The classic story of superfluous paperwork *involves* (deals with, has to do with) a newly commissioned Army officer irked by paper shuffling.

The major contributors feel that education can be expanded only by cutting back the emergency relief, which at present *involves the supply of* (supplies) supplementary foodstuffs to 866,000 refugees.

There are extremists who insist that every job *involving* (that has to do with) growing and processing of forest products needs to be handled by a graduate forester.

involved is often unnecessary and should be left out:

Governor Wallace indicated he would favor keeping the three Birmingham schools (*involved*) closed as long as there is dangerous violence.

This is Washington and, therefore, the Presidential succession is being discussed in terms of (*the*) personalities (*involved*) instead of (*the*) principle.

Nothing I have done has been done solely for the thrill (*involved*) or for the publicity . . . ."

I don't think Mr. Albee has succeeded in presenting his characters in depth, but he has assuredly had splendid co-operation from the actors (*involved*).

This is not a question of the merits of segregation: it is a question of the rights of citizens to educate their children in a segregated school if they wish to pay the added expense (*involved*).

The cast (*involved*) in this darkly hued play is continually rewarding.

Mr. Halaby said Soviet air officials "swore that the TU-114 was not only safe but that it had never been (*involved*) in a fatal accident."

He had been (*involved*) in public life, most of the time as either a Congressman or Senator, for more than 30 years.

inwardness is an old-fashioned literary word: "This is the *inwardness* (true meaning) of the so-called 'opening to the Left.'"

-ion is the most common ending of abstract nouns; too many *-ion* words are a warning signal that your style needs improvement. Change them whenever possible:

The two Wapshot brothers, Moses and Coverly, also trace a *declension* (decline) in their fortunes . . . .

Central to the therapeutic program would be the effort to provide the offender with more mature mechanisms for dealing with the psychological *tensions* and *compulsions* (drives) that presumably played a role in *the production of* (producing) his criminal behavior.

The ingestion or injection or inhalation of (Ingesting, injecting or inhaling) any agent taken or given to alter a person's usual mental and emotional equilibrium must be looked upon as a medical procedure.

Precision in the definition of international reserves has been impaired by the evolution of the gold standard into a gold exchange standard under which great varieties of credit instruments are counted as official reserves. (The gold standard has become a gold exchange standard under which . . . . This has made statements of international reserves less precise.)

See also ABSTRACT WORDS, -ATE, -ATION.

ipso facto is a Latin phrase that's often unnecessary: "Any book on a tedious subject (*ipso facto*) is damned at the outset before reading."

is or are? It's typical of a sloppy writer that he occasionally uses the singular instead of the plural verb:

Attempts to redraw the houses' individual rate structure *is* (are) expected to fail.

This gives substance to the widespread suspicion that there *is,* (are) in the United States, two kinds of justice, one for the rich and one for the rest of the citizens.

Two companies, Premier Albums and Documentary Unlimited, each *asserts* (assert) that *it was* (they were) first on the market.

His material on homes for the aged, which marvelously details the systematic mortification of the personality and the tenacity with which even dying persons hold on to the shreds of human culture left to them, only intermittently *make* (makes) its claimed connection between institutional dynamics and interpersonal relations.

. . . these plus countless other refinements by the leading pioneer in the development of color *adds* (add) up to one simple fact—perfected Color TV is here!

Plans for a "court of inquiry"—a legal left-over from the state's frontier past—*was* (were) somewhat up in the air.

The luminous phrase, the controlled dynamic, the elegant tone, *was* (were) ever present.

It isn't always easy to distinguish between sheer sloppiness (which accounts for most of these examples, I think) and a feeling that in certain sentences the singular sounds more idiomatic than the plural. Here are some examples that are, in various degrees, defensible—and may some day be standard English:

Every one and his brother *has* a gastric freezing machine.

The Department of Labor said that 20 per cent of all young Negroes, or one in five, *was* out of work.

Although bias and prejudice still *exists* to some degree in this country, in my opinion, *it is* far less than *it was* 30 or 40 years ago.

Postwar affluence and a general liberalization of attitude *has* improved the conditions of the working class and tended to encourage social mobility.

Savings deposits in the Berlin banks, which *is* the most certain and sure index of public earnings and public confidence which anybody can tote up, *are* far and away the highest in the city's history.

The psychological mechanics *is* very similar to overeating.

Does civil rights have anything to do with some Southern opposition to the nuclear test ban treaty?

See also ARE.

-ism is sometimes wrongly used instead of *-ity:* "He has a puritanical obsession about showing *sexualism* (sexuality) on-stage."

issue. *Take* or *join issue* is a pompous phrase. The verb *issue* is also often used pompously:

This Voucher, *issued* (made out) in your name in appreciation for your interest in the Council's publications, gives you the following extra Dividends . . . .

In January 1957, when Sandys was at the peaks of his career and a dark-horse prospect for Prime Minister, Diana announced their separation, *issuing* (giving) no reason.

-istic should be shortened or left out whenever possible:

The sex scenes were almost *animalistic* (animal) and I was shocked.

Even Erle Stanley Gardner might envy the *legalistic* (legal) ingenuity of the plot.

For most American girls the *familistic* (family) lessons of their childhoods are merely reinforced by their later education.

it lends itself easily to pompous writing:

It is not to be denied (I won't deny) that, in the homogenized mumbling chatter outside, witticisms are essayed and assayed . . . .

It will be recalled (Perhaps you remember) that the words of the 86th Psalm proclaim that . . . .

The loss of Howard K. Smith's program of comment is to be deplored, and it is hoped that perceptive and incisive news analyst will soon get a television half hour of his own again. (I am sorry about the loss of Howard K. Smith's program of comment and hope . . . .)

It is hereby vigorously urged that (I strongly suggest) you make space beside your copy of the Plays and, after enjoying Mr. Rowse, place his volume there.

See also I, ONE, PASSIVE VOICE.

ITALIAN WORDS, like all other FOREIGN WORDS, shouldn't be dragged into English prose unnecessarily, as in this sentence: "A peek behind the scenes of Washington's *la dolce vita*—as the Romans call 'the sweet life'—begins with the maligned private clubs."

Even where an Italian word is called for, there's always the danger of making a grammatical mistake:

Menotti hasn't written the great American opera, but he has written some of its greatest scenes and probably the best *opera buffo* (opera buffa) by a living composer.

Their singing was musical enough, goodness knows, but they had a great deal of trouble with the tricky *fioriture* that *is* (are) the life-blood of such music.

The politician—always the *Pagliacci* (Pagliaccio)—must smile when he wants to cry, must go on display when he needs solitude.

ITALICS. If you don't use italics, you're missing one of the best resources of writing; if you use too many, you spoil the effect you're after. The basic rule is to underline (for italics in print) the words or phrases that would get heavy natural stress in speaking—and not to shy away from the colloquial sentence pattern that calls for such stress. Here are some nice examples:

Frank and Eleanor Perry, who set a new high in quality for independent low-budget movie-making last year with "David and Lisa," have *not* done it again.

When you're doing experimental work of this nature you can't figure *every* part of it to be a success.

It's only $2,650 plus, so the three-way deal makes it a real economy, I *hope*.

But she wasn't sure if the stocks he had selected were the best ones available for *her* circumstances.

Now look at some smothered-in-italics prose:

The age of shaving comfort dawned the day that Norelco rotary blades were born. They introduced the *third* way to shave—the most *comfortable* way to shave close and clean. Norelco rotary blades whirl round at an incredible 3500 revolutions per minute. They never change direction. They *stroke* off whiskers so gently your face actually feels *soothed!*

Each photographic plate is accompanied by an architectural note. *There is also a map with each plate showing the structure's exact location in New York today.*

More significant, however, than either of these reasons for the decline of reading as a reflex action is that *relatively few people grow up seeing around them the kind of books that human beings of any age turn to naturally.*

-ity words are a symptom of too abstract writing; what should have been said simply has been said with cumbersome abstract nouns. Sentences with *-ity* words should be rewritten in various ways:

A partial explanation of Sen. Goldwater's poorer standing with the Eastern delegation is *the proximity of Gov. Rockefeller and Gov. Scranton* . . . . (the fact that Gov. Rockefeller and Gov. Scranton are nearby . . . .)

They come out like frantic figures in an animated cartoon who have just discovered *their own two-dimensionality* (that they are two-dimensional) and are having nervous breakdowns about it.

Mr. Black also urged that the United States Supreme Court

be given a case to test *the constitutionality of determining* (whether it is constitutional to determine) the educational future of children of underprivileged backgrounds through the use of intelligence and aptitude tests.

Cancer *mortality was* (deaths were) at a somewhat higher level in 1963 than in 1962.

So far as fiction is concerned the list records a *catholicity of* (catholic) taste.

It still stands, for all its familiarity and after all its mis-treatment through the years, as a sublime testament to the art of musical *expressivity* (expression, expressiveness).

The Administration has shown little understanding that the *validity* (rightness) of a given solution depends on a frame-work of purpose.

The *growing propinquity* (clustering together) of one-stop stores (*to each other*) has discouraged the very thing that the idea sought to establish.

What happened in 1940 revealed *the nullity of France as a military power* (that France as a military power was no more).

-ive.   Don't fall into the bad habit of saying *it is -ive of* when a simple verb will do:

The reluctance of Congress to act on that issue may well *be reflective of* (reflect) the plain hesitation and fears of the people themselves.

This long lapse *was indicative of* (indicated, showed) re-sistance, in the highest echelons of the Church, to reform.

In such a broad spectrum of conduct, the reading of GOOD HOUSEKEEPING would be clearly within the area *productive both of* (producing both) self-appreciation and (*of*) other, consequent, outer-directed actions.

But while we find this argument persuasive, we are unable to *consider it dispositive* (agree that it disposes) of the case before us.

Mr. Goodman has written a book *provocative of* (that pro-vokes) thought without assisting in the thought process.

Anyway, it's a good idea to stay away from *-ive* words as much as possible:

At his command was immediate *obliterative power* (power

to obliterate), more power by far than had ever been collected in one place at one time.

In later life as husband, he must be the sturdy oak, the protector, *supportive to* (the support of) his wife and family, gentle and kind, but a leader.

Perhaps *the most genuinely contributive program now on the air is* (the most genuine contribution by any program now on the air is made by) "Faith to Faith" . . . .

The mom, the nagging, domineering mother, (*the castrative wife,*) is the mother who lives through her husband and children.

-ize, -ization. Whenever you're tempted to form a word ending in *-ize* or *-ization,* don't. There's always a better way of saying it:

Harry Rubin, as the elderly sage who is *martyrized* (martyred) by an avaricious duke, has a sonorous voice and a fine rabbinical face.

It signals the continuation of a relentless trend toward *"decimalization" of the world's currencies* (making the world's currencies decimal).

The story is *capsulized* (pinpointed, put in a nutshell) by the comment of a statistician for the International Ladies' Garment Workers Union.

Tompkins' guilt feelings are *therapized* (treated) with "flak juice" and man-to-man talk.

Bucky was a hopelessly poor executive and as much of a fool about money as he had been at Harvard—living wildly beyond his means and rapidly *laocoönizing* (entangling) himself in debts and superdebts.

See also BURGLARIZE, HOSPITALIZE, INSTITUTIONALIZE, UTILIZE, VANDALIZE.

J

JINGLES. It's a basic rule of style that you should write for the ear rather than the eye. The least you can do is avoid jingles like these:

Rabbi Maurice Nathan Eisendrath does not *quail* before the fury of a religious or social *gale.*

The *object* of the *project* will be to extend present services of the *association* and to establish new offices throughout the *nation*.

And a *thug's smug* explanation was too pat . . . .

The invitation is *not expected to be accepted*.

RIA's current report on the impact of *automation on the nation* . . . .

It's been part of last week's *spec*trum of *spec*ulation about Mr. Wagner.

The defendants were proven to be as *malicious* as they were *vicious*.

The facts in the case show *no evidence of negligence* . . . .

Early this month son Jeff, offered a blank check by a rich widow for saving her child's life, named his *reward* as a new children's wing for his father's hospital after a visit to a crowded *ward*.

joust is too medieval a word for a modern sentence: "The airframe builders, plus Pratt & Whitney, General Electric and Curtiss-Wright, which are *jousting* (competing) for the engine business, have rebelled against sinking this much company money into such a fluid program."

juncture. *At this juncture* is pompous; say *now:* Hinman contends that liberalism is not dead, but only sleeping, in California *at this juncture* (now)."

jurist is not really a synonym for *lawyer* or *judge* and shouldn't be so used: "Mr. Gompers did not choose to test Justice Van Siclen's willingness to jail him. *The jurist* (Van Siclen) later, in a public statement, said . . . ."

K

kid. There's no standard English word that means someone who is no longer a child but not yet an adult. Some writers use artificial words like *youngster, teenager* or *youth,* but these are not what people say. People say *kid*.

Here are some examples to show that *kid* is on its way to being accepted as standard English:

Yet as other Americans reach new heights of affluence and

aspiration, slum *kids* are made to feel all the more worthless by their poverty and the color of their skin.

What Scarsdale does for its *kids* today, Mrs. Lear contends, other places will do for their *kids* tomorrow.

The thing started presumably with a spontaneous clash between American and Panamanian high-school *kids*.

He's 35—far from middle-aged, but still, no *kid*. Profound ideas have been expressed by younger writers.

Training, placement, subsidized work, remedial reading, writing and English—everything designed to show a *kid* if he wants to, he can make a living doing useful work.

In the events that interest American *kids* the United States athletes performed creditably.

kin is a word used only in headlines and in pompous literary prose:

CUSTODIANS' *KIN* (RELATIVES)
TO FACE INQUIRY

If one would generalize, the faults of the internationalist —in his attitudes toward the United Nations as on some other issues—are *kin* (akin, related) to the virtues of his positions.

kind of, in the sense of *rather* or *somewhat,* is now a common idiom. I see no reason for avoiding it:

She was either dressed in a housecoat or an apron and she *kind of* let herself go.

"I was getting *kind of* worried," his mother said.

"I figure half will go for taxes," he said. "That *kind of* kills it."

kindly shouldn't be used as a synonym for *please*.

L

lachrymose is old-fashioned: "Why the *lachrymose* (tearful) nostalgia?"

lack is a stiff, unnatural word. It's more natural to use an ordinary negative verb: "The building is reported to *lack* (have no) central heating and private toilets and to be in extreme disrepair."

lacuna is an unnecessary Latin word: "In such an otherwise full and satisfying book one may carp over *lacunae* (gaps)."

lad sounds affected; say *boy:*

He lives here today with his children, ranging from 17 (an athletic *lad* [boy]) to 17 months (a small girl)."

The *lad's* (boy's) service as a gigolo to the wife of an elderly rug merchant is neither amusing nor wholly believable.

lag is a headline word. Try *slow:*

TAX CUT HELD NO SOLUTION TO *PAYMENTS LAG* (SLOW PAYMENTS)

DEMAND STILL *LAGS* (SLOW) IN TAX-EXEMPTS

largesse is pompous journalese:

Many outfits that normally dispense *largesse* (gifts) are instead contributing to a charitable cause this Christmas.

The *largesse* (bonus, stock dividend) arrives in reverse order. The rights offering will be to holders of next Feb. 10.

Obviously, this sort of mass *largesse* (generosity, grant) has made the husky Armsey a big man on campuses all across the country.

lass sounds just as affected as *lad*. Say *girl:*

Precocity is a wonderful thing, and Miss Caroline Glyn, that chubby, pretty *lass* (girl), to judge by her photograph, is full of it.

Let us drink to the *lass* (girl) who is the main figure in "Hello, Dolly!", at the St. James.

Latin shouldn't be misused to mean *Latin American:*

LATIN (VENEZUELAN) GRANDMOTHER BEARS QUINTUPLETS

LATIN PHRASES. It's a good style rule to avoid FOREIGN WORDS in general, but it's particularly important to avoid Latin words and phrases, since they always sound snobbish. There is no Latin phrase that can't be put into English:

In toto (Altogether), this destructive force represented the equivalent of 30,000 pounds of TNT for every human being on earth.

In the moment of *extremis* (despair) Robert F. Kennedy, so much of whose life had been fiercely dedicated to his older brother, stoically avoided public tears or outcry.

She was responding to one of the most distinct *indicia* (signs) of the racial caste system.

I have become convinced that a substantial portion of the "political" obstacles to more effective national economic policies arises precisely because the policies *ab initio* (from the start) do not project in their content or presentation the galvanizing force of sufficiently ethical and social objectives.

Kempton also reintroduces us to those allegedly "middle class" workers who can so suddenly be dropped by automation and other *ex cathedra* (arbitrary) changes in the economy into paralyzing insecurity.

The price paid by Rome for the destruction of Carthage was to wreck herself as well; and, if this was the fate of the victor in a pre-atomic war, it would be his fate *a fortiori* (even more) now in atomic warfare.

Also, there's always the possibility that your Latin may be rustier than you think, e.g.: "The story begins *in medias res*." (The Latin phrase means *into the midst of things* and is in the objective case; you can say "The story *plunges* in medias res" but not "The story *begins* in medias res." Better stick to English: "The story begins in the middle of things.")

See also ALMA MATER, BONA FIDE, RARA AVIS, SANCTUM SANCTORUM.

LATIN PLURALS. Use English plurals rather than Latin plurals for such words as *formulas, indexes, appendixes, Gladioluses.*

latter is a stilted, bookish word. Change it to *this, he* or *she,* or repeat the noun:

While Wilson's anger at this discrimination is understandable, he plainly did fall into his situation with IRS because of obliviousness to the present-day world, and *the latter* (this) weakens his credibility as a social critic.

Delegates and colonialism experts at the United Nations said they were worried about areas seeking independence rather than those that have already attained it. Many of *the latter* (those) also have some of the same problems.

My trip cost me $7,043, excluding meals and incidentals, but including $166.04 in excess baggage charges. *The latter* (This) was an expense I strongly advise prospective world travelers to avoid.

In such a climate of opinion, democratic self-government appeared as the natural and inevitable political counterpart to modern science and technology. *The latter* (These) were the fine fruit of human reason applied to physical nature.

One committee member got an appeal on this subject from one of his most trusted political supporters at home, and also—on behalf of the oil-depletion allowance—from a friend and business associate who was the local representative of a major oil company. *The latter* (This man) acknowledged frankly that he was only calling at the behest of company headquarters in the state capital.

The co-sponsoring auto company had objected to a scheduled Sinatra appearance because of *the latter's* (his) since-resolved problems with Nevada gambling authorities.

If taxes are taken up first, and they are much less controversial than civil rights, then *the latter measure* (civil rights) would not reach a showdown before March.

It is incorrect to compare corporate financing with that of the Federal government and say that *the latter* (Federal financing) is better because it did not increase its debt as much as did the private sector in the economy.

Surveys show that most consumers don't care whether turkey is fresh or frozen, *the latter* (frozen) being widely available.

Now one of the Latter-Day Saints' "Twelve Apostles," the top ruling council, the former Agriculture Secretary was favored to become a "counselor" second only to President David O. McKay. But *the latter* (McKay), who picks the church's two counselors, is having second thoughts.

See also FORMER.

laud is a bookish word. Say *praise*.

lawmaker is a childish synonym for *Congressman* or *Senator*. Avoid it:

Mr. Celebrezze's contention . . . didn't satisfy Rep. Curtis.

"This is the same old Kennedy story," *the GOP lawmaker* (he) said.

Sen. John G. Tower issued a call here for physicians to get into politics. . . . *The Texas Republican* (He) issued his call at a meeting. . . . He told his audience . . . . "If you don't show a lively interest in these battles," *the conservative lawmaker* (he) warned . . . .

less. Orthodox grammarians insist that *less* shouldn't be used with the plural and should be changed to *fewer*. But *less* is now common usage:

Even assuming that Ecuador elects a genuine reformer, the U.S. could expect *less* restraints on communists, less willingness to follow U.S. recommendations . . . .

No matter how we felt in the past about paying high taxes, the President convinced us that the only way to save the country was to pay *less* taxes to the government.

-less sometimes looks odd when used to form unusual words: "Enter the first non-character on the carefully arranged *scenery-less* (empty, no-scenery) stage to light a cigarette and intone . . . ."

lest is no longer part of ordinary spoken English and sounds pompous in writing. Change it to *that, or, so that not,* etc.:

This means a good deal of repetition, *lest the reader* (so that the reader won't) suddenly feel like Ariadne deprived of her clue.

Now, *lest enthusiasm* (so that enthusiasm won't) seem to be bubbling too high in this report, let it be said right here that not all the sketches in TW3 were absolutely first-class.

Lest you (To make sure you don't) doubt that the story of the murderous Chicago mobsters is running parallel to the history of Hitler's rise in Germany, brief reports of the actual Nazi record are thrown on the curtain from time to time.

"We are deeply and perennially concerned," says Mr. Pusey, *"lest* (that) we are producing people unworthy of the great opportunity for high achievement given them with the gift of life."

We are in the 1960s, and we must search our minds *lest we* (or we'll) accept unexamined the assumptions of the postwar years, *lest we* (and) act on the reflexes which were conditioned in another age.

The most articulate of the drama's theoreticians, he can lay down the law for his disciples about the necessity for avoiding the weakness of emotional involvement in the theater *lest it be* (so that it won't be) turned into an esthetic opiate for the audience . . . .

Young Ray is an idealist so disgusted with the ugliness of everyday life that he lives a hermit-like life in an attic, never venturing out *lest he* (so that he won't) become contaminated.

The real Gaullist view is that West Germany . . . is a big, deeply perturbed invalid who must be nursed, guarded, and tranquilized *lest he* (or he'll) relapse into his old illusions.

lethal is an overblown word for *deadly* or *fatal:* "Then, to save his tax bill from a possibly *lethal* (fatal) entanglement with a Southern filibuster on civil rights, he set priorities on the two key measures for the first time."

level is often misused as an unnecessary filler word:

Maternal mortality was at a record low (*level*) of little more than 3 per 10,000 live births.

Mr. Lippmann's article is an admirably concise statement of a major challenge—and a beautiful example of adult education *at the highest conceivable qualitative level* (of the highest conceivable quality).

George Orwell may have hit on a profound truth when he assumed that the present political chaos is connected with the decay of language, and that some improvement might be brought about by starting *at the verbal level* (with words).

The accreditation proposals represent an interesting effort to improve (*the level of*) public relations practice . . . .

level (verb) is a stuffy synonym for *bring* or *make:*

The validity of the truth of such charges as the Russians have *leveled* (made, brought, raised) against Prof. Barghoorn never worries the Kremlin.

It is vitally important to scrutinize the demands that the Negro leaders are *leveling* (making) against white society . . . .

It accused the Soviet leader of rocket-rattling and war-mongering, the very charges he has *leveled* (made) against China.

levy is a word now used solely when a writer doesn't want to repeat the word *tax:*

The proposed repeal of the 10 per cent Federal theater tax was rejected by the Senate today, 59 to 33. Proponents were encouraged, however, by the size of the vote to eliminate the *levy* (tax).

The consequence of the presuure for a pre-budget tax reduction is that many in Congress who favor *lowering the levies* (it) are drawing back from a plunge into a deficit pit without a visible bottom.

libation is now used only humorously, but is no longer funny: "You can throw a wedding party, complete from Smorgasbord to Prime Ribs, plus *libations* (drinks) and Wedding Cake, for only $9.95 a head . . . ."

lieu. *In lieu of* is a legalism for *instead of:*

You have two weeks within which to pay a non-recurring membership fee in amount of the quarterly cost and *in lieu* (instead) of the quarterly payment now in course of collection.

He dramatized the union's position on TV yesterday by tearing up a copy of the TA's latest economy proposals made Friday *in lieu* (instead) of an increase.

like. Most grammarians insist that *like* should never be used as a conjunction (with a verb-clause after it), but millions of Americans do it every day. Should you stick to the textbook rules or follow the current idiom? The answer depends on the particular sentence:

First, there's the case of *like* used instead of *as.* In some idioms *like* sounds more natural:

Teenagers need teen-age books *like* they need a hole in the head.

They don't seem to be coming to the theater *like* they used to.

You can say this for those ready mixes—the next generation won't have trouble making cake *like* Mother used to make.

Like, rather than *as,* is also idiomatic when you make a factual comparison:

Working in Italy is *like* it used to be in Hollywood before the unions took over.

In Jamaica, you have an excuse to stare. Faces *like* you've never seen before.

And the people were out shopping. They are out this year *like* they never have been out before.

King says that a white American must ask himself, "Are Negroes being treated *like* you would want to be treated?"

We have always gotten along with a Democratic President, just *like* Democrats have gotten along with a Republican President.

Dr. Louis S. B. Leakey, the British anthropoligist who collects fossils in East African gorges *like* some people collect seashells on the beach, displayed a group of old fossil bones yesterday . . . .

But when the comparison is abstract or theoretical, *like* should be changed to *as:*

With treatment a woman simply ages gracefully *like* (as) a healthy man does.

It's also better to change *like* to *as* in the phrase *like I said:*

It's *like* (as) I said—"Gratitude has a short memory."

Well, *like* (as) the librarian says on Saturday afternoons at those kiddie hours, it all started like this . . . .

Second, there's the case of *like* used instead of *as if.* Again, you have to distinguish between different types. *Like* is now thoroughly idiomatic in such phrases as *look like, sound like, feel like, seem like:*

Mr. Stockdale commented that the President was "afraid the loan could make it *look like I was* finagling around with the FHA."

If you listen to a man like this, it *seems like you are* in another world.

Sounds like it might almost put you to sleep.

Asked how it felt to be in the White House, he replied with a smile: "I *feel like I have* already been here a year."

The Republican leader said he told the Speaker, "It *looks to me like it's* awfully late."

Sen. Javits noted that "it *sounds very much like President Johnson is* to be all things to all men."

It *looks like all roads will soon lead* to Nairobi.

The ratings determine whether you get cigars or mud in your eye. This season it *looks like I get* the cigars.

Originally, Rockefeller asserted, the estimated cost of the program was $17 million. "Now it looks *like it will be* $40 million," he declared.

"I never know what slick means," said Massey. "And then you can go and do some shoddy damn highbrow business which *looks like it's been* mocked up in a barn—and they'll pin medals on it."

Aside from these set phrases—*look like, feel like, sound like, seem like*—*as if* is generally better and more idiomatic than *like*:

Natalie Wood and Arthur Loew Jr. are acting *like* (as if) those stories are true about them getting married very soon.

It was *like* (as if) I was floundering in deep water.

It was *like* (as if) the whole world had shut me out.

I got out of my car and took Lepke right by the wrist *like* (as if) he was a little boy and walked him over to John Edgar Hoover's limousine.

It was *like* (as if) he didn't know what I was talking about.

DRIVE IT *LIKE* (AS IF) YOU HATE IT

Third, there's the case of *like* used instead of like what. Change those sentences by adding the word *what*:

They'll leave behind something cheap *like* (what) their wives wear.

Mr. Beame said his proposal for purchase and resale of tickets was "something *like* (what) we do at Lewisohn Stadium now."

Fourth, there's the leaning-over-backwards mistake of using *as* instead of the correct preposition *like*:

Good French words are now being used *as* (like) the English words they resemble in violation of their true French meaning.

likely is idiomatically used as an adverb meaning *probably*:

Widick defines the problem of power and weakness in such a way that the reader sees why the extension of democracy in unions will not *likely* lead to changes in the labor government.

Forty-four per cent said they would definitely join the boycott; 45 per cent said they would *likely* join; 9 per cent said they would *likely* ignore the boycott; and 2 per cent said they would definitely ignore the boycott.

likewise sounds affected; say *so* or *also:*

Surely, former President Truman would *likewise* (also) subscribe to this.

"Jamie McPheeters" is considered iffy; *likewise* (so is) "The Price Is Right."

limitation can often be shortened to *limit.*

limn is sometimes used as a fancy word for *describe:*

POLITICS *LIMNED* (DESCRIBED)
IN DOCUMENTARY

It spills over with succulent tales of brazen chicanery and cool derring-do, *limns* (spans) the gamut of portraiture from the ascetic to the eccentric . . . .

line. Avoid the awkward compound particles *along the lines of, along these lines, in line with:*

Evidently whatever future the animated cartoon film has, *will be along lines much simpler than those of* "Fantasia" (it will be much simpler than "Fantasia").

He had spoken to me about *his desire along these lines* (such a desire) previously, to allow more time for his family and for his law practice.

He said *public comments he had made along these lines* (the public comments he had made) were aimed at certain labor leaders.

liquid refreshments still crop up when a writer is desperate for a synonym for *drinks:* "This steady clientele is attributable to Michael's large, emphatic, adroitly-brewed drinks of considerable repute. These *liquid refreshments* (drinks) which have made the Pub a buzzing groggery in the late afternoon Martini hours . . . ."

LISTS. When you list a number of points or items, make sure they're all grammatically parallel and each one is complete in itself. If they're not parallel, you get mixed lists like these:

Persons who have seen the Wolff design said it included the following:

- ¶ Establishment of a band of schools on the Bronx side of the Harlem River for grades 4 to 6 only . . . .
- ¶ *In less concentrated and massive areas than Harlem, areas or complexes of schools would be paired* . . . . (Pairing of areas or complexes of schools in less concentrated and massive areas than Harlem . . . .)
- ¶ Reorganization of junior high schools . . . .
- ¶ Combining three junior high schools . . . .

etc.

The two sides settled the major issues between them by:

- ¶ Allowing taxpayers to continue to deduct gasoline taxes . . . .
- ¶ Curbing the maximum amount that Americans living abroad for three years or more can exclude . . . .
- ¶ Restoring much of the benefits of the tax-free sick-pay provision in the present law . . . .
- ¶ *Deleted* (Deleting) a Senate-written deduction for political contributions . . . .
- ¶ *Eliminated* (Eliminating) another Senate change . . . .
- ¶ Removed (Removing) a proposed deduction . . . .

etc.

Unique triple-action cream . . . . It's extra effective because it works three ways:

1. Special soothing action speeds relief of tormenting itch.
2. Special de-scaling action works fast to remove scales, without skin irritation.
3. *Helps control recurrence of new scales with continued use on the affected area* (Special control action to prevent recurrence of new scales with continued use on the affected area).

If each item in your list isn't complete in itself but depends for its meaning on some word or phrase in the introductory statement, you're apt to be misunderstood as in this example:

There is no proof, he told a meeting of the World Medical Assembly, that:

Stress is responsible for the development of hypertension, or high blood pressure.

Salt in the diet is a causative factor in the disorder.

Mortality from primary hypertension has declined since the advent of drugs aginst it 12 years or so ago.

Antihypertensive drugs are really effective, as many authorities say. (The average reader of this list will probably miss the point that the speaker called each of these statements untrue.)

little. The words *a little* (like PRETTY and RATHER) often have a snobbish air of British-type understatement, as in "This record of aggression, committed and planned, has made the argument for UN universality (*a little*) uninviting."

loan (verb) is now a common idiom: "This priceless heritage was *loaned* to us to use, enjoy and pass on unspoiled to all generations to come."

locality is just a long word for *place*. So is *locale*.

locate shouldn't be used as a stilted synonym for *find*:

Federal investigators have *located* (found) no bank accounts under Oswald's name . . . .

A young woman wanted desperately to *locate* (find) an uncle who lived somewhere in the Middle West.

In the investigation of a big burglary, one of the routine steps is to *locate* (find) and question known burglars whose M.O.s fit the job.

Sometimes *locate* should be changed to *settle*: "Mr. Benson will *locate* (settle) in Frankfurt, Germany . . . ."

Often *locate* should simply be left out: "Although Dr. King's home and office are (*located*) here, he has refrained from personal involvement in Atlanta anti-segregation activities . . . ."

location, like *locality,* is overused as a synonym for *place*.

LONG SENTENCES. The average sentence in a current newspaper, mass-circulation magazine or popular book runs to about 15 to 20 words. This doesn't mean that every sentence over 20 words is too long, but it does mean that there's a limit to the number of words you can make a reader take in without a break. My list of horrible examples starts with a 47-word sentence and winds up with two 98-word monsters:

If as indicated by experimental and clinical experience the central nervous system is indeed in some patients the only reservoir of the last few remaining leukemia cells follow-ing remission induction with chemotherapy, the possibil-ity of cure in acute leukemia exists today by means of the combined approach. (47 words)

As Representative Willis of Louisiana pointed out, the section of the bill banning racial discrimination among ap-plicants for the services of privately owned places of public accommodation would re-legislate a statute passed by Con-gress in 1875 that an unreversed Supreme Court decision struck down as unconstitutional in 1883. (48 words)

"The Hand of Mary Constable" is described as a suspense novel in which Alexander Hero, a British psychical re-searcher—he previously was featured in Mr. Gallico's novel, "Too Many Ghosts"—prevents an American nuclear physi-cist from joining the Communists by utilizing his knowledge of the occult and the recent death of the physicist's daugh-ter, Mary. (55 words)

The love affair with Broadway that Moss Hart is supposed to have had and that he wrote about with brazen fervor in his autobiography, "Act One," is made to appear a dismal set-to of a bloodless kid and a weary muse in a dull back room, in the film that Dore Schary has made from the Hart book, which opened at the Trans-Lux East last night. (66 words)

For example, although the generals who took power in South Vietnam this week insisted that they had done so to block a Gaullist plot to neutralize South Vietnam, Presi-dent Johnson and his associates have been emphasizing to the press that Washington had no evidence that the French Government was actually conspiring to overthrow the former South Vietnam Government, and that the United States had nothing to do with the coup d'état. (71 words)

In the introductory chapter, "What the Historian Thinks He Knows," Hughes surveys in condensed form the ideal-ist and positivist currents of historiography in the 19th and 20th centuries, pointing out that the tendency in the best recent historical writing has been towards a pragmatic blending of stringent standards of scientific research with an openness to the discoveries of other disciplines and an unapologetic sense of the crucial role which the historian's own situation plays in his choice of both materials and methods for his study. (85 words)

It is this latter triad of motifs—the Negro as postmoral man, the hipster as contemporary hero, and existentialism as weapon and deliverance—that has come to subsume all of Mailer's concerns and that stands forth as the triple ground where his followers find him most energizing but where, from a vantage point outside the mystique, his capacity for evocation and for the destruction of stereotypes is seen to clash most angrily with his limited powers of analysis and his solipsistic thinking about the world. (85 words)

Palmer is, to be sure, a phenomenal athlete and he will be winning championships for at least another decade, but his trouble at the moment, if I may hazard a concerned guess, is that, for all his rare physical endurance and mental stamina, the pace he has kept up for the last three years has worn him down to the point where his remaining supply of nervous energy is quickly expended, along with his powers of concentration, when he attempts to subdue a tough, penalizing course with a major title at stake. (92 words)

The five understandings would provide that the treaty did not involve recognition of East Germany, that it did not limit the use of nuclear weapons in case of war, that it did not require that United States to wait for the 90 days provided in the treaty's withdrawal clause to resume testing if the Soviet Union violated the treaty, that future amendments would be subject to Senate ratification and, finally, that the ban on tests would not prevent the use of a nuclear explosion to build a sea-level canal through Nicaragua if Nicaragua approved. (94 words)

Where the taxpayer enjoyed a period of abnormally high earnings and then suffered a depressed level of earnings which began at a time several years prior to and thus remotely related to the base period and such condition continued on during that period because of a chain of events and circumstances which were of prolonged duration throughout the 1930's and not of a temporary nature, held, that the business of the taxpayer was not depressed in the base period because of temporary economic circumstances unusual in the case of such taxpayer, within the meaning of subsection (b)(2). (98 words)

The foregoing, however, is not to be taken as an attack on,

nor as a depreciation of, the virtues and the advantages of Standard English, for this, the accepted form of English, with its national scope and its national use, with its rich and varied vocabulary, with its often subtle and, for the most part, flexible syntax, with all the historical associations inevitably and naturally garnered in the course of centuries, and these and other associations enriched by successive generations, is the inestimably precious inheritance of the English people, as any such language is of any ancient people. (98 words)

See also DANGLING PHRASES, LOST THREAD, SENTENCE STUFFING, SHORT SENTENCES.

LONG WORDS. Short, common, concrete, specific words are better than long, rare, abstract, general words. Sheer length is not the most important of these distinctions, but if you're one of those people who enoy the sound and sight of polysyllabic words, learn to suppress the urge. Here are some examples of long-word addiction:

Sordi, as a patent-leather-haired snob, is marvelously hysterical . . . gallantly skittish toward his wife, *oleaginous* (oily) in his dignity toward her lover.

Facts also do not back Mr. Rossant's claim that inflation has had drastic *distortionary* (distorting) effects on the economy . . . .

Far from being mutually *exclusionary* (exclusive), the two themes are inter-dependent.

Dr. Greenfield called the rising reluctance—or inability—to seek necessary medical care a kind of *hypochondriasis* (hypochondria) in reverse.

This book covers those years when General Motors became the largest industrial concern in the world and a showpiece and showcase of American *entrepreneurial* (business) versatility.

My conviction was based, less on confidence in the Keynesian *armamentarium* (bag of tricks) as politically feasible medicine, than on the surmise that the war had taught Americans the lesson that wars cure depressions . . . .

The historian often finds himself wishing he were presented with clear alternatives for his *self-conceptualization* (choice of a label).

See also ABSTRACT WORDS, GENERAL WORDS, RARE WORDS, SHORT WORDS.

loom (verb) is a pompous word usually meaning nothing at all; get rid of it:

> Two of the most important men (*looming*) in this field *include* (are) Robert B. Anderson . . . and Donald C. Cook.

> Four years later another Pittsburgh appearance *loomed* (came up) . . . .

> As of early November it appeared the reforms may have been sacrificed in vain, for *the strong possibility loomed* (there was a strong possibility) that the tax bill would not be passed until early 1964.

> It is evident that the slowness of customers to adopt a new product *looms as* (is) a severe constraint on the expansion of over-all demand through innovation.

LOST THREAD. If you make it a habit to write long, complex sentences, then it's inevitable that sooner or later you'll commit sentences that don't properly hang together. In the following examples I have italicized the point where each sentence went astray:

> The more we continue to ride in automobiles and sit at ladies' aid societies or bridge tables and sip coffee, *our bones become* more and more demineralized.

> What time, in its centuries of darkness, has done with a remarkable felicity of touch for the Venus de Milo, so that some spirit of the Venus seems always on the point of breaking out of her, *so does the inner soul* of unending generations break out, too, in all religious faiths.

> When a man must maintain not one but two homes; when he must contribute beyond his real means to every charity "because it is expected of him"; when he must educate his children and run expensive campaigns for reelection— *this man is* an economic victim in an affluent society.

> If I were a bright young girl who could not go to college, or the parents of such a girl, I would give the most serious consideration to a career *for such a girl* in the military or in one of its nursing and health services.

> This requires not only recognition that "a page of history is worth a volume of logic"—in Holmes' phrase—but also *to perceive* that the future is history.

What he has done, as co-author as well as director, is merely place these people—an edgy, snarling husband, his cool and calmly critical wife and a surly and sassy young hitchhiker whom they have picked up en route to their boat—within the controlled confinement of a trim little sailing sloop and *there has them* work out their aggressions and their sly sexual rivalries.

It was slow and in its sentiments it sometimes seemed repetitious, yet this listener had a sense of frustration because the performance, late in starting and the oratorio so long, *he was unable to stay* for the last act and therefore to hear the music devised for her final martyrdom.

See also DANGLING PHRASES.

luminary is too grand a word when something simpler will do as well: "Here we are in 1963, and Mr. Waugh has been asking himself what had happened to these aging *luminaries* (leaders) of the Bright Young People."

luncheon is one syllable too long; say *lunch*.

-ly. There's a trend toward using adverbs without -*ly*—for example, *quick* and *slow*. The following sentence is now idiomatic:

The first primary comes in March and Republicans must get busy *quick*.

In contrast, this sentence now sounds wrong:

When the opposition is deep-seated and widespread throughout the country, Congress is inclined to go *slowly* (slow).

So-called link verbs like *turn, taste, become, grow, seem, smell, look, feel* are followed by adjectives (without -*ly*) rather than adverbs (with -*ly*). Mistakes are common:

Only the large fleshly nose stood out *whitely* (white).

Dialogue is the basis of drama, and Bernard Shaw proved that a comedy can be all talk and virtually no action and turn out *delightfully and powerfully* (delightful and powerful), although he was certainly capable of offering physical action, too.

He told his audience that "you can rest *easily* (easy) for a little while now as far as Medicare is concerned because it probably will never get out of committee."

Dr. Bacon's and Mr. Bandel's findings were based on the

same statistical sources, but came out *oppositely* (opposite) through selectivity, emphasis and interpretation.

See also -EDLY.

M

mad, in the sense of *angry,* is now standard American usage:

The market is near record highs and that means business is good. So what's everybody *mad* about?

The average person who feels he's denied the right to vote is so damned *mad* that unless you have a person of gentle temper helping him, you've got a fight.

People come up to me in the street, *mad* at me for leaving the program.

magisterial is a pompous word for *masterly:*

This *magisterial* (masterly) biography by Isaac Deutscher assures him of his place in Russian history.

All of us have been grateful to our new President for the *magisterial* (masterly) way in which he took hold of his responsibilities.

magnitude is a long word meaning *size:*

The *magnitude* (size) of the spot problem from the advertisers' standpoint was illustrated in the case of Procter & Gamble . . . .

An engineering business of extremely large *magnitude* (size) is therefore hanging in the balance.

Of the first magnitude is a silly cliché: "Granted that if Carol Channing weren't already a *star of the first magnitude* (top star), 'Hello Dolly!' would make her one."

major, majority can often be changed to *most:* "I very much fear that when we come to what we might call the bottom of the barrel, we shall find that, *for the major part,* (most of) those colonies are very small . . . ."

male shouldn't be used as a noun when referring to people: "Only 37 per cent of the *males* (men) questioned said they'd vote against a woman for the Presidency."

mantle is now used solely as a pompous figure of speech:

> Vernon recently cast aside the *mantle* (disguise) of disinterested scholarship.

> Mr. Rattigan's suave craftsmanship . . . *confers a mantle of credibility on* (gives an appearance of credibility to) "Man and Boy."

> As manager, Yogi will take a pay cut of perhaps $10,000, and *the mantle of dignity rests a bit awkwardly on his bulky shoulders.*

mar is a headline word; the normal word is *spoil:*

> Rain showers earlier *marred* (spoiled) the ceremonial welcome for the monarch and queen . . . .

> The East German gesture was *marred* (spoiled) by an announcement that East German border guards shot and killed a Hamburg laborer . . . .

> Their new film, "Ladybug, Ladybug," lacks both the sensitive perceptions and fine acting that distinguished its predecessor and is overloaded with the pat propagandizing, psychological clichés and overt symbolism that *marred* (spoiled) it.

masterful means domineering; don't use the word when you mean *masterly:* "His playing was fluent, imaginative, sensitive and completely *masterful* (masterly)."

On second thought though, it's probably too late to insist on that distinction.

materialize is a long, awkward word that can usually be changed to *work out, turn out, come up,* etc.:

> There are bigger plans afoot for her here next season. One can only pray they *materialize* (work out).

> Lots of what Mr. Baker heard and saw *materialized as* (turned into) fantastic paper profits to himself and others.

> The effects on religious thought and on the strongly organizational habits of religion have been slow to *materialize* (come).

> No candidate against him for the problematical Presidential election in 1965 has as yet *materialized* (turned up).

> If plans *materialize* (work out), I should have a book sometime in 1965.

This issue, as *materialized* (expressed) in the differing appropriations and allocations sought by the President and the Passman forces, will be adjusted in the House-Senate conference . . . .

Plans Ben-Gurion conceived won't *materialize* (work out, take shape) under his command.

matter. The phrase *in the matter of* is often unnecessary: "This gift is reinforced by uncanny inventiveness in (*the matter of*) instrumental color."

matutinal is a stilted Victorian word referring to *morning:* "Reactions of New Yorkers as they are passed by former President Truman on one of his frequent *matutinal* (morning) constitutionals."

maximize is often used where the simple word *raise* or *increase* would do:

These difficulties have led to the questioning if income or welfare *maximizing* (raising, increasing) assumptions and of current "rational" methods of planning . . . .

Traditionally the question has been whether a firm's sole obligation is to *maximize* (raise, increase) its profits or whether it should expend some of its resources on improving the general quality of life in society.

maximum is now a fad word. There is no sentence where it can't be easily changed to *top, most, longest, biggest,* etc.:

He demonstrates, with *maximum* (greatest) impact, how other species must feel at the receiving end of man's behavior.

In the depression days of the 1930's, the economy had *maximum* (more) freedom, less government and less bureaucracy.

Barring last-minute changes, the *maximum* (longest) distance between elementary schools paired in a Princeton Plan zone will be one-and-a-half miles . . . .

The drawing shows Buddy Werner of the United States in the perfect but unnatural ideal for *maximum* (top) downhill speed.

Reflecting essential design changes, the estimated *maximum* (top) gross weight has crept up and now is calculated to approach 300,000 pounds.

may or **can?** *See* CAN or MAY?

me. The old argument over *it's me* versus the unnatural *it is I* has long been decided in favor of *it's me.* Here are a few random examples of current usage:

> "*Me* drink sherry?"
>
> Don't let another girl help you in the kitchen. Shows "poor little *me*" tendency.
>
> *Me,* I never watch the game.

NIXON IN 1964: NOT *ME!*

> The only good reason for rushing into print with a report on something called the First International Girlie Exhibit . . . is that everybody else is doing it and we had better go on record before the thing is exhausted. (*Me,* I'm tired of it already.)

See also BETWEEN YOU AND I, HER, HIM.

media is a Latin plural, but is now commonly used as a singular: "There have been other histories of *this media,* but not one of them is as full of the flavor of the times . . . ."

medic, medico are journalese words for *doctor:*

> *MEDICS (DOCTORS) RELATE BALDNESS HOPE*
>
> Miller uses other couples as a sort of counterpoint. One is a spiritless *medico* (doctor) and his fading wife.

mentality is overused as a pompous synonym for *frame of mind* or *outlook:* "Our foreign policy, grounded in a 'social study' *mentality* (frame of mind, outlook), was not set in simple geographical terms . . . ."

message. Too bad this good old word has been taken over by the advertisers: "We are directing this *message* (ad) to a small group of successful research directors who are not actively seeking new assignments . . . ."

METAPHORS. *See* MIXED METAPHORS.

metamorphose. Is this word necessary? "Although Johnson *metamorphosed* (changed) from a slim, dapper man with a long, narrow head into a bear with a profusion of lips and double chins, his style remained much the same."

milieu is a French fad word for *surroundings* or *environment:* One feels that he was trying to escape from his *milieu* (environment), but undoubtedly he was surrounded by Yiddish-speaking people.

Bernard observed, "Health comes from harmony between the external *environment and the internal milieu* (and internal environment)."

minimal shouldn't be used when *small* or *very small* would do: "My investment in stocks and bonds is *minimal* (very small)."

minimize shouldn't be used as a pompous synonym for *cut down, lower, brush off, underrate,* etc.:

What then can be done to *minimize* (cut down) the risk of damage to the babies whose conception and birth we cannot or do not prevent?

Here are some recent tax developments the early filer should keep in mind to *minimize* (cut down) his tax liability.

These have a vital bearing also on the question of maintaining business confidence, or at least *minimizing* (holding down, lessening) business uncertainty, in the event of the recurrence of such a tragedy . . . .

The American State Department has studiously *minimized* (brushed off) suggestions that the revolution in Zanzibar might have been organized entirely by outside elements . . . .

There should be no *minimizing* (underrating) what the Soviets have already done.

Can Vietnam, Cuba, Panama, Cyprus, China really be downgraded as much as Mr. Johnson *minimized them* (did)?

minimum should usually be changed to *least:* "He showed remarkable talent for translating vision into reality with a *minimum of* (the least) error and waste."

mirthful sounds stilted and artificial: "Its premise is amusing; its unfolding seemingly takes forever and is not nearly as *mirthful* (funny) on the whole, as are some of the situations concerned."

mix instead of *mixture* is on its way into standard English:

The secret is the *mix* of frequencies in the sound pulses, a formula that Lockheed copied from the porpoises.

Yet, as some senators wistfully recalled, Johnson had somehow made that unlikely *mix* produce.

MIXED METAPHORS. Sloppy writers don't pay any attention to what they're saying and produce a wonderland of mixed metaphors:

A clash of wills between the White House and the Southerners *jelled* after Rep. Smith postponed hearings until 1964.

This view is echoed by hundreds of doctors who have sent protests to the FDA.

The oddly encircling triangle may also be a source of discomfort.

When the fuss has settled, the Senate will probably outline a code . . . .

As with any dynamically successful new product or service which promptly begins to *pull a bandwagon* of adherents, the matter of standards quickly becomes an important element in the marketing process.

Naturally, there were *aspects* of his musicianship that his one concerto *left unanswered.*

Reading the book again, many years later, it is clear that *sex has,* as usual, *wrecked the perspective.*

In Saigon, Mr. Lodge *left the door wide open to a draft.*

It seems that *the fox has risen to the bait.*

The mainspring of this new outlook was the belief in a natural order for social arrangements based upon the nature of man, natural law, and natural rights.

The same *groundswell* that a hundred years earlier had *culminated* in what another martyred President had called a fiery ordeal was beginning to make its tremors felt.

The Harris poll shows . . . that *the political cost* of the Cuba failure *may plummet* out of control.

An even greater amount of *red ink,* $450,000, *went gurgling down* with "Tovarich". . . .

The Senate Judiciary Committee *laid the groundwork* today *for a possible clash* between Congress and the Supreme Court over the apportionment of state legislatures.

Perhaps my capacity for moral indignation *lessens with the gray in my hair.* . . .

It's a situation I don't have to cross at this point.

So *the tangents reaching out* from his influence *are all covered.*

But don't for a moment imagine that this 110 per cent adopted Hoosier wears *rose-colored blinkers.*

The protest is *a straw in a windstorm.*

And he will also liquidate much of his problem in this area by having *a dagger at the throat of the anti-Communist situation which President Macapagal seeks to strengthen* in the Philippines itself.

mode is a highbrow little word for *way, method, mood:*

The traditional *mode* (way) of thinking about international conflicts is in terms of a struggle for power . . . .

Anger is not a useful *mode* (mood) for a critic.

modicum is a fancy Latin word for *some:*

Medical care for the aged is finally getting *a modicum of* (some) attention on Capitol Hill.

There was *a modicum of* (some) interest in the distasteful determination of the Texas Junior Chamber of Commerce to push Miss Jeanne Amacker (Miss Texas of 1963) into her chance at Atlantic City . . . .

modus operandi is a longish Latin phrase; the English word is *method:*

The subcommittee hearings disclose that principles basic to a practical and otherwise sound *modus operandi* (method) are emerging.

A few years ago I re-read the story of Jack the Giant Killer and was struck by the highly questionable ethics of Jack's *modus operandi* (method).

What would we not give to have a similar documentation of the esthetic attitudes and creative *modus operandi* (method) of Bach and Beethoven?

modus vivendi is defined by Fowler as "any temporary compromise that enables parties to carry on pending settlement of a dispute that would otherwise paralyze their activities." But people who use the phrase to show off don't care about its exact meaning:

The *modus vivendi* (way of life) is casually chic: the expectant divorcee can reside at the luxurious four-story lodge ($50 a day with sun deck) or at one of the Tyrolean cottages . . . .

The general purpose of these books is presumably to draw a picture of a certain form of society, a certain way of life—

the modus vivendi (that) of a small and ancient Massachusetts port . . . .

mom is a word that's not fit to print:

A CBS-TV SHOW FOR JFK'S *MOM* (MOTHER)

moment of truth means the climax of a bullfight—the moment when the matador kills the bull. But in current American writing the fad phrase *moment of truth* may mean almost anything:

The supposedly perfect love affair between Mac and Phoebe collapses at the *moment of truth,* and the reader is left wondering why.

MOMENT OF TRUTH ARRIVES FOR N.J.
SCHOOL UNBEATENS

A dental patient's first *moment of truth* arrives when he is escorted to the contour chair.

Legislators, like matadors, face their *moment of truth*—how to cut down onrushing government costs by the thrust of well aimed tax programs in 1964.

monarch is now strictly a standby word for people afraid of repeating *king* or *queen:* "Banner headlines relayed Buckingham Palace's announcement yesterday that the 37-year-old *monarch* (queen) will give birth next year."

more than one is illogically but idiomatically used with a singular verb: "*More than one* family *has* been distressed when the city assessed taxes in a new development that ranged as much as $20 a month in excess of estimates."

moreover, like FURTHERMORE, is a ponderous way of getting from one paragraph to the next. The best way to deal with *moreover* is to cross it out wherever it crops up. Here are two examples of paragraph transitions made smoother by this method:

. . . And thereafter General Motors' leadership is never challenged with enduring success.

As the story unfolds, (*moreover,*) every detail of corporate strategy, every method and innovation and interrelationship is carefully explained in the same stolid but lucid manner . . . .

It does not matter, in truth, whether the slum areas are mainly inhabited by Negroes or white people. What matters is that the schools in such areas are almost invariably poorer in every respect, with meaner playgrounds, worse buildings, fewer and less qualified teachers, and so on, than the schools in the same city's middle-class areas.

This is the case, (*moreover,*) although the schools in the slum areas have a vastly bigger job to do. . . .

most, for *almost,* is a common idiom:

Most anyone with an interest now can have a say in what kind of local air service he would like to see in the future.

"We were lucky," he said. "People all around us were dead, *most* all of them."

Europe's rich have been getting richer but so have the workers and *most* everyone else in the Common Market countries.

motivate, motivation are fancy fad words; try *cause* or *reason:*

Sultan feels that it is concern over their jobs that *motivates* (causes) labor leaders to respond negatively to pleas for more democracy.

Although he is not aware of his *motivations* (reasons), your nephew may be using you to communicate the hostility he feels for his father since his father is your brother.

Mr., Mrs. It sounds unpleasantly genteel if you refer to your husband or wife as *Mr.* or *Mrs.:*

"I want to emphasize," he said, "that *Mrs. Block* (my wife) and I did not want anything for ourselves."

"Of all the boys involved," Leas said, "only one has had the courtesy to apologize to *Mrs. Leas and myself* (my wife and me)."

"I might say," said Dr. Durant, "that the writing about the salons in this new book is almost entirely the work of *Mrs. Durant* (my wife)."

multitudinous is a long word; *many* will often do: "The program showed the *multitudinous* (many) jobs performed by women in the Soviet Union."

mum is a silly headline word:

ESTIMATE BOARD *MUM* (SILENT),
BUT SOLD ON FLUORIDES

Elizabeth Taylor and Richard Burton, *mum* (silent) on their plans for the next few days but shopping on a grand scale in the meantime, were still here as day dawned today.

Harvard was *mum* (silent) on what happened at the "wild parties" Monroe referred to.

must (noun and adjective) is common usage now, but most writers think they have to put quotation marks around it. Don't.

The filibuster would stop action on such outstanding *"must"* (must) legislation as foreign aid, an $11 billion tax cut and a host of appropriation measures.

It is an exhibition of bang-up painting and sculpture that makes the new galleries, through November and December, a small museum that should go on everybody's *"must"* (must) list.

See also QUOTATION MARKS.

myself shouldn't be used when *me* is enough: "It soon became only too clear to my husband and *myself* (me) that our mere attempts to explain the Sullivan Law and how it operates were making us suspect."

mystique is, by definition, an indefinable something. It's a great fad word now, used constantly and casually: "A peace, like a war, has its own *mystique,* tone and cycle of behavior."

One way to improve your style is to avoid the word *mystique.*

N

nadir is a bookish word for *low point:*

Very probably the *nadir* (low point) of the year's humor is Stewart reading Henry Miller's "Tropic of Cancer" straight through . . . .

There's no place to go but up in '64 now that "The Prize" is with us to hit what might well be sustained as the nonsense *nadir* (low point) of the year.

nagging backache is perhaps the most tiresome cliché in English.

NAME DROPPING always sounds unpleasantly snobbish: "There is a new style in our foreign affairs that owes more to *Jomini* and *Clausewitz* than to *De Callières* and *Czartoryski.*"

See also ALLUSIONS.

NAMES. The first style rule about names is to spell them right. The second is to stay away from the headline habit of using nicknames:

ROCKY (ROCKEFELLER) OPENS BRIDGE
AND FORESTS

PRESIDENT TO *BOBBY* (ROBERT KENNEDY)
—STAY ON

What should you do when you don't want to mention someone's real name? Don't try to tell your story without using *any* name:

One day almost two and a half years ago, *a financially troubled widow* entered the Wall Street offices of an investment counselor. *The woman* had money—about $240,000 in stocks. But *she* also had three children . . . . (This sounds awkward and unnatural.)

Don't use stock "anonymous" names like *Smith* or *Jones:*

Take the man who asked the question—*let's call him Jones* . . . . Now consider the circumstances of the man to whom the question was addressed. *Smith* is the head of a small but very profitable wholesale drug house . . . . (Dull and textbooky.)

The solution is to use natural-sounding fictitious names. Here are some simple ways of introducing them:

A year ago a 46-year-old housewife *we will call Agnes Gentry* suddenly fainted.

As an example of one effective procedure, *take the case (much oversimplified) of Fred and Ruth A.* who disagreed violently over the disciplining of their 7-year-old son.

A more formidable obstacle is the attitude of the teachers. *I recall, for example, Miss Jeffers (that is not her real name).*

We have these friends *we'll call the Shaws.*

To show this, *there is the case of Henry and June, who are real people and live in New York* and have a very fine marriage except that Henry steals money from her.

narrate is a bookish word for *tell:*

The story has a true-to-life background, *narrating* (telling) the adventures of a girl Robinson Crusoe . . . .

The story is *narrated* (told) by Maugan Killigrew, the oldest son (but illegitimate) of Sir John Killigrew, governor of Pendennis Castle on the Cornish coast.

narrative shouldn't be used as a clumsy synonym for *story:*

Mr. Kurnitz has handled the rather easygoing *narrative* (story) skillfully.

Caroline's highly personal *narrative* (story) spins along with naturalness and freshness.

Taking a deceptively simple little story about the early marital problems of a young bride and groom, with no complicated plot devices to confuse it, he has presented *his narrative* (it) with such unostentatious wit, grace and charm . . . .

Nevertheless, the first part of the *narrative* (story) does succeed in generating progressively greater interest in the last paintings of Matthew Tresilian.

nary. Don't decorate your sentences with archaic English. Say *not one:* "That made a Lewis brood of six boys (one adopted) and *nary a* [not one] girl."

natatorium is a word that crops up when a writer is desperate for a synonym for *swimming pool:* "The pool was the largest indoor *natatorium* (swimming pool) in the city."

native shouldn't be used as a synonym for *born* since it still carries an overtone of contempt: "Father Hoa, *a 55-year-old native of Southwest China* (who was born in Southwest China 55 years ago), has been fighting communism since before World War II."

nature, like CASE and CHARACTER, is often abused as an empty filler word. Cross it out:

The *secret nature* (secrecy) of the FBI search was indicated by the fact that detectives of the Charles St. Pct. told The Post they knew nothing of the hunt.

It was this careful avoidance of several potential climaxes, which I thought were (*of a*) virtually obligatory (*nature*), that kept me from joining in an otherwise unanimous critical enthusiasm . . . .

His snore is *a roar of such a nature* (such a roar) that when people hear it they feel themselves assaulted . . . .

naught is a bookish word; change it to *nothing:*

Mark Robson, who directed, hasn't looked at a lot of old Alfred Hitchcock pictures for *naught* (nothing).

The encouragements evidently have come to *naught* (nothing).

The many constructive steps taken during the Kennedy administration toward the business community went *to naught* (for nothing) under the continued harassment in other areas.

nay is a piece of old-fashioned rhetoric; make it *no:*

In New York alone, 408 viewers phoned the network to say yes in emphatic terms, while 233 others called to say *nay* (no) in stricken terms . . . .

Since "The Nylon War" was written, my interest—*nay* (no), preoccupation—with the interrelation of disarmament, foreign policy, and domestic policy has become still more intense.

There are artisans . . . *nay* (no), artists! . . . who can create a hair piece that will look natural on you.

ROCKEFELLER DECLARES—*YEA & NAY* (YES & NO)

near future. Instead of the pompous phrase *in the near future*, say *soon:* "But such hopes may not be fulfilled *in the near future* (soon)."

needless to say is usually unnecessary and should be left out: "*Needless to say, both* (Both) agencies are heartily in favor of this merger because of the tangible benefits that we believe will result for clients and the respective organizations."

needs (adverb) always sounds bookish: "His reputation is based as much on taste as on success—despite an occasional lapse in deference to a deodorant or detergent that one *must needs* (has to) promote, proudly."

nefarious sounds old-fashioned; try *vicious:*

He tried to paint Latex as a parvenu which had the *nefarious* (vicious) plan of cashing in on Goodrich's years of research . . . .

Where does white colonialism figure . . . in the caste system within India that is as ancient as it is *nefarious* (vicious)?

negate is abstract and formal; try *deny, contradict, rule out:* "The decision to buy, whether it be a house or cooperative apartment, may be *negated* (ruled out) by insufficient immediate capital and a limited monthly allotment for housing."

negative is often a pointless circumlocution for *no:*

"I still feel," said Senate Majority leader Walter Mahoney, "the verdict will again be *in the negative* (no)."

Mr. Reuther's answer was *negative* (no).

If the bulk of the windfall goes to those with low incomes, *the effect on unemployment will be negative* (there will be no effect on unemployment).

Having scoured the lawbooks, counsels for the defense found exactly the text quotation they wanted in support of the argument that *both questions should be answered in the negative* (the answer to both questions should be no).

negative (verb) sounds terrible: "Time and again such skills as he possessed were *negatived* (canceled out) by perilous indiscretions, vain and foolish improvisations."

neighborhood. For *in the neighborhood of* say *near* or *about:* The total loss—dead, damaged and defective—is *in the neighborhood of* (about) one hundred per thousand.

President Johnson's new budget will be *in the neighborhood of* (near) a record $100 billion.

nemesis is the name of the ancient Greek goddess of divine retribution. It's not a word to be used casually: "Whom should he find ensconced in the tropical splendor but his erstwhile *nemesis* (enemy) who has gone native . . . ."

neophyte is a big word. *New* or *novice* will usually do: "A *neophyte* (new) secretary, innocently directing proper strangers to the improper address. . . ."

-ness. Don't give in to the temptation of using unusual *-ness* words. There's always a simpler way of saying it:

He had read everything in the papers about Ambassador Lodge's conclusions about the *repressiveness* (dictatorial methods) of Diem's brother.

The author sets himself the task of telling exactly what happened, no *fanciness* (fancy), from the time people began hounding him to announce for the nomination . . . .

Children don't need all that *mommyness* (motherliness).

The *organizational massiveness* (massive organization) by which a military machine is characterized . . . .

The act alone would give the unregistered Negro a feeling of *somebodyness* (being somebody) in casting a vote.

We feel that a little social worker may have more *worth-whileness* (worth, significance) than many of the Who's."

In Steinberg's interpretation, the music's *picaresqueness* (roguishness) and its poignancy were only mildly projected.

-nesses sounds awkward and can usually be avoided: "There is a lack of grip, and it seems to adversely affect the Wapshot books in two main ways: it leads to unredeemable *carelessnesses and loosenesses* (carelessness and looseness) of construction . . . ."

new departure is just a long way of saying *new:* "The financing arrangement for these sales to the Communist countries *does represent a new departure* (is new)—the United States government and the tax-paying citizens of this country are assuming full credit risk for these sales."

nigh is an example of heavy-handed would-be humor:

Male heavyweights are flexing their political muscles as election year draws *nigh* (near).

Director Mervyn LeRoy lets the pace lag from time to time, but relief is ever *nigh* (near).

But it's only a moment in *nigh on to* (almost) an hour and a half of stale stuff . . . .

no is often used with unnecessary quotation marks:

When the subcommittee bill came up, Lindsay and three other liberals voted *"no"* (no).

Of 157 departments queried, 99 answered *"no"* (no) as to whether the food requirement was enforced.

non- always makes ugly words; try to say it differently:

He sees a need for a *nongovernment* (private) agency to judge the truthfulness of advertising.

These two points—*nonproliferation and nonaggression* (no proliferation and no aggression)—would probably have to be included in any new package.

It is with great sadness that I realize the *nonfulfillment* (dashing) of these high hopes.

Breaking the old monotony of statesman portraits, Mrs. Kennedy's undertaking has brought to the White House many *fine nonportrait* (other fine) paintings.

Atracta, having been fired for *nonfeasance of* (not fixing) breakfast, goes to law against her former employer.

Mrs. Lloyd-Jones told them she thought it was high time they stopped being accepting, *non-judgmental and non-moralistic* (and refraining from moral judgments) in their relationships with students.

none other than is an old-fashioned figure of speech that doesn't fit into modern prose:

The promoter offering snowbound Northerners easy-payment terms on modern Florida homes was (*none other than*) the United States Government and its Federal Housing Administration.

And who became the incarnation of the Argentine tango and Argentine Gaucho? *None other than the* (The) handsome young Italian boy Rudolph Valentino.

nonexistent is as ugly as it is common. It can be avoided in various ways:

Often dinner is a hamburger served in a paper bag; *books are nonexistent* (there are no books); home is a rooming house . . . .

While lung cancer is rare among nonsmokers—and almost *nonexistent* (unknown) among nonsmokers in rural areas—it is less rare among cigar and pipe smokers . . . .

Since the element of suspense is *nonexistent* (absent), the result is fairly tame . . . .

Bundy had worked on a couple of books about Henry Stimson and Dean Acheson, but *his experience in the field of his responsibilities was almost nonexistent* (had almost no experience in the field of his responsibilities).

That *nonexistent* (imaginary) entity that so glibly is called "The South" . . . .

This is somewhat similar to a corporate pattern in Japan, where employment is for life, advancement is by seniority, and dismissal is almost *nonexistent* (unknown).

The immoderate size of the tax cuts could have been offset by reforms. But *reforms are nearly nonexistent* (there are almost no reforms).

Ordinarily, a burglar will not enter occupied premises, so he will ring doorbells, and if his rings are answered, will pretend to be collecting money for charity or looking for a *nonexistent* (fictitious) Mr. Scott.

nor is a tricky word. Watch these pitfalls:

America, Dr. Gould told the conference of the Educational Records Bureau, prepares its students neither for independent thought, *life nor for peace* (nor for life nor for peace).

Neither attitude—Kerr's *nor* (or) Kefauver's—is typical.

The American people should not have to choose, *on the one hand, between* (between, on the one hand) an all-powerful government dominating our lives . . . *nor* (and) on the other hand, a Federal government committed to withdraw from free world leadership and roll back the clock on social gains and human progress.

normalcy has been derided by grammarians but fills a need:

The establishment of such a force in Europe would enable us to restore *normalcy* to our relationship with the Continent.

Perhaps the most startling and revealing figure of the new *"normalcy"* of Berlin is the sudden increase in real estate values.

not un- is annoyingly pompous:

Kaysen's effectiveness was *not unconnected with* (partly due to) his relative obscurity.

To pursue its unique and *not unambitious* (ambitious) object, the Center has assembled a staff . . . .

Not unexpectedly (As you would expect), the essays vary considerably in acumen and felicity of style.

Macapagal's urgent promotion of his reforms has *not been unaccompanied* (been accompanied) by scandals of the sort that seem to plague every Philippine President.

The outbreak of this rebellion just now is *not unconnected* (connected) with the high and, as a trend, rising rate of unemployment . . . .

His problem in following Kennedy is *not entirely unlike* (somewhat like) Truman's problem of following Roosevelt.

Sen. Hickenlooper is *not widely known for his reluctance* (always ready) to take a good, hard partisan whack at the Democrats whenever he sees a chance to do so.

notwithstanding is much too ponderous for everyday life. Say *in spite of* or *despite*:

It was the consent given to the sale of wheat to the Soviet Union and other Communist countries, *notwithstanding* (in spite of) the "cold war."

It can be reported that the Senator's health has nothing to do with his decision *notwithstanding* (despite) scare stories from the Washington rumor mill.

This was held to be personal expense, *notwithstanding* (despite) the fact that the property involved was of a business nature.

Currently the light of publicity is focused again on our fantastic burial customs, which have sprung up in a large part to pretend that the dead have not died, *all practical evidence to the contrary notwithstanding* (in spite of all practical evidence to the contrary).

nowhere near doesn't make much sense but is an accepted idiom: "*Nowhere near* enough American women are checked for cervical cancer by their doctors."

NUMBERS. *See* FIGURES.

numerous shouldn't be used where *many* would do: "During his career Dr. Bartlett developed *numerous* (many) methods and tools to modernize the work of tree surgeons."

nuptials is a pompous synonym for *marriage* or *wedding:*

> MISS NIEBLING, WHEELOCK '64,
> PLANS *NUPTIALS* (WEDDING)

For the Wapshots can't really marry people: they are born married to their land, their traditions. Further *nuptials* (marriages) are bigamously transitory.

objective (noun). Why not *aim?*

That his *objectives* (aims) had not been achieved at his sad and untimely death was a matter beyond his control.

Dr. Erhard, in an interview, explained the *objectives* (aims) of his visits.

obtain. Why not *get?*

The following year she *obtained* (got) a license to fly heavier-than-air machines.

If you order now, you can *obtain* (get) your own and your Christmas present copies at a special saving.

When, immediately after a big burglary, detectives arrive at a burglar's home in the middle of the night, the burglar knows that without a search warrant they may not legally search the place, or even enter it, against his will, and that at that hour they probably haven't gone to court to *obtain* (get) one.

Sometimes *obtain* can simply be left out: "But this process is distorted in the case of a homogeneous product, such as a household bleach, produced under conditions of oligopoly, (such) as *(obtain)* in the liquid bleach industry."

obviate sounds pompous and academic; try *do away with, cancel, prevent, forestall, blot out, meet:*

My own feeling was that the threat of a boycott had been sufficiently successful to *obviate* (prevent) the need for such action at this time.

But inadequacies of the vision that were incidental only, by *obviating* (forestalling) measures to prevent wage-slavery and control business cycles, brought discredit upon it.

Now, the fact of one viewer's disappointment scarcely *obviates* (cancels, blots out) the towering virtues of this excursion into antiquity.

To *obviate* (prevent, forestall) any hesitation a Negro might feel in speaking freely to a white researcher, almost all the interviewers were Negro.

occur seems a harmless little word, but *happen* is usually better:

The Gross National Product is high and the depression or the recession did not *occur* (happen).

Changes in Chinese attitudes are not likely to *occur* (happen) soon.

odium is an unnecessary Latin word: "If the fine art of animation is to live and preserve its dignity in the culture of motion pictures, where the economic strictures are so great and where it has to *endure the odium* (take the blame) of guilt by association with endless cartoon commercials on television, then it must be practiced by artists who can bring great imagination and devotion to their work."

oe. The trend is toward using *e* in such words as *ameba* and *fetus*.

of is a weed that should be pulled out of all sentences where it doesn't belong:

> Of the 15 millionaires who used this charity provision to avoid paying taxes, eight *(of them)* made their charitable contributions to their own private foundations.

> Of all the objections everybody had to giving me the part, not one *(of them)* was because I was too pretty.

> The process of being born is one of the most hazardous *(of)* medical episodes in America today.

> He emphasized his belief in the right of self-expression, leaving ambiguous the issue *(of)* whether spitting, pushing and placard-throwing were covered by his call for the articulation of deep convictions.

> The only remarkable thing about Goldwater's explanation *(of)* how he and Senator Javits might find a way of living with each other is the fact that he made it.

> There is no earthly explanation *(of)* why.

See also ALL OF, OFF OF, QUESTION OF WHETHER.

If you use many abstract nouns, you're apt to fall into the *of-of-of* style—like this:

> The advisability *of* making extensive changes in the nature *of* the dietary fat intake *of* the people *of* this country has not been demonstrated.

> But to the obvious difficulties *of* persuading the electorate *of* the desirability *of* such a program must be added the problem *of* our own reaction to the achievement *of* rapid growth in the underdeveloped areas.

See also ABSTRACT WORDS.

It's silly to deliberately misspell *of* for *have* when you're quoting an uneducated speaker; both words are pronounced *uv:*

> They're so calm . . . . If that had happened to white folks, we'd *of* (have) moved in and tore the place apart.

> "You should *of* (have) heard that thing when it hit the wall in the station house," a cop said.

of course, like EVERYBODY KNOWS, sounds annoyingly snobbish when referring to matters widely unknown:

Mr. Bernstein ran the risk *(of course)* of comparison with Stravinsky's own recorded performance of the scores.

There are the great archetypal bad dinners *(of course)*, the Thyestian banquet and Grendel's feast in Hrothgar's hall.

There has *(of course)* been a federal program in existence for vocational education since 1917, when the Smith-Hughes Act provided for sharing costs with the states.

of late sounds bookish. Say *lately* or *recently:* "But *of late* (lately) this famous swan-fleet has been sadly dwindling, because no little cygnets are being born."

off of. Cross out *of:* "Simple Simon says, hands off (of) eyes."

oftentimes, ofttimes. Say *often:*

How far can a writer venture in embellishing the *oftentimes* (often) spare details of Biblical stories with his own descriptions and dialogues?

The head of a powerful arm of American Reform Judaism called on Jews tonight to reassess Jesus and to revise an "*ofttimes* (often) jaundiced view of Him in whose name Christianity was established."

oh is a pet word of arch columnists:

Oh, how (How) we laughed when Baroness Hilla von Rebay, back in the 'thirties, kept buying Kandinskys by the hundred . . . .

But *(oh,)* how bitter the opposition. Mrs. Harold Lifvendahl, of Larchmont, says she always enjoyed my columns until . . . .

oldster is an ugly invention. Stick to *old man, woman, people:* "So it was fitting that the *oldsters* (old people) began by not appearing in the sundeck press room, where they were to have told the press how it felt to be old and going to Europe."

-ology is sometimes added unnecessarily by long-word addicts:

Our children are growing up not knowing the Christmas *hymnology* (hymns) of the church.

In all cases the onset of the illness was signaled by psychotic *symptomatology* (symptoms).

one sounds clumsy in such sentences as "The task will not be *an easy one."* Why not "The task won't be easy?" If you too have the *a-one* habit, get rid of it:

The Napoleonic lode is *(a)* seemingly inexhaustible *(one)*.

The position of Richard Nixon in California political calculations is *(a)* curious *(one)*.

There is a complaint to be made, but you must be the judge of whether it is *(a)* valid *(one)*.

Anne Boleyn's story is *(a)* superb *(one)*, practically unmatched for drama, pathos and irony.

Don't use *one* as a synonym for *I*, implying that you've appointed yourself spokesman for humanity at large:

One guesses (I guess) that this book will emerge as one of the few classics directly produced by World War II.

One questions (I question) why this young man who saw you at work daily never showed interest at that time.

One gathers (I gather) from the Russian retreat that Khrushchev needs Kennedy's good will even more than Kennedy needs Khrushchev's.

One wishes one (I wish I) could welcome "Bicycle Ride to Nevada" more warmly, for its aspirations are as honorable as they are serious.

One could not listen (I listened) to his performance of Schumann's "Symphonic Etudes" and *not come* (came) away convinced he could bring the same strength, poise, attention to detail, understanding and musical imagination to Beethoven for instance.

See also I.

Sometimes *one* should be changed to *you* rather than *I*:

Continuing down Reitschul Gasse, *one enters* (you enter) a passageway and *emerges* (emerge) in Josefs Platz . . . .

One needs (You need) to vary *one's* (your) sentence length; to amplify *one's* (your) vocabulary; to diversify *one's* (your) tone.

The one . . . the other, like THE FORMER . . . THE LATTER, should be replaced by names or simple pronouns: "His novel is more in the line of George Macdonald and C. S. Lewis. If it has ancestors at all, they are the unjustly neglected 'Phantastes' of *the one* (Macdonald) and 'Perelandra' of *the other* (Lewis)."

one of. "It is really *one of the nicest things that has* happened to me." Grammatically, the word *has*—instead of *have*—in this sentence is a mistake, but the idiom is firmly established:

> *One of the things that makes* conservatism too damn hard to sell is that its exponents make such violent and foolish statements.

> It is about nothing at all. That is *one of the things that makes* it so attractive.

> If you're *one of those people who doesn't* know the difference between a 27 per cent depletion allowance and a 50 per cent override . . . .

> By *one of those strange coincidences that seems* to be the life blood of the current music season . . . .

ongoing is academic jargon. Try *active*: "The psychiatric and moral-legal views of criminal responsibility are similar in that both involve an imperative, a calling to account and an intervention in an *ongoing* (active) pattern of living."

onus is the Latin word for *burden*. Often the best English translation is *up to*: "*The onus is on* (It is up to) the young man to present himself before the draft board."

operational is sheer pomposity: "A liberal is a man who cultivates the skills that make freedom *operational* (practical)."

operative is now the fashionable long word for *key, active* or *at work*:

> The Nixon candidacy, long quietly *operative* (active) in fact, now must totally change in strategy.

> The *operative* (key) factor is fear of failure.

> As a result, Marxism as an *operative* (active) political philosophy is waning in the West.

> Strongly *operative* (at work) among us is the aspiration to establish justice.

opine for *think* is hopelessly old-fashioned humor: "Where Aristotle *opined* (thought, believed) that all men pursue the good, Kant believed that all men pursue duty."

opprobrium is an unnecessary four-syllable Latin word for *reproach* or *blame:* "I fail to see why France should suffer any more *opprobrium* (reproach, blame) than Norway, Pakistan or Great Britain, who are NATO members."

opt is a silly fad word. Say *choose:*

> Even Walter Heller thereupon replied that, if this was the real situation, he, too, *opted for* (chose) a tight budget.

> There are teachers and artisans and businessmen and doctors and clergymen and lawyers who have *opted for* (chosen) a locale in which they can acquire a civic identity.

optimal is a pompous word for *best:*

> We cannot, however, live lives built around the level of stress and then all of a sudden switch off the stress factors and expect to continue to function *optimally* (at our best).

> The more we grapple with planning problems, the more uneasy we are becoming about our ability to make *optimal* (the best) choices for the future.

optimum. *Best* is better.

opus is the Latin word for *work.* Say it in English: "And that's about the nicest thing anyone can say about Mr. Lemmon in this nasty little *opus* (movie)."

-or sometimes makes long, awkward words: "Nor can *the appreciator of* (anyone who appreciates) modern art be far removed from the exploring temperament of those who create it."

oral comes from the Latin and means *by mouth.* It does *not* mean *by ear:* "The State Education Department had recommended that the newer audio-lingual method stressing *oral comprehension* (speaking and listening) be taught in preference to the older methods stressing writing and reading." *See also* VERBAL.

orb is a poetic word for *eye.* Don't use it in prose.

order. *In order to* can always be shortened to *to:*

> *In order to* (To) achieve his dream he had to contend with some surprising problems.

> This was the radical revision of investment priorities the Soviet leaders so obviously need to make, *(in order)* to improve the declining Soviet rate of economic growth . . . .

> *On the order of* should be changed to *about:*

> Last year's Chinese Communist grain crop was *on the order of* (about) 182 million tons.

> There is neither equity nor honor in this brazen species of

handout—which already costs *on the order of* (about) $1.8 billion a year.

other than sounds bookish and legal. Usually the thing to do is to push the word *other* forward:

The school achievement of a child is strongly affected by *factors other* (other factors) than native intelligence.

This means that Mr. Macmillan can, with good grace, retire for *political reasons other* (other political reasons) than the Profumo affair.

Sometimes *other than* should be changed to *except* or *aside from:*

These cases are not secret, however. It is just that no one *other than* (except) those concerned generally pays any attention.

These gains were achieved despite the fact that P. & G., *other than* (aside from) taking advantage of the advertising economies, has carefully avoided changing the Clorox operation.

ourself. When you use the editorial *we,* you'll sooner or later find yourself saddled with the silly word *ourself:* "We are happy to offer *ourself* as an opinionated, expert, entirely uninvited arbitrator."

See also WE.

oust, ouster are strictly headline words. Try instead *drive out, expel, expulsion:*

CONGO *OUSTS* (EXPELS) ENTIRE
RED EMBASSY

The Baathists were ousted (driven out) earlier in an army coup d'état.

Cronin's statement also hinted that Finley's *ouster* (expulsion) from the league might be considered at a later date.

outcome is sometimes used as a fancy synonym for *result:* "A study indicated that a weight gain of one pound per week during the last half of pregnancy was associated with the most favorable fetal *outcome* (result)."

outline (verb) shouldn't be used as a synonym for *describe:*

The Washington Star *outlined* (described) the profitable

financial dealings Mr. Baker had with the Mortgage Guaranty Insurance Co. of Milwaukee.

Secret documents *outlining* (describing) the plans and operations of the cartel were obtained by the Herald Tribune.

Dr. Pusey had her to dinner in Cambridge and *outlined* (described) his plans for the institute.

over-. Don't yield to the temptation of using fancy words with *over-*: "The first ingredient would be *an overarching* (a chief, main) concern for the values comprising a good life."

overall is much overused instead of *whole* or *total:*

The council fathers still must vote once more on the *overall* (whole) document.

The *overall* (total) infant mortality rate for the United States in 1962 was 25.3 per 1,000 live births.

But, *overall* (on the whole), we are attending a school-masterish exercise on a blackboard.

overestimate. *See* DIFFICULT TO OVERESTIMATE.

owing to seems to be used often by people who are afraid of saying *due to:* "*Owing to* (Due to) the tragic events of the last weekend, nearly all of New York's night spots remained dark through Monday."

own (verb) is old-fashioned in the sense of *confess* or *admit:* "There is at least some evidence that Johnson's reputed hostility to 'intellectuals' has been exaggerated, but he himself has *owned up to* (admitted) a preference for the concrete rather than the abstract."

P

pace. "This latinism," says Fowler, "is one that we could very well do without in English." So, even if you know how it is pronounced (PAYsee) and what it means *(in spite of what So-and-so says)*, you'd better leave it alone. Example: "Earls, even with long blond tresses and *(pace Dr. Rowse)* [in spite of what Dr. Rowse says] a really odious face, like Southampton, do not commonly excite such torrents of sound and feeling."

pachyderm is no longer funny as a synonym for *elephant:* "It is impossible to find *pachyderm* (elephant) parking space in Bangkok."

package is a current fad word in sentences like this: "The Russians were interested in striking a *package* deal sponsored by Washington."

I have a hunch that *package* in this sense is here to stay.

palpable sounds bookish. Try *obvious, visible, clear:*

Cavanagh's most *palpable* (obvious) fault is ducking tough decisions on key personnel.

More often, that legislation is being demanded by the national interest, a *palpably* (clearly) different thing.

The underlying fact of the new diplomacy is that in a shrunken world, foreign affairs have come to exert a *palpable* (visible) impact on the day-to-day lives of average men.

paradigm is the current fad word for *model:*

Monsignor Joseph Clifford Fenton is editor of the *paradigm* (model) of American Catholic conservatism, the American Ecclesiastical Review.

As General "Buck" Turgidson, chairman of the Joint Chiefs, Scott is the brash, boyish *paradigm* (model) of technological knowhow . . . .

PARAGRAPHS are a convenience to the reader: it's always better to have too many paragraphs than too few. When in doubt, start a new paragraph.

For example, look at this 200-word paragraph:

In that atmosphere, the Administration's task is particularly difficult. Beating back the subcommittee bill in the full committee is hard enough; the more so as Southern Democratic members may abstain, or even vote to approve the subcommittee bill, confident that it would be easy to whip on the floor of the House or in the Senate. Moreover, it is not sufficient simply to defeat the subcommittee bill. An agreed substitute must be available, otherwise the 35-member Judiciary Committee would have to do the drafting job all over again—a process that would take months. The only certainty at the week end was that the search for an acceptable substitute was on, with a vote in the full committee scheduled for day-after-tomorrow. Except for the civil rights issue, the Administration's $11 billion tax reduction measure would now be enjoying plain sailing. It passed the House last month by a sizable majority. In the House Ways and Means Committee, most of the controversial reform measures were knocked out; and the Administration has ceased to press for the others. Thanks to the "O'Brien majority," even the Republican demand for matching prescribed budget against the tax reduction was handily beaten on the House floor.

Now look at the same piece of prose, cut into seven convenient paragraphs:

In that atmosphere, the Administration's task is particularly difficult.

Beating back the subcommittee bill in the full committee is hard enough; the more so as Southern Democratic members may abstain, or even vote to approve the subcommittee bill, confident that it would be easy to whip on the floor of the House or in the Senate.

Moreover, it is not sufficient simply to defeat the subcommittee bill. An agreed substitute must be available, otherwise the 35-member Judiciary Committee would have to do the drafting job all over again—a process that would take months.

The only certainty at the week end was that the search for an acceptable substitute was on, with a vote in the full committee scheduled for day-after-tomorrow.

Except for the civil rights issue, the Administration's $11 billion tax reduction measure would now be enjoying plain sailing. It passed the House last month by a sizable majority.

In the House Ways and Means Committee, most of the controversial reform measures were knocked out; and the Administration has ceased to press for the others.

Thanks to the "O'Brien majority," even the Republican demand for matching prescribed budget against the tax reduction was handily beaten on the House floor.

paramount shouldn't be used as a pompous synonym for *first*: "*Paramount* (First) in importance is the relation of world trade to world peace, since the communication and understanding between nations implicit in trade is basic to peace."

PARENTHESES can be used to make a point softly but effectively:

> Blackburn was a famous character in and around Gloucester for the next thirty years, but, unlike many such characters, he had no flaw in him; he was hungry for neither notoriety nor money. (Indeed, he gave away in his lifetime something like fifty thousand dollars to the poor and unfortunate.)

> He was one of the great originals of the romantic era, and his music comes across today with no lessening of its vitality. Now, if only someone would take a look at that Ugly Duckling of the Big Five, the F major . . . (It's really a swan, you know.)

> Simultaneously, other surgeons installed shunts of plastic tubes to carry the blood that should have passed through the inferior vena cava to the jugular veins in Bingel's neck. A second group stood ready with a heart-lung machine in case Patient Bingel needed it. (He didn't.)

part. *On the part of* is a cumbersome preposition. Say *from* or *of:*

> Sound in an orchestra requires creative ability *on the part of* (from) the conductor; the ability to say what has not been said before.

> It seems to me this large mandate *on the part of* (from) the voters merely reflects the fact that a fallacy seems to be very popular.

> He attributed much of the speed and the noise to the desire *for fun and excitement on the part of the ambulance drivers* (of the ambulance drivers for fun and excitement).

partake of is a bookish phrase; it's simpler to say *share, have, use:*

> That style *partakes largely of* (uses a lot of) twelve-tone techniques, but of the rather conservative side of the school.

> The owner sets the counterweight according to the weight of the bird he hopes will *partake of* (use, share) his hospitality . . . .

> These are representative figures in contemporary writing, and there are scores of others that *partake of their* (share their, have the same) quality, which is to reduce the sexual encounter to rape or the degradation of the sexual partner.

partially can always be shortened to *partly.*

PARTICIPLES. *See* -ING.

passing as a euphemism for *death* is usually out of place: "Mr. Michaels has had the grace to spare us the details of his *passing* (death) but he has depicted the relationship between Dylan Thomas and his wife, Caitlin, as a most lively one . . . ."

PASSIVE VOICE. The most common fault of style is overuse of the passive voice. Change to the active voice whenever you can:

> Continuous maintenance and continuing improvement of our striking power *is insisted upon by Mr. McNamara.* (Mr. McNamara insists upon . . . .)

> The situation *was being viewed by experts in transit labor* as the most serious in the last 15 years. (Experts in transit labor viewed the situation as . . . .)

> *The point may be made* (Let me make the point) by a citation from Milovan Djilas's "Conversations with Stalin."

> We are, of course, deeply sorry to see the Western Edition go. *Every effort is being made* (We are making every effort) to find new jobs for the several dozen persons whose livelihood depended on it.

> The tendency to blame the failure to get the U.S. economy moving again on so-called "political" difficulties beyond the reach of national leadership *cannot be said to be* (is not) pointless.

> Thanks to the inventions of man, instantaneous communication throughout the world *has been made* (is) possible.

> *See also* IT, THEREBY.

paucity is just a fancy way of saying *little* or *few*: "In a time when there is *a paucity of* (little) fine, new drama, explore the wealth of the past."

pecuniary. Be straightforward: say *money*.

peer group is educational or sociological jargon for what used to be called *friends*:

> Everybody in the industry has been forced to become an authority *in his peer group* (among his friends) on the subject.

> It cannot but help as well to influence beneficially other multiple sources that lead to anti-Semitism, which involve

the complex interaction of the home, school, *peer group* (friends), neighborhood and mass media.

pen (verb) sounds old-fashioned and shouldn't be used as a synonym for *write:*

The material was written by Peter Cook . . . who founded The Establishment night club in London and *penned* (wrote) much of the Broadway hit titled "Beyond the Fringe."

RED-TRAINED OKELLO *PENS* (WRITES) SCRIPTS FOR AFRICAN GRAB

True enough, the poet *penned* (wrote) no memoirs, he merely left us Shakespeare's Complete Works.

pending shouldn't be abused as a preposition meaning *until*

He was safely protected *pending* (until) arraignment and trial.

BRITISH POSTPONE SALE OF 12 JETS TO DOMINICANS *PENDING* (UNTIL) STABILITY

For the moment, and *pending* (until) any more sinister disclosures, l'affaire Rometsch has largely served to enliven the investigation . . . .

Jacques Tine of France said after the vote that he, too, favored postponement *pending* (until) further consultations.

per annum. Say *a year.*

per cent. Don't use *per cent* as a synonym for *profit:* "To lay stress on the gross total of profits without regard to whether individual companies are making a satisfactory *per cent* (profit) on their investment is to confuse the issue."

per diem. Say *a day.*

per se means *as such.* It's better to say it in English:

Mr. Baker's business activities *per se* (as such) will not be condemned.

Its hallmark is a ruthless use of the emotional appeal exercised by children *per se* (as such).

I don't consider hardening of the arteries to be a manifestation of aging *per se* (as such) at all.

peradventure. Now *there's* a pompous word: "My reading of the American segment I have seen in the past 12 days is that America does not as of now belong beyond *peradventure* (doubt) to either party."

perchance. Say *perhaps* or *maybe.*

peril shouldn't be used as a substitute word for *risk:* "This single policy can be written to protect your family from almost every property *risk and liability peril* (and liability risk)."

PERIODS mark the end of a sentence, but they can also be used *within* a sentence. This is an effective punctuation device, but like everything else, it can be overdone. Here's an example of two sentences chopped arbitrarily into eight pieces:

News comes in bits and pieces. But we think it doesn't have to come to you that way. So we take the many sides of every important news story. Get the facts. Look at them in relation to yesterday. And with an eye toward their effect on tomorrow. Then mold them into an intelligent, understandable story. Like the one above.

In contrast, look at some fine examples of rhetorical periods used with just the right effect:

Exactly who reads collections of occasional criticism? The victims, I suppose, if they still survive. Other critics, perhaps. And devoted students. But how about the ordinary reader . . . .

Although he sticks to one film, he doesn't confine himself to one shot of a product, situation or animal. Instead of taking only one picture of apples he takes hundreds. A single apple. A pair. A trio. A basketful. An orchard. An apple cider mill. A sliced apple. And so on.

Mr. Friedman digs deeper into his fiddle than Heifetz, and comes out with a ravishing, full-blooded tone that soars and sighs, with just the proper measure of restraint. One might almost say Kreisler. Kreisler with a nervous edge.

When young Madame Sarabhai was invited by the Institute for Advanced Studies in Theatre Arts to train American actors and actresses in Kathakali (ancient dance drama), she arranged for a rather distinguished baby sitter. The chairman of space research in India. Her husband.

See also AND, BUT, SHORT SENTENCES.

perpetrate does *not* mean whatever it's supposed to mean in this sentence: "There is the idealistic, cotton-candy attitude still *perpetrated* (taught? spread?) in many schools which sees public life as a step below heaven, where selfless altruists labor tirelessly in the public interest."

persons. Don't say *persons* when it's more natural to say *people:* "The fact sheets are aimed primarily at the 6 million *persons* (people) whose tax liabilities aren't adequately covered by the paycheck withholding system."

persuasion. The phrase *of the such-and-such persuasion* sounds genteel and Victorian:

Richard Rovere was the first journalist *of the Eastern persuasion* (from the East) to render Taft justice.

Combs is *an observer of politically liberal persuasion* (a politically liberal observer).

pertain is a formal word that can be simplified in various ways:

Re your editorial *pertaining to* (about) the Port Authority destroying the downtown business area . . . .

Of the five, only Richard Frantzreb . . . had read the book. He thought it had a basis of truth, "but I felt like I was outside looking in. It *didn't pertain to* (wasn't about) me."

It was our statement to the Secret Service that any arrangements *in so far as they pertained to* (about) the security of the President was their affair and not ours.

We will take a searching look at both the laws and law-enforcement machinery *as it pertains to* (covering) organized gambling.

peruse shouldn't be used as a fancy synonym for *read:*

MANY EXPECT SMOKING TO BE
INDICTED—7,000 REPORTS HAVE BEEN
PERUSED (READ)

"Passwords" is a proper present for all people who want a book that they can *peruse* (read) with pleasure.

phenomenon is a long, awkward word. Whenever possible, say *thing* or *fact:*

The craze is expected to gross $60 million this season and one toy executive says: "It's the biggest *phenomenon* (thing) ever to hit the trade."

But Wilson is not a prophet; he is an eminently lucid, thoroughly balanced man, a skilled interpreter, a commentator for whom complexity in *phenomena* (facts) has always called forth a matching complexity of understanding.

philosophy is much abused as an impressive synonym for the simple word *idea:*

The plea that Captain Rickenbacker will make in his crusade will follow the lines of his past *philosophies* (ideas).

The *philosophy* (idea) seems to be, the bigger the burden the government assumes, the more likely it will be that private companies can provide adequate insurance.

These are the men who will reflect the *philosophies* (ideas) of the President and carry out his wishes.

picture shouldn't be used as an all-purpose word. Be specific: "His situation, of course, is complicated by the Vice Presidential *picture* (race)."

place (verb) isn't any better than *put*. Say *put*.

plaudits is old-fashioned; say *applause:* "Judy Garland's daughter, Liza Minnelli, earned *plaudits* (applause) in 'Best Foot Forward.' "

plethora is the Greek word for *fullness*. Why not say it in English?

How come *the plethora of* (all those) films about prostitution and brothels which have been given Code seals?

It was a happy thought on Mrs. Vining's part to write a novel round Donne's eventful life. Though there is *a plethora* (plenty) of critical writing on his work . . . .

PLURALS. *See* ARE, IS or ARE, LATIN PLURALS, THEY.

politico is journalese for *politician:* "Any *politicos* (politicians) who dream of some comfortable compromise on the central issues are deluding themselves."

polity is a rare word sometimes used in the same sense as *policy*. Since most readers will probably take *polity* as a typographical error, you might as well say *policy* to begin with: "Heavily concentrated in the upper Midwest, the Brethren are mostly German in national origin, differ in theology and *polity* (policy) from the Methodists only in small detail."

Pollyanna is now commonly used in the sense of super-optimist, as in: "At the weekend, only an optimist could retain any real hope of getting a civil rights bill past Congress at this session. And only a *Pollyanna* could fail to see in the turmoil on Capitol Hill portents of much more significant trouble for the whole movement toward racial equity in this country."

Actually, Pollyanna, the heroine of the famous girls' book by Eleanor H. Porter, did *not* stupidly expect everything to work out fine, but showed people how to put up philosophically with misfortune.

But I guess it's too late telling people that *Pollyanna* doesn't mean what they think it means.

pontiff is now used solely as the standard substitute word for *pope*. My advice is, say *pope:* "Pope Paul VI, in the first specially recorded message ever made by a *pontiff* (pope) for British television, said tonight . . . ."

portend sounds portentous. Say *show:* "While this falls short of a proposal for neutralization, it does *portend* (show) a willingness to seek a political solution."

portent sounds just as portentous. Say *sign:* "There are encouraging, although remarkably diverse, *portents* (signs) on the horizon."

portion shouldn't be used as more formal synonym for *part:*

A large *portion* (part) of the leaders in the public relations field have been subscribers of Public Relations News since it was established . . . .

Desertion in the lower-income groups now accounts for a significant *portion* (part) of the public welfare administrator's chronic case load.

portray, portrayal shouldn't be used as fancy synonyms for *act, play, part, role:* "Miss Kaye, whose previous acting experience was limited to video *portrayals* (roles, parts), proved to offer even more than Universal executives had bargained for."

positively is often unnecessary and should be left out:

He *(positively)* boasted that he was withdrawing from the race to put men on the moon.

The means by which he arrives at this view can, in specific cases, make *(positively)* appalling reading.

POSSESSIVES. *See* -'s, -s' *or* -s's?

posterior to is a clumsy circumlocution for *after*.

postprandial is an example of heavy-handed would-be humor. Say *after dinner*: "Bankers have an uncanny habit of turning into *postprandial* (after-dinner) literary critics *manqué*."

postulate (*verb*) means *assume, claim, take for granted*. It shouldn't be used instead of *state* or *base*:

> While *postulating* (explaining, stating) the theory that high living standards produce poor distance runners, he clenched his left first. . . .

> . . . the reluctance to examine and question the premises on which we *postulated* (based) our more advanced ideas and programs, including the ideas which sustain our most advanced and radical art.

posture is now the fad word for *attitude*, and is wildly overused:

> Confident that the President of the U.S. is virtually stalemated into (*a posture of*) inaction, foreign governments feel free to pursue their disturbing policies without fear of reprisals.

> The reticence of the industry's spokesmen seems to be a result of a joint decision by the six major producers to *take a low posture* (lie low).

pray for *please* sounds old-fashioned and arch:

> Talk all you please about the way character grows when midnight snacks are eschewed, but *pray* (please) don't talk about it to me.

> And where (*pray tell*) do they intend to put the bars?

pre-. Go slow in forming words with *pre-*; usually the results are ugly:

> In view of the recent evidence of *pre-coup atrocities* (atrocities before the coup), I find it increasingly difficult to sympathize . . . .

> *Gov. Wallace issued a pre-dawn executive order* (Before dawn, Gov. Wallace issued an executive order) to keep 20 Negro students out of five other Alabama public schools.

precipitate, precipitous are long words. *Rash, sudden, hasty* are shorter and better:

The political fortunes of Sen. Barry Goldwater have taken a *precipitate* (sudden) drop.

To make an outright contribution to TV public service that might involve hundreds of thousands of dollars, he said, cannot be undertaken *precipitously* (hastily).

predecease, even in legal documents, should be changed to *die before.*

predicated has four syllables. Why not use the one-syllable word *based?*

I once read a story, whose title and author I have long since forgotten, which was *predicated* (based) on precisely this premise.

The effort is *predicated* (based) on the belief that Mayor Wagner cannot be persuaded to run this fall against Sen. Keating.

predominantly has five syllables. How about *mainly* or *chiefly?*

One ward is *predominantly* (mainly) Polish, so we ran a Polish boy down there.

The plan calls for *predominantly* (mainly) middle-income housing.

pre-empt is much too formal for many sentences: "There is a great deal to be learned here, with one factor *pre-empting* (topping) all others in importance."

prejudicial is a long, awkward word. Try *harmful.*

preliminary to is a clumsy compound preposition. Say *before.*

premier (adjective) sounds fancy and bookish: "One cannot help but think that our *premier* (foremost) literary critic . . . is a bit of a dope."

premises smacks of law and police. Say *building* or leave it out: "Will Steven Armstrong has conceived a set which revolves to represent (*the premises of*) a mental hospital."

preparatory to. Don't use this phrase as a compound preposition meaning *before:* " 'Arturo Ui' will have a series of low-priced previews *preparatory to* (before) opening Nov. 14."

prepared to sounds pompous. Say *willing to:*

Despite such words of caution there have been many wishful thinkers outside the government *prepared* (willing) to believe a truly new era in United States-Soviet relations is in prospect if, indeed, not already arrived.

Yet the question remains: What social responsibilities are our corporations *prepared* (willing) to assume, and what are the consequences of such an interpretation of the corporate role likely to be?

In retrospect, however, this corner is *prepared* (willing) to concede that concern with the derivative nature of "T.W.T.W.T.W." perhaps is not as vital as it may have seemed . . . .

preponderance, preponderantly are used by long-word addicts instead of *most, many, mostly, largely, mainly, chiefly:*

But Zanzibar-like events also demonstrate the *preponderance of* (many) unrelated reasons for the fratricide that shames the world.

As in the House hearings, *the preponderance of* (most) pleas come from private-interest spokesmen . . . .

These types of cuts are wholly or *preponderantly* (largely) wasteful, even as economic stimulants.

PREPOSITION AT END. Yes, you *can* end a sentence (or phrase) with a preposition, and very often you should. Look for instance at these three unidiomatic sentences by superstitious writers who didn't dare put the preposition after the verb:

But *on whose side should we get* (whose side should we get on) in a situation where neither is right?

When Mr. Wallace read his mild editorial, viewers may well have wondered *on what facts his opinion was based* (what facts his opinion was based on).

The poison *to which I refer* (I refer to) is the American monopoly of nuclear weapons in *NATO.*

If you need encouragement, here's a little collection of sentence-ending prepositions at their finest:

Her temperament is such that she does vigorously *whatever she is concerned with.*

"The toughest ones are *the easiest to get along with,*" Mr. Bernstein once said.

One Congressman thought the headwaiter's presence at the NATO conference *the "damnedest thing" he had heard of.*

Five times in the last two weeks *the office has been broken into.*

The Secretary General, more than anyone else, is aware of the insecurity in the Congo, *what it could lead to and the conditions it stems from.*

Many fingers were crossed, and strong men went looking around the building's modernistic interior *for wood to knock on.*

"I agree with a large fraction of *what he agrees with,*" Friedman explained.

He said that Mr. Mahoney "might not know about it, because the committee perhaps has not reported to him yet, but *the proposal is being worked on.*"

At one West Side school last week a teacher was heard to say, quietly, *"There is nobody left to integrate with."*

Whatever the salutation, letters addressed to the UN that are obviously not diplomatic or personal are *theirs to cope with.*

Here is a high-school senior willing to spend his father's money in a restaurant his father has always regarded as *too expensive to take his mother to.*

presage (verb) is a bookish word; try *foreshadow* or *mean:*
A. H. Raskin of The New York Times warned in a recent magazine article that the challenge may *"presage* (foreshadow, mean) nothing less than the eventual disappearance of unions as we know them."

France officially recognized Communist China yesterday in a move which almost certainly *presages* (foreshadows, means) a strong fight for Peking's admission to the United Nations this year.

His most illustrious ancestor was a woman, Transcendentalist Margaret Fuller, whose strong-minded individualism *presaged* (foreshadowed) Bucky's own.

prescient is a rare word; the ordinary word is *prophetic:* "In his *prescient* (prophetic) book, *The Lonely Crowd,* David Riesman said that adult educators would have to serve as 'leisure counselors.' "

PRESENT TENSE. Strict grammarians insist on a rigid sequence of tenses in English, but idiomatically people often use the "ungrammatical" present tense because it sounds more lively:

> Underlining this is the fact that many companies told McGraw-Hill they would spend more if the economy *is* stimulated by a tax cut.

> "And then," Morris continued, "he gave a long spiel about how the Mayor *is* trying to ruin him personally."

presently. The standard dictionary meaning of *presently* is *soon*, but most people use it as a pompous synonym for *now*. Better stick to *now*:

> Mr. Nitze denied categorically that he advocated this either in 1960 or *presently* (now).

> The report said that of nearly 19,000 restaurant liquor licenses in the state, "most are bars only and sell substantially less food than *presently* (now) required under State Liquor Authority regulations."

> As *presently* (now) written, the averaging formula does not provide much help for such persons.

> Some writers vary *presently* with *at present* or *at the present time*. But none of these variations is as good as *now*: "Contrary to the beliefs of many, private insurance plans cannot economically write health insurance for the aged *at the present time* (now)."

prestigious is now the fad word for what used to be called *honored, distinguished, well-known, famous*:

> A blunt rejoinder came promptly from Manhattan's *prestigious* (famous) Sloan-Kettering Cancer Center.

> Last week the *prestigious* (distinguished, famous) American Jewish Committee accused 50 of the country's top utility companies of discriminating against Jews in hiring and promoting top executives.

pretty lends itself to snobbish understatement: "Let me go on to say that Mr. Simon's comedy is *pretty* jolly."

prevail often sounds formal and stiff:

> The circular motif *prevails* (appears, shows up) throughout the building which is basically one great circle intersected by smaller ones.

> It is likely, however, that a taxpayer claiming a similar deduction will have to go to court to *prevail* (win, succeed).

preventative means exactly the same as *preventive;* strike out the unnecessary extra syllable.

previous to shouldn't be used as a compound preposition; say *before:* "Not two days *previous to* (before) receiving the Feb. 7 issue, I searched in vain for information . . . ."

previously is much overused. It's better to say *earlier:*

Previously (Earlier) he had visited Alma-Ata, capital of the Soviet Republic of Kazakhstan.

Previously (Earlier) two Democrats considered "sound" had been named to the subcommittee.

principal (adjective) is a longish word often used instead of *main* or *chief:*

Scientific studies have been undertaken in various countries and their *principal* (main) result has been to implicate cigarette smoking . . . .

The abstentions were *principally* (mainly, chiefly) by Communist countries and their sympathizers.

prior to. There's no excuse for using the stilted phrase *prior to* instead of *before:*

Once when all the comics had been "on," they were requested kindly to be quiet, just *prior to* (before) filming a commercial for the picture.

These strips constitute Tristan's only arable land, and *prior to* (before) the departure of its population one of them was the site of the island's only settlement.

Defendant Pace has admitted that *prior to* (before) the commencement of this action, he did not even intend to call plaintiff's case for trial.

As the sales force of a client company stepped out to the veranda for cocktails *prior to* (before) an auto presentation, they were confronted with the spectacle of an unbelievable horse, painted blue from head to hoof.

pro is now standard English and doesn't need quotation marks: "He is respected as a '*pro*' (pro) in the art of getting action on controversial legislation."

probe is strictly a headline word. Say *investigation:* "The Senate (*investigation*) subcommittee resumes its *probe* (investigation) of the controversial TFX warplane contract . . . ."

proceedings is sometimes used humorously, but the effect is weak: "Estelle Parsons demonstrates her delightful gift for humor as the one girl in the *proceedings* (show)."

procure, like OBTAIN, shouldn't be used as a pompous word for *get.*

prohibit is a formal legal term; change it to *prevent* or *forbid:*

The State Department has cautioned Spain that her rapidly expanding economic relations with Cuba may lead to the invoking of legal provisions *prohibiting* (forbidding) United States aid to countries that help the regime of Premier Fidel Castro.

The provision *prohibits* (prevents) Federal regulatory agencies from requiring utilities to pass along benefits of the investment tax credit of 1962 to consumers in the form of lower rates. (Better: The provision says Federal regulatory agencies mustn't force utilities to . . . .)

Mr. Worthy yesterday hailed the Federal Appeals Court action in declaring unconstitutional the Federal law that *prohibits* (prevents) a citizen from leaving or entering the country without a valid passport. (Better: . . . the Federal law that says a citizen mustn't leave or enter . . . .)

It may be that these judges were not *prohibited* (prevented) from enjoying such hospitality, but perhaps they should have been.

proportion, proportions are used in many wordy circumlocutions:

Serious programs to develop new and backward old nations have been largely left to the United States by other Western peoples with the financial capacity to undertake *them in greater proportion* (more of them).

An "explosion" in color-casting, in short, now seems a great deal less likely than a slow recognition by the ABC and CBS networks that the size of the color-watching audience is *attaining more significant proportions* (getting bigger).

proven is getting old-fashioned. Say *proved:*

None of this has *proven* (proved) to be in the slightest bit true at all.

I think we've *proven* (proved) something to everyone.

provender for *food* isn't funny. Say *food:* "We chose among the

good German *provender* (food) a jumbo pig's knuckle with
wine kraut, $2.25."

provide is an overformal word that should be changed to *give,
say, have, offer:*

> The way in which the President met the challenge *provides*
> (gives, offers) a clue to the way in which he is likely to
> work with Congress in the months ahead.

> It is the second question that *provides* (gives, offers) the
> author (*with*) his most effective ideas.

> Prior to 1960 Section 373 of the General Business Law
> *provided* (said) that if usury had been charged, the
> creditor could not recover if he sued to recover the amount
> of the loan.

> The oratorio *provides* (has) a sympathetic fellow-Christian
> in the person of Irene . . . .

> An IEY *provides* (offers) a means for real international
> medical cooperation.

Often *provide* can be left out altogether: "Equally interesting
sections are (*provided*) by J. B. Segal on Sabian mysteries, by
E. D. Phillips on the vanished Caspian region peoples . . . ."

provided and **providing** should normally be changed to *if:*

> Actually, when the time comes, I anticipate that men will
> have far less trouble filling up their empty hours than the
> alarmists predict, *provided* (if) they have adequate incomes.

> He said he accepted, in a letter sent yesterday, *provided*
> (if) he can participate in the outline of a stage-by-stage
> city-wide desegregation.

prowess is archaic. Try *skill, talent:* "Mr. Seferiades' literary
prowess (skill, talent) came to notice in the mid-1930s . . . ."

proximity is a circumlocution for *close* or *near:* "They believe
that future stores must be *in close proximity* (close) to their
markets so that there can be both fast turnover of goods and a
maintenance of quality."

PUNCTUATION. *See* APOSTROPHES, COLONS, COMMAS, DASHES,
DOTS, EXCLAMATION MARKS, HYPHENS, PARAGRAPHS, PERIODS,
QUOTATION MARKS, SEMICOLONS.

purchase should normally be changed to *buy:* "She said Mr.

Baker and Mr. Novak initially *purchased* (bought) two city blocks in Ocean City."

purport (verb), **purportedly** sound stiff and legal; try *said to, supposed to,* etc.:

These reports *purported* (were said) to contain derogatory information on Mr. Reynolds's background . . . .

Some of the documents and lists *purportedly* (supposedly, were said to have) wound up in Mr. Eastland's dossiers in Washington.

The program *purportedly was* (is said to have been) prepared with the assistance of professional educators.

purpose. *For the purpose of* and *with the purpose of* shouldn't be used as pompous synonyms for *to:* "The Governor is entering the New Hampshire primary *with the purpose of winning* (to win) the nomination, not *with the purpose of throwing* (to throw) himself in the path of an onrushing Senator Barry Goldwater."

pursuant to is legalese. Try *under.*

pursue is a formal word that can often be changed to *follow, carry through, do:*

Qualified sources said that West Germany's "flexible" policy toward the Communist East . . . will be *pursued* (followed, carried through).

Obviously, the investigation that is justified in the public interest should be *pursued* (carried out) regardless of the consequences . . . .

When Mr. Ben Gurion unexpectedly resigned as Premier last June, he announced that he would settle here to *pursue* (do) all the leisurely reading, writing and meditating that his official responsibilities had denied him for many years.

purvey, purveyor are far-fetched synonyms for *supply, supplier* or even simpler words:

Whatever heights Massenet may later have risen to as a *purveyor* (supplier, composer) of a certain kind of sociable, sentimental melody, he didn't have it in 1881 . . . when he composed "Herodiade."

Reports that the toy *purveyor* (store) was for sale have persisted for the last few months.

Q

qua. Why use a Latin word? Say *as*.

question. Don't use the ugly police-blotter phrase *the . . . in question:* "This is a story sad to write, for it is about someone who had become a good friend. Alexander Rorke Jr. (*the friend in question*) is missing somewhere in the Caribbean . . . ."

question of whether, why, how. Cross out the unnecessary *of:*

The offender's illness has nothing to do with the question (*of*) whether (*or not*) he is "free" or "responsible" in the traditional sense.

There is the question (*of*) whether Harris invented sex episodes in the hope of increasing sales or heightening effect . . . .

As the competitive justification has become muted, the question inevitably has begun arising (*of*) why all the urgency in the lunar project.

Therefore the balance of payments deficit raised the question (*of*) how far it should be allowed to go before being checked by a corresponding reduction in domestic liquidity.

The question (*of*) how much stretch a stretch fabric should have was cited . . . as one of the industry's "most serious problem areas."

See also AS TO, OF, WHETHER OR NOT.

quondam is an unnecessary Latin word. Try *former* or *once*.

QUOTATION MARKS should never be used to apologize for informal words and phrases. Have the courage of your own language and save the quotation marks for someone else's:

Many styles that had their origin in women's wear have found their way into children's apparel where they have become "*hot items*" (hot items).

Have you learned how to make managing your home a joy, instead of being "*tied down*" (tied down) by it?

Then their partnership was incorporated and they "*went public*" (went public).

If you're in the 30–to–40 range—and have neglected to

keep *"in shape"* (in shape)—you may think it risky to start exercising again for fear that it will *"strain"* (strain) your heart.

Potentially, U.S.A. has the greatest number of *"top flight"* athletes in the world—so it's *"up to us"* to develop these talented men and women who will then have the *"stuff"* to become winners in every possible event at the Games. (Potentially, U.S.A. has the greatest number of top flight athletes in the world—so it's up to us to develop these talented men and women who will then have the stuff to become winners in every possible event at the games.)

See also AD, MUST, PRO, SHORTENED WORDS, SLANG, UP TO.

QUOTATIONS. Misquotations are common, but I wouldn't worry too much about them. Less common is the super-correct, carefully verified quotation, which is always pompous:

"Ill fares the land, to hastening ills a prey / Where wealth accumulates and men decay," mourned Oliver Goldsmith in one of his deepest moods of Celtic melancholy, probably after a bad night at the gaming table.

It's much better to use a vaguely remembered quotation just as it comes naturally to your mind, frankly admitting that you didn't bother to look it up. Here's a nice example:

We think it was in "Nicholas Nickleby" (and if it wasn't, somebody will tell us by return mail) that a character remarked sadly how it never conceivably happened that the "Help Wanted" advertiser in one column got together with the "Job Wanted" advertiser side by side with it.

See also ALLUSIONS.

quoth is archaic and doesn't belong in a modern sentence: "Did that mean Liz Taylor would also join the cast? 'Absolutely not,' *quoth* (says) Huston."

R

rapport is a current fad word, meaning an understanding of someone else's feelings. It's much overused:

He's the only man who can hold an endless *rapport* with ignorant children in foreign lands . . . .

You would think there would be some *rapport* with this show, which is weekly trying to demonstrate the value of the simple life.

rara avis is Latin for *rare bird*. Why not just say *rare?* "A company of 30 had assembled for a musical not 'based on,' 'adapted from' or 'biographical of'—a musical, in other words, that will be *a rara avis* (rare) among Broadway shows."

RARE WORDS. If your vocabulary is bigger than that of your readers, that's nothing to be proud of. On the contrary, it is a liability, since it forces you to watch yourself carefully so you won't inadvertently sound like a show-off. Here are some examples of words that came naturally to the writer but were probably unknown to most readers:

The young Edmund Gosse found the aging Christina a decidedly formidable and unattractive personage, and complained that her *subfusc* (drab, dingy) appearance was particularly "hard to bear from the high priestess of Pre-Raphaelitism."

Mr. Geismar sets about its sentinels with a critical *knobkerrie*. (A knobkerrie is a heavy club used by African Hottentots. *Bludgeon* would have been a better word.)

Words are used like *tesserae* (squares, pieces) in a mosaic.

MacDougal and Bleecker is the *epicenter* (center of the earthquake).

Much early Auden was taxingly *hermetic* (occult, obscure), as though he were writing in a private language for a handful of friends.

I gave the writers of these sentences the benefit of the doubt. But there's no question that the writers of the following sentences knew better. They deliberately picked rare words for their readers to puzzle over:

The Rugantino of the affair, as played by Nino Manfredi, seems to have some *patellar* (kneecap) difficulty that prevents him from moving around as picaresquely as we might expect.

Laundered by a benign autumnal sun, Manhattan last week seemed renewed, inviting, *lithically* (stonily) radiant.

The largest retrospective of abstract expressionism's most inventive practitioner traces the *phylogeny* (history) of a style.

Onstage or on-camera, she can somehow suggest the sort of skirted *arachnid* (scorpion) that bites through everything in its path.

Rufus' great-great-grandmother, *edentate* (toothless), gibbering, gaunt, propped up in her wheelchair . . . .

When she wishes, she can be extremely funny, after a slightly *ophidian* (snakelike) fashion.

Assistant U. S. Attorney Charles A. Stillman yesterday identified the lady with the *hirsute adornment* (wig) as Mrs. Grace Patricia Simone, 36, of Miami . . . .

Next to that of advertising, the jargon is surely the ugliest and most intellectually *viscid* (sticky, gluey) in existence.

When he had completed celebrating the diminutive, airborne *ungulates* (reindeer), Dr. Hadas was asked how he felt about Dr. Moore's beloved corn.

The ultimate in the look-at-my-big-vocabulary game is the rare word thrown in just to prove the writer knows it:

The tonal aspect of his work gives it a propulsiveness (—*a teleology, to use an increasingly stylish term*—) that is never found in the work of atonal composers.

Reversal of fortune (*or peripeteia, as I have a habit of calling it*) has to do with any unexpected shift from the norm.

Sooner or later, every rare-word user becomes a victim of his own vocabulary:

Certainly two handsome men with prettier profiles than Mastroianni and Perrin you would be hard-pressed to find, but the *eugenics* of their brotherhood defy belief. Mastroianni is dark, brooding, unshaven . . . while Perrin is titian-haired, fair of skin . . . . (*Eugenics* is the science of improving the human breed. What the writer should have used instead of the rare word *eugenics* is the common term *genetics*.)

See also DEFINITIONS, EXPLANATIONS, FRENCH WORDS, GERMAN WORDS, ITALIAN WORDS, LATIN PHRASES.

rate means a number that shows a ratio or percentage. The word is sometimes misused as in this example: "One out of every 20 babies now born in this country is born out of wedlock. Since 1940, according to the Population Reference Bureau, *the illegitimacy rate has* (illegitimate births have) tripled. The bureau estimates that there were 89,000 illegitimate births in 1940, 141,000 in 1950, 224,000 in 1960."

rather, like A LITTLE and PRETTY, is sometimes used for pompous understatement: "Mr. Cheever has one fine surprise when he stages a riotous Easter-egg hunt that is (*rather*) rife with slapstick waggery."

rationale is now a great fad word. It is pronounced in half a dozen different ways and may mean *theory, thinking, reason, reasoning, basis, ground, plan*. Each of these words is better than *rationale:*

> Two months earlier, in August, the FAA bureaucracy, after weeks of feverish activity, produced the broad outlines of a *rationale* (plan) under which the project would proceed within the 75-25 percent cost-sharing formula.

> It means selling the idea of constitutional government to men like a leader in the Dominican Republic who gives this *rationale* (theory, basis) of Latin American politics: "There are only three ways to handle people in Latin America: kill them, jail them or have drinks with them . . . ."

> Certainly the big Announcement enclosed speaks very much for itself, but it does seem that a few words might well be added about the *rationale* (theory, basis, reasoning) of the so-called "open-end" subscription.

> This arrangement not only gives us sales patterns, but also the *rationale* (reasons, thinking) behind the purchases.

> One obstacle to understanding and working with the poor has been the absence of an appropriate theoretical *rationale* (basis) and a paucity of techniques by which new theories can be applied as they develop.

> These Auschwitz scenes, with their attempt to give the Doctor a pseudo-theological and very "German" *rationale* (basis, theory) in philosophy for his frightful crimes, are pretentious and false.

re is all right for a caption, but shouldn't be used in a sentence: "*Re* (To end) the current water shortage, meters should be required in all buildings."

re-. Think twice before you form a new word with *re-;* chances are it'll sound wrong:

We can *resensitize ourselves* (sensitize ourselves again) to the reality of human pain and the fragility of human life.

I believe their faith can now be *re-stirred* (stirred again), and that the results will soon be seen on the battlefield and in the villages of Viet Nam.

reaction is one of the most overused words of current English. Try to get away from it now and then:

In somewhat similar fashion *reactions to* (feelings about) novels that are intended to be more significant because of symbolism and parallels to ancient myths vary widely.

The general *reaction* (feeling) was one of hope that network television might at last break out of its canned-film mold . . . .

realistic is sometimes misused to mean *true, correct:* "He dismissed previous estimates that there were 175 combat divisions in the Soviet Army as *unrealistic* (untrue, wrong, incorrect)."

realm shouldn't be used as an empty filler word like NATURE or FIELD: "It is true that a few assertions are made which go beyond what some readers will accept, but any overstatement seems to be *in the realm of* (due to, just) enthusiasm, a quality often lacking in psychiatric practice."

reason. Avoid compound prepositions and conjunctions with *reason.* Change *for the reason that* to *because* or *since;* change *by reason of* to *because of.*

reason is because. *See* BECAUSE.

receive shouldn't be used where *get* or *have* would do:

Pomerantz testified he had *received an injury to his hand* (had injured his hand) and that the skin on his neck was broken . . . .

For one of the most talked-about and respected writers of the century, the late German playwright has not *received* (had) much Broadway exposure.

recipient. "Can any man say that sort of thing and retain a shred of self-respect?" That was Fowler's comment on the silly circumlocution *to be the recipient of* for *get.* Almost fifty years have gone by, and the phrase is still around:

Only one other person—Sen. Herbert H. Lehman—*has been the recipient of* (got) a special award, in 1947.

As for the widow of the policeman, J. D. Tippit, who was slain while trying to arrest Mr. Kennedy's accused assassin, she *is the recipient of* (got) $50,000 in donations.

reduce, reduction. Just a reminder that *cut* is shorter and better: "Agencies whose proposed expenditures will show *reductions* (cuts) include the Atomic Energy Commission, the Department of Defense . . . ."

reference. *With reference to, in reference to* should always be changed to *of, on, about.*

reflect means to show something indirectly, as in a mirror. The word is greatly overused as a fancy synonym for *show*, even where there's no reason for stressing the indirect mirror image:

The Governor's decision not to make a similar stand at Auburn *reflects* (shows) a recognition of the futility of interfering with Federal Court orders.

It *reflects* (shows) the viewpoint of a young, competent, sharp-eyed reporter who has had a front-row seat throughout a fascinating drama.

The type of questioning engaged in by Sen. Thurmond *reflects* (shows) an attitude that is against everybody and everything which has the approval of anyone except the most hard-shelled conservative.

regale is old-fashioned; say *entertain, feast, treat, delight:* "If you want to be *regaled* (entertained) with something that might be called chrome-plated thistledown plotting, this picture could fill an idle two hours."

regard. Weed out the cumbersome prepositions *with regard to, in regard to, regarding, as regards.* Say *on* or *about:*

Think of the importance of key decisions *regarding* (on) the buying or renting of homes, the kind of insurance to buy, the management of one's own business . . . .

We disagree with your editorial *as regards* (about) a special effort.

Ed had informed me that he wanted to talk to me *regarding* (about) his continuance as chairman of the New York County executive committee.

Far too many of these youngsters were hazy, if not totally ignorant *regarding* (of) the simplest facts about the geography of their own country.

regretfully shouldn't be misused to refer to the speaker (or writer) rather than the subject of the sentence: "The Judge noted *that 'regretfully, the* (with regret that 'the) Universal Declaration provides no means of enforcement . . . .'"

See also GRATEFULLY, HOPEFULLY, THANKFULLY.

relate shouldn't be used as a formal synonym for *tell* or *say:*
  It remained for Milton Berle to *relate* (tell) that he'd recently told President Kennedy in Washington that his son Billy, now less than two, "will be the first Jewish President."
  The production that Mr. Schaefer and Mr. Yellen chose to do was to *relate* (tell) in elementary narrative the discouragement, bitterness and humiliation . . . .
  "Most of the full-time tape watchers know their business and do well," *relates* (says) another branch manager.

The word *relate* is also sometimes used instead of the simpler phrase *have to do with:*
  The dramatically conflicting views of the contents of the commission's special study . . . *do not in any direct way relate to* (have nothing directly to do with) the subcommittee's intent to castigate the commission.

Some sentences can be improved by simply leaving out *relate:* "Man finds his fulfillment only as he (*relates meaningfully and*) is in communication with a society."

related with, relating to, relative to, in relation to. Say *on* or *about:*
  Among the papers he culled from the files were those *relating to* (on) pricing agreements.
  In a recent issue you made comment *relative to* (on) the John Birch Society.
  I would be more than willing to pay for any article *related with* (about) the terminal.

relative is sometimes misused for *relatively:* "Enthusiasm for the reduction among Business Council members had previously been limited to the *relative* (relatively) few who participated in the Administration-sponsored Businessmen's Committee for Tax Reduction."

relevance is sometimes misused for *connection:* "Pupils feel that there is no *relevance* (connection) between their classroom textbooks and what they see in the world around them."

relocate sounds overformal. Try *move:* "The merchants have insisted that most of them would be ruined if they had to *relocate* (move)."

remark shouldn't be used as a synonym for *said:* "Agreeing that there may be some waste in both, he *remarked* (said) that in a war, all expenditures are a waste."

remittance shouldn't be used as a euphemism for *money, cash, payment:* "You needn't send *remittance* (money). We'll bill you later."

remuneration. Another common euphemism for *pay*.

render. Try *make*.

repast. Hopelessly old-fashioned. Say *meal*.

repel from is unidiomatic: "He is *repelled from* (discouraged from, put off) reading by fatuous primers about 'nice' children . . . ."

REPETITION OF WORDS. The average American has a morbid fear of repeating words in writing and considers this the greatest sin against the rules of good style. Actually, it is a very minor matter and a thousand times less obnoxious than the mechanical use of synonyms for the sake of variation. Consider for instance the following paragraph in which the word *cheese* is used five times:

> Clifton Fadiman, who has written some of the best essays on wine and food, once noted that if a cheese was well and truly made, there was, for the dedicated cheese lover, no such thing as a bad cheese. The cheese might be disappointing; it might be dull, naïve or oversophisticated, but it remained cheese—"milk's leap toward immortality."

Did the repetition of the word *cheese* bother you? I'm sure it didn't. Nobody ever notices the natural repetition of the natural word.

And now, having said this, I'll quote a few exceptional sentences where the repetition of a word *was* bad and should have been corrected:

> His cheerful young niece is got with child by, of all things, a plumber's *helper*. He decides he must *help her*. (Change *plumber's helper* to *plumber's mate*.)

Any move for a *sweeping* inquiry is likely to be *swept* under the rug. (Change *sweeping* to *large-scale*.)

CHIANG *BREAK* CALLED *BREAK* FOR FRANCE (Change second *break* to *lucky*.)

See also JINGLES, SYNONYMS.

replete is a pompous word for *filled* or *full*:

This is a vast subject, *replete with* (full of, filled with) difficulties and resistant to brief review.

He has lived a fascinating existence *replete* with (full of) incident.

reportorial is a ponderous word. Try *reporting* or *reporter's*:

As a *reportorial* (reporting) medium, TV must cover such news . . . .

Miss Dawkins has a *reportorial* (reporter's) eye for the mechanics of life in America.

represent, like CONSTITUTE, is much abused as a stately synonym for the simple verb *be*:

Families with incomes of $15,000 or more received 23.7 per cent of the total family income although they *represented* (were) only 7.3 per cent of all families.

Homosexuals who are identifiable probably *represent* (are) no more than half of the total.

The TV commercials employed this year may well *represent* (be) a classic example of an industry's response to public opinion.

The project *represents* (is) a novel advance in astronomy.

The South Vietnamese Embassy here confirmed that it had received bills from hotels and stores around the country, *representing* (for) charges by Mrs. Ngo Dinh Nhu.

republic is so pompous by now it can hardly be used with a straight face: "This is one of those moments when there is reason to wonder whether the Congressional system as it now operates is not a grave danger to the *Republic* (country)."

require is not as good as *need* or *call for*: "It will *require* (need, call for) only a moment of map reading to understand what has happened."

requisite. Try *needed*.

reside is pompous English for *live*: "For a period, she *resided* (lived) with Mrs. Michael Paine, in Irving, Tex."

residence. Say *home, house, apartment*—anything but *residence*.

respect. Don't use *with respect to* or *respecting* as circumlocutions for *on* or *about*: "The guarded optimism in the Rockefeller camp *with respect to* (about) New Hampshire is based in large part on these assets . . . ."

respective, respectively are words used by timid souls who have a horror of the slightest possible false reference. If you're a habitual *respective* or *respectively* user, you'll be surprised to hear that these words can always be safely left out:

The popular guess is that the foursome discussed plans for Liz and Richard to obtain their (*respective*) divorces before they leave Mexico.

Not only are the prices of these wines about double what they would have been five years ago, the curious thing is that they do not reflect any comparable shift in the (*respective*) economies of France or Germany.

In a Presidential year, New Hampshire and Wisconsin hold the first primary elections—March 10 and April 7 (*respectively*).

Some of his speech writers have given a wrong comparison of the way the Federal government and private business (*respectively*) handle their debts.

Farewell, au revoir and *auf Wiedersehen* are ways of saying "good-bye" in (*respectively*) English, French and German.

Those sets would not be equivalent, of course, to the set of dimes in a dollar or the set of wheels on a car, because the cardinal numbers of those sets are 10 and 4 (*respectively*).

Two young professors have written books about him—Messrs. Wiley and Meixner of (*respectively*) the University of Wisconsin and the University of Kansas.

His latest pen and wash drawings and a collection of his oils recently went on exhibition in separate, one-man Madison Avenue shows, at the FAR and Grippi galleries (*respectively*).

respond, response are pompous synonyms for *answer*: " 'I respectfully disagree,' Mr. Gilpatric *responded* (answered)."

result. Change the cumbersome preposition *as a result of* to the simpler *because of*: "Orwell hazarded the guess that the German,

Italian and Russian languages all deteriorated *as a result* (because) of the word jockeying that ensued as soon as dictatorship in one form or another fastened itself upon these peoples."

retort shouldn't be used as a fancy synonym for *answer:* "The Maharaja of Jaipur *retorted* (answered) from Bombay that the choice of this ancient princely city for the winter meeting of the All-India Committee of the Congress party was a mistake in view of a famine in Rajasthan."

reveal shouldn't be used as a pompous synonym for *show:* "Our probing of similar occurrences recently tends to *reveal* (show) a pattern of spontaneity." *See also* DISCLOSE.

rise. *Give rise to* is a roundabout way of saying *raise:* "This situation *gave rise immediately to* (immediately raised) a fundamental question involving set theory."

ROMAN NUMERALS. Avoid Roman numerals:

> GALLUP POLL: ROBERT KENNEDY
> TOP CHOICE FOR NO. *II* (2) MAN

roseate. The normal word is *rosy:* "That is the *roseate* (rosy) prediction of Dr. Grover W. Ensley, executive vice-president of the National Association of Mutual Savings Banks."

round doesn't need an apostrophe: "A truly refreshing gift idea . . . . one that will be enjoyed all year *'round* (round) as a new surprise."

ruler shouldn't be used mechanically as a synonym for *king* or *emperor:* "The *ruler* (emperor) has been the object of United States admiration since 1936, when *the emperor* (he) made a dramatic appeal to the League of Nations."

RUN-ON SENTENCE. *See* COMMAS.

S

-'s. In modern idiomatic English the possessive case with *'s* can be used only for people—*John's, my sister's, the President's, the neighbor's dog*—but not for things or abstract nouns. All the following examples sound artificial and wrong:

The president of the American Medical Association carefully cemented *his organization's alliance* (the alliance of his organization) with the drug industry at an industry luncheon here yesterday.

THE MARCH'S MEANING (THE MEANING OF THE MARCH)

TV'S RICHARD BOONE (RICHARD BOONE OF TV) HURT IN CAR CRASH

At *war's end* (the end of the war) he was in Okinawa.

The main business is to prepare for the hardest challenge to *Christian Democracy's 14-year rule* (the 14-year rule of the Christian Democrats) in West Germany.

On Long Island, the price of land has gone from 10% of *a house's cost* (the cost of a house) to 25% in five years.

TIN'S (TIN) PRICE RISES TO A 13-YEAR HIGH

The reasons for *friction's predominance* (the predominance of friction) are easily understood.

Moreover, there is now a new dimension to *the bill's woes* (the woes of the bill).

The *school's authorities* (authorities of the school) believe that a well-rounded education must include a knowledge of music and dance.

Socrates said this at *Athens' end of a creative period* (the end of a creative period in Athens).

Since Chinese dinners run to eight courses, one should never be the first to take food from a new dish or eat much of what is served at *meal's end* (the end of a meal).

OBSCENITY'S PRICE (THE PRICE OF OBSCENITY)

INTEGRATION'S VICTIMS (VICTIMS OF INTEGRATION)

There is still comparatively little knowledge of events taking place outside the Vietnamese capital and of *the American military's role* (the role of the American military) in those events.

He based his conclusions on an exhaustive study of the *Common Market's growth* (growth of the Common Market) by

Munich's prestigious Institute for Economic Studies (the prestigious Institute for Economic Studies at Munich).

-'s or -s's?   When a name (or a noun referring to a person) ends in *s*, *z* or *x*, the normal way of forming the possessive is by adding *'s*:

His scale of living is considerably more modest than *Jones's*.

It does my heart good to think that my children may be able to reap the fruits of Dr. *Gross's* diligence.

Over the years complaints piled up about *Leibowitz's* court.

By attacking outgoing Democratic Gov. Bert *Combs's* executive order outlawing segregation in state-licensed businesses, Nunn piled up votes . . . .

Present at the hush-hush conference were *Liz's* lawyer, Mickey Rudin . . . and Dickie's attorney Aaron Frosch.

LANOUX'S NOVEL WINS PRIX GONCOURT

It sounds wrong and unidiomatic when the possessive is formed by just adding an apostrophe:

"Nobody blocks at all," Fat *Thomas'* (Thomas's) brother was saying the other day.

Joe *Louis'* (Louis's) wife seems to be Liston's lawyer now.

He wants to marry the *boss'* (boss's) daughter.

Early today, *Lewis'* (Lewis's) associates were pointing up the fact that he'd seldom had a loser in 29 motion pictures.

John Williams will play the *actress'* (actress's) ex-husband who left her 29 years before.

The only exception to this style rule is what might be called the abstract possessive—a possessive that refers to abstract relationships rather than physical possession or family ties. Here are some examples where the apostrophe-only form looks and sounds more natural than the added *'s:*

He was intrigued by Dr. *Argyris'* assertion that the average employe works at only about one-third his productive capacity.

BARRED *GOMPERS'* UNION STRIKE

She finally turns on the unlucky messenger who has had to carry *Titus'* decision to her . . . .

The truth is that *Moses'* role as president of the World's Fair Corporation cries out for investigation.

Krips' Schubert was not profound and it was not even *gemuetlich.*

SEEKING *HOLMES'* LONDON

FAR CRY FROM *DEBS'* DAY— SOCIALISTS ENJOY A LAUGH

The rejected Gov. Richard J. *Hughes'* plans for the state's fiscal future . . . .

said. There are two basic rules about so-called speech tags like *said.* First, don't break the rhythm of the sentence you're quoting. Second, don't go out of your way to find variations of *said, added, answered.*

Here are some examples of speech tags in the wrong place:

"We must," he said, *"recognize the duality of the two."* ("We must recognize the duality of the two," he said.)

"What," we asked Ho Thong Minh, *"is the next step in South Vietnam?"* ("What is the next step in South Vietnam?" we asked Ho Thong Minh.)

"We cannot," he says, *"become a factory."* ("We cannot become a factory," he says.)

And here are some choice specimens of far-fetched synonyms for *said:*

"The morning mail is running maybe 99% in my favor," he *blushes* (says).

"Governor, you look good," Zaretzki *barbed* (said).

"It wasn't a movie," your correspondent *needled* (said).

"Keep breathing," she *dimpled* (said).

Tch-tched (Said) Florida Senator George Smathers: "Shameful for an ex-Senator."

"They think I'm too old!" he *grumped* (said).

"You never been in clinic before?" the Negro clerk *looks up* (says) suspiciously.

"I'm not as informed probably on many aspects as you are," he *ventured* (said).

"My thoughts, I guess, are bitter," *allows* (says) Mignon McLaughlin.

"If I don't make it," he *shrugs* (says), "I can always find something to do."

"Suddenly all these Brooklyn homes become like gems," *glooms* (says) Phil.

See also INVERSION, SYNONYMS.

salient is a bookish word; try changing it to *important*: "The whole question of religious art grows increasingly *salient* (important), urgent and confused."

same should never be used as a pronoun: "Only Ruark would write such a miserable and low article and it was very regrettable that a paper of your category *did print same* (printed it)."

sanctum sanctorum is Latin for *holy of holies*. The following sentence illustrates the dangers of using Latin: "The temptress, Eve, is permitted and encouraged to invade her sweetheart's *sanctorum* (privacy) every Saturday for 12 hours."

sanguine is a pompous word for *hopeful:*

G. E. is *sanguine* (hopeful) about future export possibilities in the developing countries of the world.

Mr. Truman added *sanguinely* (hopefully), "Business men don't elect Presidents any more. The common people elect them."

sans is one syllable shorter than *without,* but that's no excuse for reviving this obsolete word:

This five-flight walkup is a one-room void with annexes: a postage-stamp bedroom *sans* (without) a bed, a bathroom *sans* (without) a tub . . . .

His columns drifted toward the mawkish—rhapsodizing about young lovers, old buildings, the sights and smells *sans* (without) the sounds of the Métro.

sartorial is a fancy word referring to tailors and their work. Change it or leave it out: "With that Cortes thrust forth his arms, revealing his exquisite cuffs, patted the pristine handkerchief in his breast pocket and departed in (*sartorial*) splendor."

sated is far-fetched for *satisfied:* "Mr. Adams has never *sated* (satisfied) an appetite as he moved through the history, sights, tastes, and leisures of San Francisco."

satisfied is often abused as a long word for *sure:* "Senate Democratic leader Mike Mansfield said he *has satisfied himself* (is sure) that present key employees of the Senate Democratic majority have no sideline interests that conflict with their jobs."

savant is no longer the common word for a *scientist, scholar, expert*: "Erasmus Darwin had already staked out a reputation for himself as one of the chief *savants* (scholars) of the day as well as a successful poet."

save, in the sense of *except,* is wholly obsolete, although many writers seem to consider it decorative or elegant. It isn't:

Our least known and, *save* (except) for some naval victories, least triumphant armed conflict must surely be the one called the War of 1812.

Changes in transportation and communication are lessening the dependence on the urban core, *save* (except) for a decreasing group of contact-oriented activities.

savvy is overused as an adjective meaning *smart, knowing, shrewd*: "By 1934, he was *savvy* (knowing) enough to ask his friend Albert Einstein a prophetic question: could man unlock the atom's energy?"

scant is a bookish word; say *little* or *only:*

There is *scant* (little) prospect that the tax bill now in Congress will much improve the situation.

When the great day came, Kaunda had *scant* (little) time to rejoice.

A scant (Only a) few minutes after her arrival she was hurriedly called down from her box to backstage.

It was not until September 24th, *a scant* (only) three weeks before opening night, that the four members of his company's executive committee voted to underwrite the new "Aida."

scion is a pompous, vaguely Victorian word meaning a descendant of prominent ancestors. *Son* or *heir* will usually do:

Bright scholars have driven out dull *scions* (heirs).

What *scion* (son, heir) of what wealthy family wants to court and marry her?

Sometimes *scion* can simply be left out:

WALTER LIEBMAN, LAWYER, *(SCION)*
OF BREWING FAMILY

scoff at sounds bookish. Try *laugh, make fun of:*

The Arizonan *scoffed at* (made fun of) Mr. Johnson's spending cut.

He *scoffed at* (laughed at, made fun of) the notion that the legislators, having been to sea free, would prove susceptible to changes in the Banking Law desired by the mutual savings banks.

scribe, scribbler, scrivener shouldn't be used as arch synonyms for *writer:*

Johnny Carson moved Roy Kammerman over to the "Tonight" show as chief of the staff *scribes* (writers).

Norah Lofts looked like a lady, not a *scribbler* (writer), in antique jewelry, pale blond coiffure, Paris tweeds.

This *scrivener* (writer) never matriculated in the write-like-you-talk school, and does not believe in it.

sculpt is being objected to by some, but is now fully established:

"It was like *sculpting* a face in the dark," she says.

Jacques Lipchitz is *sculpting* a bust of Charles Revson, head of Revlon.

secondly can and should always be shortened to *second*.

secure (verb), like OBTAIN and PROCURE, is much abused as a pompous synonym for *get:* "He has two instant tasks. One is to *secure* (get) an astute campaign manager."

seem. Don't say timidly *it seems* when *it is. See also* APPEAR, WOULD SEEM.

select (verb) is usually too formal. Say *pick* or *choose*.

sell is now standard English in this sort of sentence: "Supporting Mr. Shriver in attempts to *sell* the program was Walter W. Heller . . . ." *See also* BUY.

semantic is a current fad word, used for almost any kind of reference to words and their meaning:

The Vatican made public summaries in various languages. . . . An important *semantic discrepancy* (difference in meaning) was noted.

In the light of the current movie vogue for titillating titles, one must be grateful to "Love with the Proper Stranger" for its *semantic* (verbal) decorum.

semi- should be used with care. It often makes ugly compounds:

"Harris Yulin brings a restrained earnestness to his characterization of a *semi-damned* (half-damned) soul."

SEMICOLONS are a very effective style device to show the connection and interplay of related statements and ideas. Look at these examples and see how much better the semicolons are than periods:

> He was celebrated as the author of "The Three-penny Opera" which created a sensation in 1928; he was notorious as a man of Communist persuasion.

> His family is out for the money; he is pursued by threatening letters signed "J. J. J."; adventures embroil him beside which the goings-on of "Tom Jones" read like some sober government report.

> It is a perfectly wonderful ensemble. Its style is robust; its ensemble is impeccable; its tone is heavenly.

There's the same old argument about the semicolon before *and* in a series as there is about the comma before *and*. The trend is toward lighter punctuation before *and:* just as the comma is changed to no punctuation mark, the semicolon is downgraded to a comma:

> Other resolutions indorsed the upgrading of qualified Negroes for civil service posts, particularly in the Post Office Department; scored discriminatory practices in hiring personnel in Catholic hospitals, and asked Catholic Inter-racial Councils to give urban renewal programs high priority among their concerns. (Note the comma after *hospitals*.)

> The acceleration of the pace may be traced to three important factors: the need, which is global; the success of the single oral contraceptive now generally available, and the profit motive. (Note the comma after *available*.)

See also COLONS, COMMAS, PERIODS, SHORT SENTENCES.

senior citizens is a silly euphemism heartily disliked by most of those so called.

SENTENCES. *See* COLONS, DANGLING PHRASES, LONG SENTENCES, LOST THREAD, PERIODS, SEMICOLONS, SENTENCE STUFFING.

SENTENCE STUFFING is one of the worst sins of current writing. It's true that you can't always limit yourself to one idea per sentence, but you *can* try to give information as simply and clearly as possible. The more facts and ideas you pack into a sentence, the harder you make it for the reader. Here are some horrible examples:

At the same time a blustering Fidel Castro was demanding that the U.S. call off its economic blockade of his hurricane-ravaged island, the State Department charged yesterday that a jet "presumed to be Cuban" strafed an American-owned freighter just 13 miles off the Cuban coast.

With Pope Paul VI participating in a ceremony of the type last held in 1870, when the dogma of papal infallibility was handed down by the first Vatican Ecumenical Council, the 2,200 churchmen are expected to authorize changes in the liturgy to permit the use of vernacular languages, including English, in parts of the mass and sacraments.

Elected yesterday to succeed Pakistan's Muhammad Zafrulla Khan as the 18th Assembly session's presiding officer, Dr. Sosa-Rodriguez will take up duties more engrossing than those he already complained do not give him enough time for reading and for his favorite sports—motoring and swimming.

A scant 14 seconds separated the football forces of Cornell from their third Ivy League defeat and their fourth overall yesterday when they came up with a touchdown and a two-point conversion for an 18-17 triumph that busted the hearts of Columbia's Lions before an estimated 13,000 at Schoellkopf Field.

Mrs. Marlene M. McIlvaine, married to a gas worker, mother of two children, aged 2 and 3, and daughter-in-law of a cop, was the first woman picked to sit as a juror at Thompson's trial for the murder of his heiress wife, Carol, last March 6 in St. Paul.

The most popular finalist in years was the toy group winner, a white Maltese, Ch. Co-Ca-He's Aennchen Toy Dancer, handled by the owner, 16-year-old Anna Maria Stimmler, of Fairview Village, Pa., a junior at St. Joseph Academy of Chestnut Hill, Pa., where the nuns were all praying for their star pupil and her canine birthday present.

The rusty-haired little Chicago Loyola senior, pulled out by three pace-carrying but outclassed rivals in the 53rd running of the Baxter Cup at the New York A.C. games gave the enthusiastic crowd of 14,000 a taste of what was coming by sprinting the last three laps, instead of his customary two.

See also ADJECTIVES, AS, -BORN, DANGLING PHRASES, HYPHENS, -ING, LONG SENTENCES, SOURCE ATTRIBUTION, SYNONYMS, TITLES, WITH.

set forth is a pompous word for *write* or *give:* "In *setting forth* (writing, giving) its decision, the F.T.C. was careful to avoid a blanket indictment of advertising."

shakes. *No great shakes* is good idiomatic English, but this sentence is not: "Among his fellow Senate correspondents, the United Press' Allen Drury was not considered *much shakes.*"

shall and will. The old complicated rules for using *shall* and *will* no longer apply to current American English. *Will* for the future tense is now standard.

she. In old-style diplomatic language, all nations are referred to as *she.* The modern system is to use *it:*

> The Soviet Communist Party's Central Committee is pondering the grave crisis in agriculture that has made it virtually impossible for Russia to feed *itself.*

> Red China has stated flatly that *it* would never sit in the same room with Nationalist China.

> France has not made it clear how *it* will vote on that issue.

The old system now sounds pompous and often ridiculous:

> A plan for resolution of at least some of the differences between Israel and *her* (its) Arab neighbors was put forward.

> At the current session Czechoslovakia was elected to serve in 1964 on the understanding that *she* (it) would resign and permit Malaysia to hold the seat in 1965.

> Somalia has had only a token army because *she* (it) has not been able to afford a larger one.

shed is often misused as a fancy word for *give up:* "A classic contest seemed in the making between Douglas-Home, 60, Scottish aristocrat who *shed* (gave up) an earldom to succeed Harold Macmillan and the Labor Party's rapier-tongued leader, Harold Wilson, 47."

shibboleth means a *test word, pet phrase* or *catchword* of a special group, but is now generally used in the sense of *empty slogan* or *false gospel:*

It is all very well to say that the average person knows what is obscene, but this is one of those *shibboleths* that won't bear close examination.

We've spoken in partial truths, shrouding the inadmissible facts, and made a *shibboleth* of regarding the Negro problem, in the words of Gunnar Myrdal, as "An American Dilemma."

shod is obsolete: "She *is shod in* (wears) either a nurse's or Army shoes and both are more or less unfair to the female limbs."

SHORT SENTENCES of two or three words are among the most effective style devices there are. For instance:

Ultramicroscopic adenoviruses (measuring less than ten-thousandths of a millimeter) are reckoned to be likely tumor producers because they are common, variable and inclined toward latency; that is, they tend to lie dormant and then suddenly erupt. *Nobody knows why.*

Here is not only a great dramatic singer, but a superb stylist as well. Perhaps her Donna Anna makes Elektra seem like a flower-maiden by comparison, but it all adds up to one of the genuinely vital operatic conceptions of the day. *See it.*

The most interesting toast at the Elysée Palace on New Year's Day, when General de Gaulle received diplomats, was drunk privately by Soviet Ambassador Sergei Vinogradov and José Maria de Areilza, Count of Motrico, envoy of Generalissimo Franco, Spanish Chief of State. Vinogradov lifted his glass and proposed: "May this year see the establistment of diplomatic relations between Spain and the Soviet Union." *Motrico drank.*

See also COLONS, PERIODS, SEMICOLONS.

SHORTENED WORDS. Don't be afraid of using shortened words like *ad, bra, exam, gas, gym, lab, phone, pro, rhino, vet.* All these and many more are now standard English. They should be used freely without either quotation marks or apostrophes.

shun is a headline word; say *avoid, stay out of, keep out of:*

JUNIOR HIGH JOBS *SHUNNED* (AVOIDED) BY MANY

He deliberately has *shunned* (avoided) all contracts so that he can take as much time as he wants for his trip around the world.

Many businessmen claim that people working for them would be glad to *shun* (avoid, keep out of) a strike if they were not afraid of violence or intimidation.

sibling should be left to the sociologists: " 'Two Brothers' is a very personal retrospect on the author's relationship with his younger *sibling* (brother)."

side. The expression *on the . . . side* often sounds snobbish and studiedly casual: "The conductor himself shaped both scores with a fine robustness, judicious *tempos a bit on the rapid side* (but fairly rapid tempos), and a remarkable insight into the right way to balance part against part in music of this sort."

signal (*adjective*) is bookish; say *outstanding, notable.*

sine qua non is an unnecessary Latin phrase; try *essential:* "European and British motor cars that are shifted by hand would be *a sine qua non* (essential) for the hood of distinction . . . ."

sir. It is true that British baronets and knights are properly referred to by their first names, preceded by *Sir,* but it's snobbish to do that when a reference by the last name alone would be more natural:

Sir Alec will (Douglas-Home will) spend about a half hour discussing current events with Joseph C. Harsch . . . .

Sir Alec gave (Guinness gave) an hypnotic performance in New York in 1950 in T. S. Eliot's "The Cocktail Party."

Sir Guildhaume was (Myrddin-Evans was) chairman of the governing body of the International Labor Office in 1946 . . . .

sire for *father* or *ancestor* is arch and pompous: "Will you have recalled in later years, I wonder, what your Pulitzer Prize-winning *sire* (ancestor) really thought of this selection, title by title?"

situated is often unnecessary and should be left out: "The sprawling buff-colored Harriman house (*situated*) in Georgetown, Washington's fashionable, old Federal City area . . . ."

SLANG. Many people are so afraid of using slang in writing that they shy away from *any* colloquial or informal expression or use timid quotation marks around such common words as *ad, gas* or *movies.* This is absurd; many words widely considered slang aren't slang at all but good informal English.

Even genuine slang can and should be used in writing if it fits naturally into the context and is the most effective way of saying it:

Nhu *was the heavy in the cast*, the man who had whittled everything away within himself until only the naked power instrument was left.

Warner Bros. which has a huge stable of eager young contract players, has dumped a number of them into "Palm Springs Weekend," one of those tinseled, modern-youth-on-a-spree *deals*.

In that room it seemed perfectly plain that Goldwater was embarrassed by the vulgar idiocies committed by the *kooks* and cranks on his side.

See also BUY, GIMMICK, GUTS, KID, QUOTATION MARKS, SELL.

slay is a headline word; say *kill, shoot, murder:*

> DEATH OF ACTRESS HELD
> A *SLAYING* (MURDER)

> SISTER-IN-LAW HELD IN *SLAYING*
> (KILLING) OF TYCOON

It is not without significance that when Lee Oswald was *slain* (killed, shot) the overwhelming reaction was not that of a joyous lynch mob . . . .

One of the most puzzling things about the case is how the *slayer* (killer, murderer) escaped in broad daylight without attracting attention, for he must have been drenched in blood.

sleuth shouldn't be used as a fancy word for *detective:* "The same security people service Tiffany and Plummer-McCutcheon—and these *sleuths* (detectives) recognized the brunette with the wig."

so is better and more idiomatic than the more formal *so that* in many sentences:

I've written bail on people who stole money *so* they could bet on horses.

Certain chambermaids and bellhops will gladly let you into a room *so* you can rob it and split the payday with you.

How is the salesman to tell on short notice which type of person he's face to face with *so* he can adjust his pitch accordingly?

so as to sounds stilted. Leave out *so as:* "In order to justify this performance, they have tried to establish specific links among these three men (*so as*) to provide their new book with the needed cohesion."

solon is a stale joke and shouldn't be used as a synonym for *Senator* or *Congressman:* "Sen. Barry Goldwater, the vigorous and vocal *solon* (senator) from Arizona, has further complaints against me."

someplace is used idiomatically for *somewhere:* "You don't care about the rest of the passengers, you take the bus to get *someplace* and when you get there you get off."

sort of is good idiomatic English. Don't shy away from it:

> If the hard core hasn't got an audience to prance in front of, they lose their momentum and *sort of* fall by the wayside.

> I had *sort of* an opportunity to see Hoffa on a different basis.

> "Having lived in houses that I *sort of* tamed myself," said the First Lady, "I find there are not a tremendous amount of closets here, but there are enough."

SOURCE ATTRIBUTION at the end of sentences is an ingrained newspaper habit that has produced millions of misshapen, anticlimactic sentences. There's no cure for this disease but total abstention from the habit. Some prize examples:

> Capucine, the Italian film star, and William Holden are voyaging together from Las Palmas in the Canary Islands to the Bahamas aboard a luxury yacht, *island sources revealed*.

> A subtle change is taking place in the mood of the country, *is the belief of the Esquire publisher*.

> The coordinator's responsibility often starts several months before the builder gets his temporary certificate of occupancy from the city, and it usually lasts until the last of more than a hundred tenants moves in, *the broker noted*.

> However, mechanization of G. E.'s transformer plants at Pittsfield, Mass., Rome, Ga., and Hickory, N. C., together with the use of computers in designing the devices, has enabled the division to design transformers efficiently and quickly to the customer's specifications, *Mr. Sampson said*.

> A strangler killed actress Karyn Kupcinet, 23, beautiful,

brunette daughter of Chicago newspaper columnist Irv Kupcinet, *a surgeon reported after an autopsy today.*

Executors' commissions, legal fees, accounting fees and other estate administration costs can be deducted, at the option of the executor, on the estate tax return, or on the fiduciary income tax return filed on behalf of the estate *according to Bernard Barnett, chairman, Committee on Federal Taxation, New York State Society of Certified Public Accountants.*

spate is a bookish word meaning a sudden flood or outpouring. Try *flood, crop:*

The controversy started by the publication of Merriam-Webster's Third International Edition still rumbles through the press, and the *spate* (flood) of books and articles that it has produced . . . .

The only link between the German woman and Mr. Baker is a *spate* (flood) of unverified reports . . . .

As an old-timer in L. A., I have been critical of the *spate* (crop, flood) of novels about my hometown . . . .

speechify is no longer funny: "Not only did she *speechify* (make speeches) against McCarthy, in 1954 she voted to censure him."

sped sounds archaic; say *speeded* or *speeded up:*

BUYING SPUR: CASH TO VETS WILL BE
SPED (SPEEDED UP)

The dynamism of U.S. culture and technology has *sped* (speeded up) the process.

SPELLING. It's good style to use simple spelling whenever you have a choice. If you're a conservative speller, try changing to *subpena, esthetic, catalog.* But don't use spellings that may annoy some readers, like *nite, tho, thru.*

SPLIT INFINITIVE. Putting an adverb between *to* and the infinitive of a verb has been condemned by grammarians as long as anyone can remember, but people keep on doing it. Why? Because in many sentences that's the best way of saying exactly what is meant. For instance:

"I want you *to really work* on this," he said.

If you saw the man once, then you would know he would not be the kind *to ever have* this zoo closed for the children.

Mr. Galamison declared "the problem here is that there is no will" *to truly integrate* the schools.

The Pentagon announced plans yesterday *to further strengthen* troop atomic firepower in Europe and the Pacific.

He was the only one of the three *to actively seek* the Prime Minister's post.

A recommendation by Birmingham's biracial committee *to immediately employ* Negro policemen came under attack in Alabama's strife-torn city.

The stage is set for the Senate *to quietly kill* a contemplated investigation of the drug industry.

It might be well to set up a research center *to better understand* the theory and principles of reproduction.

One wonders why Dr. Gove and his editors did not think of labeling *knowed* as substandard right where it occurs, and one suspects that they wanted *to slightly conceal* the fact or at any rate to put off its exposure as long as decently possible.

In each of these sentences the reader would have been briefly misled if the adverb—*really, ever, truly, further, actively, immediately, quietly, better, slightly*—had been withheld until after the verb. The only way to make the meaning quite clear was to put the adverb right after *to.*

But what about putting the adverb *before* the word *to?* you ask. The answer is that this device invariably sounds stilted and artificial. Look at these examples:

Without the copious notes which Mr. Jones provides it is unlikely that anyone except the author would be able *fully to understand* (to fully understand) the poem.

He can convey what it is like *actually to read* (to actually read) a particular book.

But *effectively to demolish James* (to demolish James effectively) needs a tone unlike that of Mr. Geismar.

I am here this morning *formally to announce* (to announce formally) my candidacy for the Republican Presidential nomination.

By failing *explicitly to differentiate* (to differentiate explicitly) the political system from one of its constituent parts —the government—Mitchell at times reifies the former concept . . . .

The 69-year-old Prime Minister, who has said he wants *personally to submit* (to submit personally) his resignation to the Queen . . . .

In the last four examples, I don't suggest that you change such awkward constructions to split infinitives, but that you put the adverb *after* the verb. After all, you can't get away from the fact that most split infinitives are ugly and should normally be avoided —as in these typical examples:

It isn't enough to *temporarily deprive yourself* (deprive yourself temporarily) of fattening foods.

We don't wish to *inadvertently miss* (miss inadvertently) a single opportunity to serve.

I believe it was a gross hoax that should cause the Labor Department to *completely re-examine* (re-examine completely) the functions of and the methodology used by its staff.

This leaves some situations where you'll have to decide for yourself whether to use a split infinitive because it brings out the precise meaning or avoid it because its ugly. Here are two pairs of examples *with the same adverb* where a split infinitive sounds right in one sentence but wrong in the other:

The report commended radio for its ability *to quickly report* major news to the world, news magazines for their ability to be clear and readable, and television for its news documentaries. *But:* Chrysler hopes to *quickly accelerate this* (accelerate this quickly) to one a week until a full fleet of 50 cars are undergoing testing.

If ever there was a dress that wasn't grown up *to adequately cover* a grown up woman, this is it. *But:* The mayors urged the President to *adequately replenish* (replenish adequately) the rapidly exhausting Federal financial aid in the fields of urban renewal, housing and other related programs.

spouse. It's true that English has no other word for *husband-or-wife*, but *spouse* just isn't part of normal English. Say *husband* or *wife:* "The permits will be limited to those with *spouses* (husbands, wives), parents, children, grandchildren, brothers, sisters, uncles, aunts, nephews or nieces on the Communist side of the Wall."

stance, like POSTURE, is now a fad word for *attitude.* Say *attitude:*

The Administration has subsequently carried its revised *stance* (attitude) into the Senate Finance Committee.

Throughout all this, he makes his own emotional *stance* (attitude) quite explicit.

A man's private affairs ought not to overshadow the entire program and *stance* (attitude) he offers the electorate.

standpoint. *From the standpoint of* is a cumbersome prepositional phrase. Cut it out:

If a good script comes up, *from the standpoint of the characteristics as they* (with characteristics that) would come across to the audience, I'd do it in a minute.

It would be a national tragedy if research programs of high quality were curtailed in a significantly serious way in order to divert funds for research which appears to be more *spectacular from a popular standpoint* (popularly spectacular).

state (verb) shouldn't be used as a formal synonym for *say:* "When questioned about the Philadelphia election at his press conference, President Kennedy followed this same approach, *stating* (saying) that he did not know there were any differences on civil rights between the two candidates."

statement, in the current fad sense of an artist's expression of his ideas, is annoyingly pompous:

Director Irving Vincent has not solved all problems of pace, but his *statement* (direction) of the play is lucid, and he conveys the tart Shavian flavor.

Carl Foreman wrote, produced and directed an epic he calls a "personal *statement* (movie)" about the futility of war.

He is one of the most authentic and powerful of American humanists, an artist who translates the American scene into a strikingly personal *statement* (expression) of sympathy for mankind.

The statement of Act II is (Act II says) that Stalin finds God, and it wrecks his love affair.

statuesque is journalese for a *tall* or *big* girl: "Linda, 22 and *statuesque* (tall), is first of Hope children to go into show business."

stellar is a bookish word for *star:* "Americans may wonder why their well-fed, healthy children cannot turn out more *stellar* (star) performances."

stem (verb) is overused as a literary synonym for *come:*

Some of the unhappiness undoubtedly *stemmed* (came) from the way the bill had been railroaded through the committee.

L. S. Simckes *stems* (comes) from a long line of rabbis.

stipend is old-fashioned. Say *salary* or *grant:* "Yesterday's ruling provides that a candidate for a doctorate degree who does no work for his *stipend* (grant) other than the research required of other students without *stipends* (grants) need not pay tax on the money."

SUBJUNCTIVE. The simple subjunctive without the word *should* often sounds stiff and formal:

Since each voter has only one vote I suggest that if he is interested in good government he *select* (should select) the best candidate regardless of party.

When Ed Murrow left CBS to head the USIA his partner and co-producer, Fred Friendly, insisted that the door marked "E. R. Murrow" *remain* (should remain) the way it was.

The Government has in effect denied a Soviet request that it *disclose* (should disclose) the circumstances of the defection.

It expressed quite forcibly his desire that the commission *proceed* (should proceed) expeditiously with its proper work of carrying out the expressed will of the Council Fathers.

See also AS IF, AS THOUGH, BE, IF, WERE or WAS?

subsequent is just a long word for *later:*

While Pugwash, Nova Scotia, was the site of the first conference, in July 1957, ten *subsequent* (later) ones have been held, at irregular intervals, in widely scattered parts of the globe.

Most concerns decided to allow the stations to carry the spot announcements at a *subsequent* (later) date.

She was divorced from Sergeant Pic's father and had two sons by a *subsequent* (later) marriage.

subsequent to is a clumsy preposition; say *after:*

The upturn that started early in 1961 has not been appreciably better than the entirely unsatisfactory upturns that followed the earlier recessions *subsequent to* (after) the Korean war.

The laws say flatly that any alien who *subsequent to* (after) entry has been twice convicted of "crimes involving moral turpitude" is deportable.

subsequently is a four-syllable conjunction that should always be changed to *later* or *after that:*

The 12-year-old Jewish girl, who described her life hiding in an Amsterdam garret in a moving diary, *subsequently* (later) died in a Nazi concentration camp.

I *subsequently* (later) saw photographs of some of the sealskin tapestries made under Father Tardy's supervision.

In 1940, the Soviets occupied and *subsequently* (later) absorbed Latvia into their union.

The girl *subsequently* (later) married a Buenos Aires accountant.

He cursed himself for suppressing it. No mistake of a similar nature, or of comparable magnitude was *subsequently made* (made after that).

substantial is much overused. Try *big, great, large, good, heavy:*

A *substantial* (big) cast change was made for the Metropolitan Opera's fifth "Don Giovanni" of the season.

Mr. Anderson said that all countries with *substantial* (large) stockpiles of gold and reserve currencies should chip in to help solve the problems of the have-nots.

A *substantial* (large) number of economy bloc lawmakers voted for an initial $400 million APW appropriation in 1962.

According to the commission, Procter & Gamble did not contend there would be *substantial* (big) economies in the production and distribution of Clorox.

Training on the Ph.D. level is very desirable, along with *substantial* (good, much) experience in operations research and computer applications.

A substantial (great) number of large advertisers had considered asking the TV industry to absorb the loss stemming from the cancellation of spot announcements during the four-day period of emergency broadcasting.

The problem will be to get the GOP rank-and-file to limit debate without *substantial* (heavy) cuts.

substantially is even more overused than *substantial*. Say *greatly, largely, much, sharply, heavily, well*:

In a modern general hospital, the over-all prevalence of infections has not fallen *substantially* (greatly, much).

Working together, the New York Stock Exchange, the American Stock Exchange and the National Assn. of Securities Dealers have *substantially* (heavily, sharply) raised the entrance requirements.

This is *substantially* (well, much) below what the negotiators have been discussing.

Sen. McCarthy is a handier writer than Mr. Truman, even if he is covering *substantially* (much, largely) the same course.

Substantially (Greatly, Much) aided by the force of President Kennedy's personality, the new Chancellor just managed to put on the defensive his tacit "Gaullist" opposition in West Germany.

substantiate.   It's simpler to say *prove* or *back up*:

The figures do not *substantiate* (prove) some sensational charges made this month about the quality of the foreign language program in the city's schools.

Mr. Debose *substantiated* (backed up) Mrs. Philipides' story. "I saw this guy on the floor near me," he said.

substantive is often used in the sense of *essential* or *relevant*. The best thing is to leave it out:

As a legislator he overemphasized his talent for adjustment and compromise at the expense of developing any line of commitment on *(substantive)* issues.

The only question is whether the author's intelligence, time and energy could not have produced findings of greater *(substantive)* significance if a less rigid role-theory approach were used.

It took 12 years for television to offer a *(substantive)* drama on the subject of the medium's darkest hour.

substitute is sometimes mistakenly used instead of *replace:* "The game of mutual disparagement is occasionally *substituted* (replaced) by an equally dubious one—that of excessive praise of foreign systems."

succor sounds too Biblical. Say *help.*

succumb shouldn't be used as a euphemism for *die:* "What did they die of? Of the cigarette smokers, 110 *succumbed to* (died of) lung cancer, while only 12 of the non-smokers did."

such. There are several common abuses of *such.* First, don't use *such* instead of *any, they, these:*

> Additional Final Tiebreaker Puzzles, not to exceed 2 more, will be employed if necessary to break ties, should *such* (any, they, these) occur in the Final Tiebreaker.

Second, be careful when you use *such* without *a* or *an:*

> The Council may promulgate one or two chapters of the schema De Ecclesia, on the nature of the church. *Such* (an) *action* could indicate . . . .

Third, change *such is the case* and *such is not the case* to *it is so* and *it isn't so:* "That would suggest confidence and ambition in a favorable job market. But *such is not the case* (it isn't so)."

Fourth, rewrite most sentences with *such as:*

> We have been informed by the Public Health Service that the scientific evidence now accumulated *is such as to remove* (removes) almost the last doubt that there are any health effects associated with smoking.

> Frederic D. Donner, chairman, said the dividend was "consistent with the corporation's policy to distribute . . . *such additional amounts as prevailing conditions and the outlook warrant* (additional amounts warranted by prevailing conditions and the outlook).

suffice is too grand a word for *be enough* or *do:* "I am reasonably sure that it is just a funny farce that will *suffice* (do) until a funnier one comes along."

sufficient, sufficiently shouldn't be used where *enough* will do:

> He expected that there would be *sufficient* (enough) revenues to meet the cost.

> Despite highly enthusiastic reviews, it failed to attract *sufficient* (enough) customers and was on the verge of closing.

Mr. Wallace said he believed his stand at Tuscaloosa last summer dramatized the Federal-state issues *sufficiently* (enough).

Panama's argument in respect to economic benefits is that her chief natural resource—her geographic shape and position—is not contributing *sufficiently* (enough) to the national economy.

Some writers go one step further and lengthen *sufficient* to *a sufficient number of*. It still means *enough*:

The prospect of moving the rights and tax bills this session was complicated by the problem of keeping *a sufficient number of* (enough) legislators on hand to transact business after mid-December.

He is simply inadequately acquainted with *a sufficient number of* (enough) cultures to grasp enough facts to write an accurately informative and dependable book on so fascinating and complex a form of human behavior as religion.

supererogation. *It would be a piece* (or *work*) *of supererogation* is a pompous phrase meaning *needless to say* or *it goes without saying*. Like those other hypocritical phrases, it should be cut out: "The play is full of effective theatrics—an encounter between Luther and his father (Kenneth J. Warren), a number of colloquies between Luther and his Augustinian mentor (Frank Shelley), a glimpse of Pope Leo (Michael Egan) in hunting garb and accompanied by various beaters, a couple of braces of Russian wolfhounds, and a pair of falcons (—*but to detail all the remarkable action and all the remarkable acting, particularly by Mr. Finney, would be, I think, a piece of supererogation*)."

surcease is archaic; say *respite* or *letup*: "During the month of mourning for President Kennedy there was no *surcease* (letup, respite) from political contention on Capitol Hill."

surmise (verb) is a fancy word; try *think, guess, suppose*:

The fault, he *surmised* (thought, supposed), lay with the majority leader.

The President recognized the challenge for what it was; he *surmised* (guessed) four days before the actual vote what the opposition might try to do.

surmise (*noun*) should be changed to *thought, guess, theory*:

"The *surmise* (guess, theory) is either that patrolman Tippit picked Oswald out as fitting the description of the suspected assassin broadcast over the Dallas police radio or that he recognized the ex-Marine and Marxist as a suspicious-looking character."

sustain shouldn't be used as a pompous synonym for *suffer*.

sustained is a bookish word for *steady* or *lasting:* "We should strive to disprove the basic Chinese foreign-policy calculation that a *sustained* (lasting, steady) commitment to national liberation struggles and local wars will force the 'imperialist' powers to yield gradually."

sway is a headline word for *move* or *influence:*

> MARITAL ISSUE *SWAYS* (MOVES, INFLUENCES) FEW VOTERS

syndrome means a set of symptoms. The word is now much overused as a fad word outside medicine. Here are some suggestions for getting rid of it:

> In many countries, Mr. Stevenson said, governmental policies "are dedicated to rooting out this dread *syndrome* (disease) of prejudice and discrimination."

> To offset this human storage-battery *syndrome* (effect), some top brass try grounding themselves with door keys, like Franklin's kite.

> A fine antidote to the anti-hero *syndrome* (books) is to be found in "With Fire and Sword," a collection of war annals edited by Quentin Reynolds and Robert Leckie.

> At first, I had feared that it might cost more to hire a baby sitter for a highly sensitive, neurotic dog suffering from *(a)* rejection *(syndrome)* than for a normal, squawling child.

SYNONYMS. One of the basic rules of style is to call things by their natural, familiar names rather than by fancy, artificial, pompous synonyms—*even at the risk of repetition*. This means total abstention from what Fowler called "elegant variation" and habitual use of repetitive words and pronouns. Here are some choice specimens from my collection:

> Once when the late Heywood Broun was writing a Mother's Day tribute to his own *maternal parent* (mother), *the columnist* (he) said . . . .

"A Requiem for John Brown" traced *the antislavery figure's* (his) life from his participation in the border warfare in Kansas to his ill-fated attack on Harper's Ferry and his hanging in December, 1859.

Jean Seberg last Saturday was married to Romain Gary, famous French writer, career diplomat and aviator . . . . "Frenchmen," *the alluring expatriate* (she) said, "think you have to break in an American woman like a horse."

During the Roosevelt, Truman and Eisenhower eras, an average of 65 Southern Democrats in the House defected from party ranks on major legislation. Under the Kennedy administration, these losses have been whittled down to an average of *35 Dixie members* (35).

To the south of Philharmonic Hall, the New York State Theater, three-quarters finished, rises to its full stature and the unfinished interior gives even a greater sense of spaciousness than did *the symphonic building* (Philharmonic Hall) at the same stage of construction.

Another is a marble figure of a little girl with an apple and a bird by Jean Baptiste Pigalle. It was completed a year before *the famous sculptor's* (Pigalle's) death in 1785 and was done to confound critics who complained that, in old age, *the artist's* (his) hand had lost its cunning.

This varies from the Administration's tax cut proposal, which would *trim* (cut) corporate rates to 48 per cent and *slash* (cut) personal taxes by $8.5 billion.

Sometimes synonyms are abused to give added information through sentence-stuffing:

Backing for Dr. Adenauer's position was looked for from Heinrich von Brentano, parliamentary leader of the ruling Christian Democratic Union, in todays talks at Cadenabbia, *the 87-year-old Chancellor's* (Adenauer's) retreat in Northern Italy.

Andy was born on March 9, 1925. *The affable, square-jawed shipping clerk, though never in robust health,* (Though never in roubst health, he) has never been afraid of work.

The young pharmacist made Miss Buck a soda. Even at that age Humphrey was loquacious, and he talked his way into a date with *the petite daughter of a local produce merchant* (her).

D. A. Wade was rugged in his cross-examination of Schafer. He called out his questions in a rasping near-shout, and *the bespectacled CCNY graduate with the high forehead* (Schafer) seemed a little cowed by Wade's aggressiveness at first.

The spectacle of high fashion and promenading celebrities on the paying side of the orchestra pit has its dazzling match on the stage in a new production of "Aida." The choice of *the 92-year-old classic* ("Aida") marked the ninth time that *Verdi's great drama* (it) has opened the Metropolitan season.

See also AS MANY, BARD, CANINE, CHIEF EXECUTIVE, DWELLING, FELINE, GENERAL WORDS, JURIST, LATTER, LAWMAKER, LEVY, MONARCH, NATATORIUM, PACHYDERM, PONTIFF, REPETITION, SAVANT, SOLON, THAT, VEHICLE, VOLUME.

synthesize is sometimes used as a pompous word for *put together* or *grasp:* "If neither you nor I could understand or *synthesize* (grasp) Resnais's "Muriel" on first viewing, this does not necessarily mean the film is a failure artistically."

T

take issue shouldn't be used as a pompous synonym for *disagree:* "Loynd *took issue* (disagreed) with the *Wall Street Journal's* assessment."

take place is a formal phrase suitable for formal ceremonies. For ordinary events, say *happen* or *go on:*

There are market technicians who insist that recent new highs in the market averages are deceptive and that some basic deterioration is *taking place* (happening, going on) despite all the excitement.

It's questionable whether what *took place* (went on, happened) on the stage of the Phoenix Theater last night qualifies as a play.

tantalize goes back to the Greek myth of Tantalus who was tormented by food and drink within sight but out of reach. The word shouldn't be used where there's no such frustration:

Whatever the rights or wrongs of Hill's suit, Baker's connection with Serv-U is *tantalizing* (intriguing).

Tantalizing (Intriguing) correlations between man's diseases and the character of the land on which he lives were discussed here today.

tantamount is a hefty word that can always be spared:

This *is tantamount to* (means, amounts to) saying: Happily, dozens of little businesses are going to be wrecked.

Bills and contracts, *tantamount to expropriation of* (expropriating) U. S. investments, are on many a Latin President's desk.

So strong is the aura of mystery surrounding de Gaulle, that harsh public criticism of him is rapidly becoming (*tantamount to*) heresy.

teen shouldn't be used for *teenage* or *teenager:*

"*Teen* (Teenage) drinkers need to feel wanted," he said.

Teens (Teenagers) worry about "holding their steady," "ostracism should they lose their steady," and "the possibility of losing out on their dates."

terminal illness sounds brutal: "Ethically, say the doctors who would let you die, they are obliged to use every ordinary means in a *terminal* (fatal) illness."

terminate, termination are long words for *end* and *ending:*

It may be that the discussion will *be abruptly terminated* (end abruptly) and the Central Committee plenum will take place as originally scheduled before November ends.

Senator Pell of Rhode Island has proposed a sensible and practical formula whereby *termination of* (ending) the cold war would be possible for both sides.

terms. The phrase *in terms of* can and should usually be shortened to a simple preposition like *of, in, by, through, under:*

It's time to think *in terms of* (of) that Thanksgiving turkey!

What would it mean to you, *in terms of* (in) social rewards and business progress, to double your present speed of reading?

No estimate of the gift was made *in terms of* (in) dollars, but it is well into seven figures.

The Reston plan was completely illegal *in terms of* (by, under) Fairfax County requirements.

True integration can only occur *in terms of* (through, with) consistently high standards and quality of education.

Sometimes an adverb is called for:

In physical terms (Physically) his playing was rather quiet, and it was reflected in the music he made.

-th in such words as *hath, doth* and *saith* has long been dead. Don't try to revive it: "It is not because rank *hath* (has) its privileges." *See also* QUOTH.

than is idiomatically used with the objective case, as in *than whom, than me, than him, than her.* A sentence like "I never met anyone with more courage *than she*" is gramatically correct, but most people say *than her.* Example: "But he divorced his wife of 31 years and married a woman 19 years younger *than her.*"

thankfully, like HOPEFULLY, and GRATEFULLY, shouldn't be used when the writer rather than the subject of the sentence is thankful:

The book is *thankfully* (happily) free of jargon.

This system, long recognized as morally wicked, is now— *thankfully* (thank God)—illegal.

that is a handy word that serves as an adjective, a pronoun, an adverb and a conjunction. The handiest thing about it is that it can often be left out. For instance:

President Kennedy yesterday signed legislation he said will sour major research. (*That* left out after *legislation.*)

He had learned 90 per cent of America's 46 million families owned no flag. (*That* left out after *learned.*)

Leaving out *that* makes for good idiomatic sentences but occasionally it's apt to mislead the reader:

Police noted (that) similar tranquilizer dart guns are used by conservationists and hunters in this country and Africa.

He insists that he did not know (that) Bioff had engaged in any illegal activities.

Sometimes an extra *that* is stuck in where it doesn't belong:

I can't believe that because I can't get everything I want,

(that) I shouldn't make a reasonable compromise for the benefit of our people.

I don't want anything I say to be construed to indicate that if efforts were made and legislation was brought up *(that)* I wouldn't bring it up in the House of Representatives as quickly as possible.

The adjective *that* is often used with a synonym where a simple pronoun would be better:

Milton M. Bergerman, chairman of the Citizen's Union, said *that group* (it) favored a general easing of restrictions on package stores.

Viewers of the festival's opening film, Luis Bunuel's "The Exterminating Angel" and *that director's* (his) earlier "Viridiana" found the subject matter familiar and the execution broad.

that or **which?** *See* WHICH OR THAT?

the. It looks pompous if you capitalize the article *the* in names or titles; put it in lower case:

So I sent $7 for a Trial Subscription to *The* (the) Wall Street Journal.

Though *The* (the) Netherlands was long thought to have no natural resources to speak of, promising pockets of gas were discovered.

Danny will simply have to improve or the folks who get him free in their bedrooms will switch to *The* (the) Three Stooges.

Dr. Kupfer also told *The* (the) Greater New York Dental Meeting about successful re-implantation of teeth that are accidentally knocked out during childhood.

Don't use telegraphic style (without *the*) where it doesn't belong:

Essence (The essence) of the private conversations was that Israeli leaders do not really think a "second round" is imminent.

Best (The best) bet right now is to use the period immediately ahead to review portfolios.

Amount (The amount) taken in the well-cased robbery during the lunch hour near the Lincoln Tunnel was estimated between $1 million and "millions."

Blame (The blame) for 95% of the victims was laid on an innocent-looking toadstool with a greenish cap known as *Amanita phalloides.*

It sounds snobbish and slightly contemptuous if you use the article *the* with the plural of proper names:

The Mailers, the Henry Millers, the Kerouacs (Mailer, Henry Miller and Kerouac) are, one presumes, proper to an age whose ear accepts with pleasure the noises of the television tout, the teen-ager-driven sports car, the jet plane.

Only *the militant Galamisons continue* (the militant Rev. Milton Galamison continues) to think that overt action, such as taking the children out of school, is the way to improve education.

See also A, AN.

their, them. *See* THEY.

thence is old-fashioned; say *from this, from that, from there:*

From there, Harris moved to the sober Fortnightly Review and *thence* (from that, from there) to The Saturday Review.

Only by forcing closure and succumbing to it can they demonstrate to their constituents that they fought to the end against hopeless odds. *Thence* (From this, From that) follows some second-grade arithmetic . . . .

thereabouts is an affectation; say *so:* "It could well happen that just about the time the first American astronauts arrive on the moon, which is to say in 1970 or *thereabouts* (so), their compatriots in the aviation industry will find themselves engaged in the fight of their lives . . . ."

thereafter is ponderous. Say *after that* or *then:*

What happens *thereafter* (then, after that) defies sanity.

To promote the independence of colonies and *immediately thereafter to* (then immediately) ignore the future of such peoples is easy to do but it is irresponsible.

There should be a booster a year later and *every five years thereafter* (then, after that every five years).

Lewis proposed to Dorothy Thompson almost on impulse after seeing her once, and *thereafter* (then, after that) continued to woo her ardently.

A correction came along the wires very soon *thereafter* (after that).

thereby always makes a stiff sentence. Change the passive voice to the active, change *thereby* to *and,* or leave it out altogether:

The assassin's gun removed the President. *An inevitable vacuum was thereby created* (This created an inevitable vacuum).

The original argument for a tax-reduction bill was that *a business recession would thereby be avoided* (it would avoid a business recession).

He can live a life of ease and splendor as a friend of the local establishment, or he can write the story as he sees it, *thereby inviting* (and invite) exclusion from all fashionable dinner parties, continual nasty harassment and possible exile.

John Nance Garner of Texas, who achieved the age of 95 this month, *thereby further strengthening* (and further strengthened) his claim to be the most venerable of former Vice Presidents . . . .

One underground cell is historically traced as the site near the manger where St. Jerome translated the Fourth Century Greek Bible into the Latin Vulgate, *thereby forming* (which is) the basis for today's Roman Catholic Bible.

It takes 67 votes, a Constitutional two-thirds of the entire Senate, to impose cloture and *(thereby)* end debate.

therefrom is stilted: "But intermission had come, and they had risen up and gone *therefrom* (away), for they were ill at ease."

therein is usually just a longer word for *there* or *in it:*

No biographer could wish for a greater compliment . . . namely, that its author might have been present at scenes *therein* (described in it).

And *therein* (there) lies the weakness of this slow, detailed and low-keyed biography of a woman.

thereof should always be changed to *of it:* "Putnam, which brought out the hardcover version, still has a sale *thereof* (of it), with a total of about 40,000 copies."

thereupon. Make it *then:*

He *thereupon* (then) outlines the familiar moral and strategic arguments against the Hiroshima policy.

And the Chief Justice, genuinely moved and touched, *thereupon* (then) consented to undertake the task which he had intended obdurately to refuse.

Thespian is a musty word that shouldn't be used as a synonym for *actor:* "The 'hero' of 'The Oscar' is an evil *Thespian* (actor) named Frankie Fane . . . ."

they is used idiomatically whenever a pronoun refers to more than one person, even though the strict rules of grammar call for *he, she* or *it.* Writers who deliberately avoid this idiom sound pompous and artificial:

We know that when a person goes shopping, *he or she* (they) will always reach for something bearing the name of a favorite.

If Aunt Ellie was a bit teched or Uncle Harry an eccentric, the family gave *her/him* (them) the big room at the top of the stairs to be kept in the background.

The idiomatic *they* is now universal and appears in print every day:

Nobody naturally likes a mind quicker than *their* own.

Everyone I have spoken to swears *they* know who the senator was who attended a lobbyist's picnic . . . .

After all, one would not trust anyone completely; it would hardly be fair to *them.*

"When students have completed a course under my direction, any one of them can stand up before an orchestra *they* have never seen before and conduct correctly a new piece at first sight."

Serbia's deadline for answering the ultimatum has passed, and everyone assumed it had been rejected. But *they* were wrong.

We have, of course, no hope of erasing this blot on our social life if we are affected by the thinking of that new and interesting cult which call *themselves* the modern conservatives.

The bipartisan Board of Elections initiated the inquiry when it forwarded to my office affidavits of registrants which *they* deemed to be irregular and incomplete on their face.

The FBI always works like this in a kidnaping case. *They* do not cooperate with local authorities.

Unfortunately, despite such statements, the charge of Jewish responsibility for the death of Jesus and *their* consequent rejection and punishment by God is still found in Catholic textbooks, sermons and liturgical commentaries.

Every Congressional district in this country that has a defense installation must understand that *they* are going to be reviewed from time to time.

But none of the three judges the 23-year-old defendant appeared before yesterday lives in that county—and *they* decided there had been sufficient adjournments.

The so-called one-stop store is on the wane, chiefly because *they* have multiplied much faster than the one-stop shopper.

See also ARE, IS or ARE?

thinking man. The old insidious cliché was "every thinking man must agree." Modern versions run like this, for instance:

The book will, I think, stir up an argument in *any intelligent family interested in education.*

Americans everywhere, *concerned with clearing the paths toward the realization of human aspiration,* will warmly welcome this book.

Every thinking person will do well to read "Prostitution and Morality."

thirdly, like SECONDLY, doesn't need -*ly*. Say *third*.

thither is archaic. Say *there*.

though is traditionally preceded by a fussy-looking comma. If you like to experiment, you might try leaving it out, as in this example: "There's no such thing as an 'Off Season' tour anymore. *There used to be though*. When people only traveled in the summer."

thrice sounds old-fashioned. Make it *three times:*

Even so, the *thrice-married* (three times married) Swedish actress thinks things have worked out all right.

Just before the vote on the Morse recommittal motion, Senator Mike Mansfield of Montana, the majority leader, *thrice* (three times) denied in a speech that he had discussed the leadership amendment with the Administration.

thus is rare in speech but common in writing. It is perhaps *the* word that most clearly distinguishes bookish English from everyday English. If you want to improve your style, start by weeding out *thus*.

Most often, *thus* should be changed to *so:*

It was not always *thus* (so).

Three years ago, when the Food and Drug Administration gave its approval to the product, the response from the firms *thus* (so) blessed was an embarrassed silence.

Because the drivers work very hard, they rarely leave their cars; *thus,* (so) a door held closed with rope or wire is no trouble either.

Thus (So) far, the only opponent to the plan on the committee is . . . .

The Civil Rights Bill is more likely to come to the House by consent of Judge Smith as chairman of the Rules Committee than to be discharged by petition and *thus* (so) it probably will not be passed before February.

As the rate of expansion tapers off, so does the need by businesses to expand their stocks of inventories and fixed capital. *Thus,* (So) a falling rate of expansion of demand during the first half of next year could lead to contraction in the second half.

With about one-tenth of gross national product devoted to military purposes year after year, there has developed a reluctance, both public and private, toward cutting back so sizable a factor of economic activity. *Thus,* (So) the very fact that makes it important to prepare for the possibility of a reduction in defense outlays—that is, the economy's heavy involvement in defense—could also make it more difficult to achieve reduction.

In other sentences, *thus* should be changed to *that way, therefore, for instance:*

By *thus circumventing* (circumventing that way) the rules and regulations of the Alliance and the criteria laid down by Congress, Senator Morse said, the State Department and the aid agency were forestalling the reforms on which the Alliance was based.

"Segregation," being a legal term, can be outlawed by courts, supported—if necessary—by armies. But courts cannot define its opposite, "integration," nor can armies enforce what courts cannot define. *Thus* (Therefore, That means) confusion—since "integration" has as many meanings as it has champions.

Typically, he is a lawyer, but he may be less sought after for his legal acumen than for his intimate knowledge of lawmaking and politics and, particularly, for his contacts on the Hill. *Thus* (For instance) he might well be an ex-Senator or Congressman or, perhaps, a former Congressional staff aide.

Occasionally a switch from the passive to the active voice is called for:

We estimate that tens of thousands of employment opportunities in such areas as teaching or research and development may be *thus* created (We estimate that this may create . . .).

Sometimes the best thing to do with *thus* is to cross it out:

The choir division normally speaks from the chancel area, and the echo division from the rear of the nave, *(thus)* providing an antiphonal effect.

This greatly desired end will not, naturally, come about by itself; *(thus)* both strategy and tactics are necessary.

However, I am not sure how seriously the whole business is to be taken. *Thus,* when (When) I pressed the matter . . . a Gaullist official with whom I was talking admitted quickly enough that France had no intention of pressing its trigger.

thusly. Even worse than *thus* is the misbegotten word *thusly:*

"While you are spending you day *thusly* (that way), you are also reliving your entire past . . . ."

thwart sounds old-fashioned; try *frustrated* or *blocked:*

Thwarted (Frustrated) afresh in his drive for salvation from the world of blacked-out teeth and mammoth powder puffs, Milton brooded.

He decided that he had been *thwarted* (blocked) by special-interest groups and their supporters in Congress once too often.

TITLES. Sentence stuffing often produces made-up titles like *"G. M. Employee* James Jamrog," *"Philadelphia subdeb* Mary Lee Davis," *"Long Island high-school teacher* George Rapport," *"Grocer* Floyd L. Simpson," *"Los Angeles Times President* Norman Chandler," and *"Crooner-actor-producer-innkeeper-*

ladies' man Frank Sinatra." Don't label people like that; if you want to tell the reader who they are and what they do, wait for the next sentence.

to. There are some pompous ways of using *to*, which you should avoid:

> If a vote were *(to be)* held tomorrow, the Administration's 1962 medicare plan wouldn't stand a chance.

> Stated in the extreme, even if White Plains and Richmond or Jersey City and Rochester *were to exchange* (exchanged) sales-controls systems, it seems probable that the drunkenness arrest figures would not show much change.

> *If we are to understand* (To understand) the real calculation behind the General's insistence on creating a French nuclear striking force, we must begin with the Gaullist conviction that because of American power the Soviet Union cannot launch a successful aggressive surprise attack.

> These are all institutional handicaps to voting. Even *were these to go* (without them), turnout would not be perfect.

> If you *were to take* (took) a course of personal instruction in a private success school, you would not have to pay $50, $75, or $100.

to wit is obsolete; change it to *namely* or *that is:* "I believe that a fact is becoming apparent, *to wit* (namely, that is): You can take the people out of the slums, but sometimes you can't take the slum out of the people."

token. *By the same token* means *for the same reason;* don't use it as a pompous synonym for *also, too,* etc.: "Mr. Lubell places no laurels on the President's brow *and, by the same token, he makes no attempt to downgrade him* (and makes no attempt to downgrade him either)."

tome, like VOLUME, isn't a synonym for *book* and shouldn't be so used: "Miss Bingham's *tome* (book) was smart-alecky and sophisticated, and concentrated heavily on dating."

too looks better without a comma before or after it:

> The Soviet performance on the Autobahn—whatever its motivation—appeared to destroy the hoax *theory, too* (theory too).

> Millions of Army men were taught to "squeeze that trigger" instead of jabbing it, in order to hit the target instead of

missing it. Same way with *photography, too* (photography too).

How your *community, too, might* (community too might) have escaped the effects of the October drought.

This kind of playing, although distinctive and very beautiful, had its *disadvantages, too* (disadvantages too).

See also COMMAS, HOWEVER, THOUGH.

-tory. Stay away from ponderous words ending in *-tory.* A simple participle will usually do:

Tryout reports on the play are generally *approbatory* (approving).

The Sonnets, when properly arranged and dated, form an astonishingly *self-revelatory* (self-revealing) autobiography.

toward, towards are sometimes misused instead of *to:*

"I'm not opposed *towards* (to) improving the lot of mankind, but . . . ."

Such study, investigation and shopping will help point the way *toward* (to) solution of a family's housing problem.

TRANSITIONS. Don't fret over how to make a transition from one topic or one paragraph to the next. Just start the next thought naturally and the transition will take care of itself. Avoid the heavy machinery of FURTHERMORE, MOREOVER, THEREBY, THUS, etc.

transmit, like FORWARD, isn't as good as *send.*

transpire literally means *become known,* but has long been misused as a pompous synonym for *happen, go on:*

What may turn out to be the year's mildest, saddest little exchange on civil rights *transpired* (happened) when Sen. Javits tried to tack an anti-discrimination rider on the agriculture appropriations bill.

"The books are completely open as to what *transpired* (happened) if anyone wants to see them," Mr. Barnes pointed out.

The Pentagon official stated repeatedly that the telephone calls concerned either business that had *transpired* (happened) before his Defense Department appointment or were simple inquiries . . . .

Here is a prize example where *transpire* (happen) was used for something that *didn't transpire* (become known):

What *transpired* (happened) at these meetings has been shrouded in unusual secrecy.

trauma, traumatic are now fad words in the sense of *shock* and *shocking:* "To the American Church and its seminaries the warning was *traumatic* (a shock); it left Catholic scholarship in a state of timidity."

trice is obsolete. For *in a trice* say *in an instant, instantly, immediately:* "Presently, along comes a dwarf who claims kinship with Miss Amelia, and *in a trice* (instantly) she is showering him with affection."

tropism, in biology, means *response to a stimulus.* Don't use this rare word to show off your vocabulary: "They *move by the tropisms of* (are moved by) power and fear in a world of reaching hands and rapped knuckles."

true facts. See FACTS.

tummy is baby talk and should never be used as a euphemism for *stomach* or *belly*.

twain is archaic; say *two:*

VILLAGE CUT IN *TWAIN* (TWO)

If you must use *twain,* at least use the plural verb: "The twain has (have) met at McCann-Erickson."

twenties, thirties, forties. See DECADES.

U

ultimate, ultimately are longer but no better than *final, finally, in the end:*

We should consider not only the short-term results of his policies but also their *ultimate* (final) consequences.

Ultimately (In the end), Washington demonstrated its loss of confidence in the Diem government by holding back funds . . . .

Even though our patience is *ultimately* (finally) rewarded, patience is required for "Therese."

un- has to be used with care. Often words with *un-* would sound better with *in-*, *no-*, *non-* or *not:*

> In keeping his film moving at a surprisingly swift pace, Mr. Malle has the assistance of an *undubitably* (indubitably) artistic and dedicated cast.

> Talk about Garbo kept cropping up all over—her clothes, her *un-hair-do* (no-hair-do), her lack of make-up.

> At the beginning of the second week, I found myself—for the first time in my *uncareer* (non-career) as a juror—on an actual case.

> *Unseen* (Not seen) by the President were five picket lines on 53rd St. and Seventh Ave.

unclad.   *See* CLAD.

Uncle Sam sounds silly when the phrase is used simply as a convenient synonym for the federal government or the U.S.:

> Why do *Uncle Sam's* (federal) outlays keep climbing relentlessly?

> The members of this small ruling class, like their counterparts in some other Latin countries, often use *Uncle Sam* (the U.S.) as a scapegoat to distract anger away from themselves.

undaunted sounds bookish; try *unafraid, undiscouraged:*

> *Undaunted* (Undiscouraged) by the lukewarm reception of variety shows on other networks this season, NBC quietly is going ahead with plans for a new series . . . .

> Siegel, *undaunted* (undiscouraged), filed a new removal application.

under the circumstances.   *See* CIRCUMSTANCES.

UNDERLINING.   *See* ITALICS.

underprivileged is a silly euphemism for *poor*. Here's a prize specimen: "In the belief that an urgent need exists to stabilize world population and thus prevent the eventual condemnation of millions of citizens to lives of *underprivilege* (poverty), misery and hopelessness, the foundation expects to expand its support of critical research and of action programs in population dynamics and population stabilization."

undersigned should be taboo. Say *I.*

undue, unduly are often used without thinking where there is no corresponding *due* or *duly* that would make sense:

> Dr. Johnson said that the combined treatment has been started on a few human patients in the last few weeks. He said they have suffered no *(undue)* ill effects.

> "The *(undue)* emphasis on advertising which characterizes the liquid bleach field is itself a symptom of and a contributing cause to the sickness of competition in the industry," the F.T.C. said.

> "I don't think it reflects any *(undue)* sense of corruption in the colleges," he says.

unfold is a pompous word; try *show, explain, bring out, happen, come about, come up, come out*s

> His individuality may be measured by the manner with which he *unfolds* (brings out, shows) tonal values as related to style.

> A series of legislative and administrative regulations covering trading in securities and commodities can be expected to *unfold* (come out) during the next several years.

> Against the background of that community, two larger experiences *unfold* (come about, happen) which give Simeon the courage to move as his conscience has been urging.

unless and until is one of those legal doublet phrases that are habit-forming for some writers. Most of the time *unless* is enough:

> It seems to me unlikely that there will be progress in the study of paranormal phenomena . . . unless *(and until)* someone hits upon methods of inducing paranormal powers in ordinary persons and sustaining them thereafter at a high level for some considerable time.

> The Southern bloc is relatively stronger in the Senate than in the House and will have the added advantage of unlimited debate unless *(and until)* two-thirds of the membership present and voting decide to invoke cloture.

> *Until and unless* (Unless) the President and the Secretary of State comprehend, if they really do not, what is so clear, the part of Rusk's news conference that states a sound principle of Government will not have the desired beneficial effect on Congress.

Sometimes, when there's little doubt of what's going to happen, *unless and until* should be cut to *until:*

> "Until *(and unless)* we learn otherwise, we assume that Wohlgemuth and International Latex, both having knowledge of the court order, will comply with the law," Jeter says.

See also AND/OR, IF AND WHEN.

UNNECESSARY WORDS are symptoms of sloppy writing. Cut them out:

> Not having seen the stage production, this writer is unprepared to say how well it was translated or in what respects it was changed *(in transition)*.

> This highly efficient plant has always made the same *(identical)* automobiles as all Studebaker owners have long enjoyed.

> The Bobby Baker case is like a *(many-colored)* kaleidoscope.

> At Macy's, women in minks jostled *(with)* girls in pedal pushers to buy costume jewelry.

> "I see black," says 38-year-old Herbert Drücker, the wiry, *blond-haired* (blond) manager of a large estate near Bonn.

> Both men suffered enormous reductions in *(financial)* income by taking government jobs.

> In Jessica Mitford's incisive indictment of the flamboyant commercialism of some funerals, told in her book entitled "The American Way of Death," there were no *(pictorial)* illustrations.

until and unless. *See* UNLESS AND UNTIL.

until such time as. Shorten it to *until*.

untimely. "When he met his *untimely* end, John Kennedy . . . ." When is death timely? At 80? 90? 100? Think about this before you use the word *untimely*.

up to is now fully respectable standard English:

> If corporations ought to be doing things they are not now doing—such as hiring Negroes on an equal basis with whites—then it is *up to* government to tell them so.

> Eventually petitioners are likely to find themselves being told at home that the matter is *up to* the Vatican.

Mr. Feldman insisted he had demonstrated de facto segregation and it was *up to* the state to prove the contrary.

What's Khrushchev *up to*?

upgrade is the fad word now and it seems hopeless to try to
bring back *improve:*

One task that Case has obviously accomplished with great
success is the *upgrading* of its product lines.

The question here is a matter of priorities, and *upgrading*
the quality of education is the first and unavoidable step in
realistic integration of the schools.

K & E BIDS AGENCIES BACK DRIVE
TO *UPGRADE* RADIO, TV

upon doesn't mean anything different from *on,* and should always
be shortened to *on.* Here's a fine example containing four *upons:*
"It will be seen then that "The Affable Hangman" is not a shocker
or *roman policier,* but a serious philosophical essay *upon* (on)
responsibility, *upon* (on) refusal, *upon the question as to whether*
(on whether), laboring under the certainty of mortality, it is
desirable or not to enter *upon* (on) the busy life of the world."

us is often idiomatically right where strict grammarians would
insist on *we:*

Now and then writing with levity, grace and warmth she
produces such a gem as "Nobody much slept here, just *us*",
a delightful little portrait of the old-fashioned house she
and her family live in.

In the words of a more courageous governor: "If not now,
when; if not *us,* who?"

See also HER, HIM, ME.

usage. Industrial *use* is shorter and better than *usage.*

utilize should always be changed to *use:*

A suggestion was broached that we would *utilize* (use)
still-frame pictures of American faces.

Postmaster General John A. Gronouski will follow prec-
edent and *utilize* (use) a Citizens' Stamp Advisory Committee for counsel on the subject matter and design of United
States stamps.

Most surprisingly, Freud did not *utilize* (use) the concept of stress, although it is a major factor in any modern discussion of mental health.

The "Adam" name was *utilized* (used) for a branded men's slacks line, which retails for $6.95 to $13.95.

The education they receive makes it possible for them to *utilize* (use) their above-average gifts to their own greatest advantage.

V

vandalize, like HOSPITALIZE, is an ugly word, but I'm afraid it's here to stay: "Like the twin-light blinking signal that had been *vandalized* (smashed by vandals) possibly weeks before yesterday morning's terrible tragedy and never repaired, several others along the city's riverbank were either out or lying on the street where vandals had wrecked them."

variety shouldn't be used in such sentences as *"The concert was of the gala variety."* Change it to "It was a gala concert."

vaunted sounds bookish. Change it to *celebrated:* "The Hallmark 'Hall of Fame' last night effected a rare and fine combination of television's *much-vaunted* (celebrated) but seldom-linked functions of entertaining and informing . . . ."

vehicle should never be used as a pompous synonym for *car:* "On a car trip from Cairo to Aswan, the *vehicle* (car) ran out of gasoline."

vend means *sell.* Why not say *sell?*

venture (verb) is old-fashioned and can usually be left out: "The Italian attempt anticipates, correctly, I *(venture to)* think, the main tendency among the masses of people on the Western European continent."

verbal comes from the Latin and means *by words,* but everybody uses it instead of *oral* to mean *by mouth:* "The details of adminstration bore him, and he obliges his ministers to give him *verbal* accounts of their activities rather than read documents."

very is now idiomatically used with the past participle of a verb; the old rule was that instead of *very* you should say *much:*

Moscoso says that he is *"very* concerned" at the danger of more military takeovers in Latin America.

"He was *very* surprised," she said.

via is Latin for *by way of* (a certain route); it shouldn't be used to mean *through* generally: "The Bank of America's billions can be translated into flesh and blood *(via* [through], for instance, its medical loans), concrete and steel *(via* [through] its building mortgages)."

viable, viability. *Viable* means *able to live and grow,* as an infant or a seed. *Viable* and *viability* are now fad words and much overused:

Over the years Congress has accumulated a number of *viable* (practical) solutions.

This new novel is a shorter and less *viable* (successful) tale.

Kennedy made the rocking chair a *viable* (workable) seat of government.

In Dallas last week, Monteverdi's rarely performed "Coronation of Poppea" proved its *viability* (durability, enduring life) by inaugurating the 1963 Dallas Civic Opera season.

The United States since the close of the war has sent $100 billion worth of assistance to nations seeking economic *viability* (growth, development).

vicinity is a clumsy word. Use *near* or *close:* "In aboriginal Australia women are believed not to conceive at all, but to be entered by a spirit-baby at a totemic center *in the vicinity of* (near) which she happens to be passing."

vicissitude is a long word literally meaning *turn* or *change.* Usually the best replacement for *vicissitudes* is *ups and downs:*

In picturing the *vicissitudes* (ups and downs) of his family the author also contrives to look back over his own career as a Harvard student, a Boston reporter, a writer of mysteries, his marriage to a no-nonsense New England girl, and his less-publicized activities as one of the busiest literary ghosts in the country.

The big, light-skinned, handsome spiritual and political leader in Harlem has survived *vicissitudes* (ups and downs) that would have wrecked many who probably consider themselves better men.

victuals is no longer funny as a synonym for *food*.

vie is obsolete; the everyday word is *compete:*

His greedy victims *vie* (compete) desperately with one another to show their love for Lahr.

The problems of the city, especially of the big city or metropolis, *vie* (compete) with those of foreign policy, race and education.

view. Avoid the compound prepositions *with a view to, in view of, from the point of view of, from the viewpoint of:*

Dr. Nahum Goldmann, termed as "wrong and misleading" impressions that Israel had become "a country safe *from the point of view of* (in) its security, strong politically and rather wealthy economically."

To make matters worse, *from the viewpoint of* (for) the male juveniles, the ratio of girls to boys had fallen to 1-to-5.

virtually shouldn't be used as a long synonym for *almost:* "*Virtually* (Almost) the first words spoken were Councilman Thomas Flaherty's motion to name Mr. Whelan."

virtue. *By virtue of* can and usually should be shortened to *by:* "He was a Kentucky farm boy who had won a host of high-placed friends *by (virtue of)* his own personality and his own well-earned athletic reputation."

visualize, like ENVISAGE and ENVISION, is a fashionable pompous word for *see, imagine, think of:*

One could almost *visualize* (see) Galbraith Defense Committees, being formed to protect him from the fury of the local Puritans and the Harvard Overseers.

Boulle has *visualized* (imagined) a planet in the system of the great star Betelgeuse three hundred light years from our own solar system.

It is such an ideal part for Boyer that it is almost impossible to *visualize* (imagine, think of) "Man and Boy" without him.

vitiate sounds bookish or legal; the regular word is *spoil:*

What was remarkable and enigmatic in the play is *vitiated* (spoiled) and attenuated on screen.

The few moments of excitement and tension are *vitiated*

(spoiled) by the trite recall of episodes in Paris and Rome
that led to domestic tension.

voice (verb) always sounds pompous; change it to *express* or
rewrite the sentence:

Professor Brown *voiced the belief* (expressed the belief,
said he believed) that for the Roman Catholic Church to
"back away" at this point from the religious liberty and
Catholic-Jewish questions would be extremely serious.

The progressives *voiced criticism of* (expressed criticism of,
criticized) the schema because they said it did not go far
enough toward the concept of bishops sharing the administration of the Church with the Pope.

volume. Only those who have no sense of style use *volume* for
book:

FAMED KENNEDY *VOLUME* (BOOK)
ISSUED IN MEMORIAL EDITION

was or were? *See* WERE OR WAS?

wax (verb) shouldn't be used as a pompous synonym for *get* or
be:

The welfare state gives Americans a grand opportunity to
wax (be, get) eloquent on their basic political philosophies.

The movement begins to *wax* (get) sluggish when Con-
stantinople is reached and the youth gets involved with his
uncle.

wax and wane is used today only by writers desperate for a
synonym for *increase and decrease:* "One subject of disagreement
is whether the number of tape watchers has increased or decreased over the years. Some brokerage houses think they are
waxing (increasing) and others, *waning* (decreasing)."

way. *In the way of* and *by way of* are elaborate prepositions that
should be cut down to *in, to* or nothing:

There are all kinds of spectacular effects in "Jennie," at the
Majestic, but there isn't much *(in the way of)* wit, style, or
content.

In *(the way of)* audience response, Miss Garland's show has been less fortunate than Mr. Kaye.

By way of guarding (To guard) against excessive disappointment if the fund got so low there was no bonus to share, the union has conducted an elaborate education campaign among its members.

way back, way off, way out look better without apostrophe.

we sounds pompous whenever it means the speaker or writer himself or some vague large group of which he has appointed himself spokesman:

We (I) remarked that *our* (my) luncheon companions had said something about a last-minute decision.

We (I) volunteered to do some doorbell ringing *ourself* (myself), and *we were* (I was) surprised at some of the reactions when *we* (I) tried to tell the people about their voting rights.

For a long first act *we are* (I was) intimately concerned with Martin Luther as tool, as a tool of elemental forces he cannot cope with physically or wholly contend with intellectually. *We do not* (I didn't) meet a philosopher. *We meet* (I met) a spiritual epileptic.

Yes, I think *we* (you) may put down "Von Ryan's Express" as one of the most enjoyable action-escape suspense stories to have come out of World War II.

We (You) must constantly keep reminding *ourselves* (yourself) that *ours* (yours) is an era of rapid social and cultural changes. (Of course, if you change this sort of *we* into *you*, your sentence is apt to sound awfully silly.)

wed is no longer used outside of headlines; say *marry:* "A 36-year-old Alaskan vowed today he would not leave the Soviet Union until he *weds* (marries) his Russian fiancee."

well-nigh sounds medieval. Stick to *almost:* "Pearson's problem is that the telephone company's image is *well-nigh* (almost) perfect."

were it not is a bookish phrase. Use a simple *if . . . not* clause: This dangerous situation would not exist *were it not that the Congress of the United States has* (if the Congress of the United States hadn't) neglected to do its duty.

We could accept their admission that their previous books needed extensive revisions *were it not that they have* (if they hadn't) strained their imagination in a quest of "newness."

were or was? The textbooks say you should say *were* instead of *was* in *if* clauses dealing with a "condition contrary to fact." But the textbooks are wrong. The current idiom uses either *were* or *was* for conditions contrary to fact, *depending on whether the idea is being suggested or ruled out.* If you ask the reader to imagine something as true, write *was;* if you ask him to dismiss it as impossible, write *were.* Here are some sentences with the idiomatic *was:*

He suggested, if credit *was* restricted to five years, the Russians would probably have to divert production from arms to other goods to pay for their purchases from the West.

"If I *was* in Manny Celler's shoes right now," one committee member said, "I'd burn the Capitol down."

I never bet, and if I *wasn't* working at the races, I would never go to them.

"No, we aren't Chrysler stockholders," Vlaha said. "I wish I *was,* now."

And here are some examples of the idiomatic *were:*

If the world *were* standing still, there would be no harm in Congress' standing still. But the world isn't.

Kennedy's programs are not the kind Mailer would introduce *were* he in the White House.

"God has given me many talents, but no great ones," she said. "If I *were* great I wouldn't have any friends."

The withdrawal symptoms for the individual who stops would be as nothing compared to those for the whole country—with its 500,000 tobacco farms and its $200 million annual budget for cigarette advertising—if smoking *were* sharply curtailed.

Demolition boss Morris Lipsett, looking on from beneath his hard hat, observed: "If it *were* art, somebody would have dug in his pocket to save it."

Writers often lean over backwards and write *were* instead of the more natural *was:*

If ever there *were* (was) an example of child wonder turned great musician, it is violinist Erick Friedman.

"I told them to see an engineer," says DiPaola. "They could check with him to see if I *were* (was) being honest with them."

The therapist, a pretty blonde with the patience of a saint, recognized that Petey would not talk unless the terrified, suffering little soul within his frail body *were* (was) reached —and reassured.

The good burglar will enter surreptitiously, and he won't disturb anything while he is searching for treasure, because if it looks as if the best jewelry *weren't* (wasn't) at home, he will come back for it another time.

See also AS IF, AS THOUGH, BE, IF, SUBJUNCTIVE.

when and if. *See* IF AND WHEN.

whence is obsolete. Say *from where*. Even worse than *whence* is the common mistake *from whence:* "This is the World's Fair Room and its single and dedicated purpose is to serve visitors to the Fair no matter *from whence they come* (where they come from)."

where. Avoid the legal *where* (in the sense of *in a case where*). Change it to *if:* "The Tax Court and the Fifth Circuit Court of Appeals ruled that sums paid an employe as reimbursement for losses on the sale of his home would be taxable income *where* (if) the taxpayer sold to move to a new location at his employer's behest."

whereas sounds stuffy. In spite of the objections of some grammarians, the common word now is *while:*

Elsewhere, "The Burghers of Calais"—perhaps Rodin's most celebrated public monument—is compared with Giacometti's "City Square," and Professor Elsen makes the just comment that although both artists show men in isolation, we at least share the isolation of the Burghers, *whereas* (while) Giacometti's figures are entirely anonymous.

She is complimented on her good sense in picking the fur *whereas* (while, although) the only good sense she had was in picking the husband or boy friend with loot to pay for it.

whereby is very formal English. It can always be changed to *by which* or *so that*, but it's even better to rewrite the sentence:

Mr. Heinlein said the bank used to pay the same rate on

school and adult accounts before it adopted split rates *whereby it paid* (with) a premium on money on deposit a year or more.

Prompt and remedial measures are being taken *whereby the temporary suspension may be lifted* (to lift the temporary suspension).

wherein is overformal. Change it to *in which, where, when:*

There is one sketch, from which the title comes, *wherein* (in which, where) some of the needed quality is captured.

Theatergoers could not recall yesterday a similar instance *wherein* (when) a single person made an outright donation.

Heaven, it is hoped, will protect innocent children in homes *wherein* (where) both parents simultaneously give up cigarets.

It is the synthesis of all interrelationships—*wherein* (in which, where, when) the result of *all* relationships finds final expression.

wherewithal is just a fancy word for *means:* "Income, since it consists of satisfactions received, or the *wherewithal* (means) to exchange for such satisfactions, tends to satisfy the recipient."

whether or not. *Or not* is usually unnecessary:

Whether (*or not*) it is the site of Leif Erickson's house can still be debated, but there are some reasons to believe it is.

The key to the argument over *whether* the Common Market produced Europe's prosperity (*or not*) may well lie with the detached view of founding father Jean Monnet.

Whether (*or not*) an unaltered psychoanalytic theory of dreaming is compatible with all these findings is a problem for further investigators.

Sen. Smith said that she still has not decided *whether* (*or not*) to give it a try.

See also AS TO, QUESTION AS TO WHETHER.

which has some handy idiomatic uses that are still frowned on by some grammarians:

"Arturo Ui" closed Saturday night, *which* I think everyone regrets.

There were five veterans who made mental errors, *which* you wouldn't believe they could do.

If it should ever be shown that one or more elements in tobacco are responsible for cancer—*which* we don't now believe—our scientists would be able to eliminate that element.

Which, when you think about it, is a natural enough question.

Which just shows that network radio can't do everything.

which or **that?** Here are two sentences with *which*:

1. Hurricane Flora, *which* killed at least 25 persons and left thousands homeless on the resort island of Tobago, pointed its 140-mile-an-hour winds last night toward Haiti, Jamaica and southeastern Cuba.

2. Institutions *which* rely too comfortably on tradition do not long survive.

Now, for the sake of experiment, leave out the *which* clause in both sentences:

1. Hurricane Flora pointed its 140-mile-an-hour winds last night toward Haiti, Jamaica and southeastern Cuba.

2. Institutions do not long survive.

You see what happened? When you take the *which* clause out of the first sentence, it still makes sense and tells the reader something. When you do the same thing with the second sentence, all that's left is nonsense. Which proves that *which* in the second sentence is wrong and should be changed to *that*.

Follow this rule and change *which* to *that* in all sentences that wouldn't make sense without the *which* clause:

In some ways, his apparent disappearance from public life may have been the best thing *which* (that) ever happened Mr. Menon.

As is well known, infections *which* (that) strike the mother during pregnancy can affect the fetus adversely.

On those few occasions when we have advertised products *which* (that) we privately despised, we have failed.

The President had inherited one of those periods of global flux *which* (that) do not lend themselves to official oratory.

Business men's requests for bank credit have been lagging behind projections *which* (that) bank economists made for the second half of this year.

The kind of character *which* (that) fills these pages is, indeed, futile.

What is becoming alarming and intolerable is a Congress *which* (that) will smother and stultify rather than debate and decide.

The leaders plan to by-pass the Rules Committee and pass the Senate-approved stopgap measure Monday under a motion *which* (that) requires a two-thirds majority.

He distinguished between those bacteria *which* (that) are always foreigners to human chemistry even when they're in human bodies sickening and killing, and those bacteria *which* (that) normally inhabit people.

The pressure to get the Mayor to say he will run against Sen. Keating is coming from the same sources *which* (that) six months ago were downgrading Wagner's possible value to the 1964 ticket.

One of the reviving influences *which* (that) periodically set to work on the English language is its adoption by somebody else.

Mr. Johnson has never believed that the fundamental issues *which* (that) divide Russia and the democratic nations can be settled by negotiation.

Mr. Dillon said the proposed reduced rate should not be put into effect unless provision is made for taxing capital gains *which* (that) are passed on from a parent to a son or daughter.

whichever is an ugly income-tax and fine-print word. There's always a way of saying the same thing more clearly and naturally:

Refund claims must be filed within three years of the time the original return was filed or within two years of the time the tax was paid—whichever was later. (Refund claims must be filed within two years from the time the tax was paid, but not later than three years from the time the original return was filed.)

Chrysler Corporation warrants *for 5 years or 50,000 miles, whichever comes first* (for 50,000 miles, but no longer than 5 years) against defects in materials and workmanship.

whither is one of the most pompous words in English. Stay off it:

WHITHER (WHAT NEXT FOR) CALIFORNIA'S GOP?

INTERNATIONAL LIQUIDITY—*WHITHER* (WHAT) NOW?

who or **whom?** The word *whom* is on its way out and now sounds pompous and wrong in many sentences:

They asked me *whom* (who) I'd been out with the night before.

The question must arise: *Whom* (Who) are they keeping the secrets from—the Russians? Or the taxpayers?

Asked *whom* (who) he would vote for, a 64-year-old machinist in Portland replied . . . .

He's someone (*whom*) the President turns to naturally and with a sense of intimacy.

In contrast, here's a little collection of good idiomatic *who*'s that would sound terrible if they were changed to *whom:*

Will they blame the Senate or will they blame me? I know *who* they will blame, so I need this program.

Shirley MacLaine's being mighty mysterious about *who* she's going to see in Ireland.

Who will the GOP nominate?

Who can the business man listen to in '64?

The old rule was to get as many people into the tent as you could possibly afford and hit them with the greatest frequency. Now it's *who* do we want in the tent.

Reporter Lester Schecter smiled sadly and tried to quip, "*Who* do I see for a job now?"

The night President Kennedy was buried, this shrine blazed with candles, and everyone knew *who* they were for.

Oddly enough, *whom* is used idiomatically in certain sentences where the strict grammarians would prefer *who*. The *whom* usage is now firmly established:

Valachi killed a convict *whom* he mistakenly thought was the mobster assigned to kill him.

The young men in their sports cars brought their girls, and a few wealthier-looking clients might be seen with ladies *whom* one hoped were their wives.

It was the first television show in months to arouse set owners to a discussion in the morning of a previous evening's program and to vivid correspondence with those *whom* they believe were suffering from a touch of Sunday-night stomach upset.

When *who* is used in such a sentence, it's apt to sound like a fussy correction of the original *whom:*

> The "mysterious American" *who* (whom?) the State Department feared was undermining its new hard-line policy toward the Dominican Republic's military-installed civilian junta turned out to be a "former" CIA agent.

> Mrs. Patricia Stanley, a housewife *who* (whom?) a Barnard College psychologist believes has the ability to detect colors with her fingertips, performed only occasionally better than chance would have allowed in tests during the last few days here.

-wise has become so well-known as a Madison Avenue cliché that it now has an established ironic use:

> "All in all, eggs have a thoroughly bad image—are obsolete, *marketing-wise,*" he said.

> "*Loot-wise,* this is going to be a lean Christmas," one agency receptionist noted.

wish shouldn't be used as a more dignified synonym for *want:* "Other members of the board said they *wished* (wanted) to evaluate the mountain of testimony put in the record during the long hearing."

wish to advise, wish to say, wish to state should always be left out: "*I wish to state that I* (I) never saw so many gates enclosing so many stores in our city."

with shouldn't be used as a sentence-stuffing device, tying two pieces of information together:

> *With* the Roman Catholic Church reporting severe shortages of priests in many parts of the world, Pope Paul VI appealed yesterday for more students for the priesthood.

> *With* an arbitrator's decision expected by tomorrow, the United States Lines has canceled for the third consecutive time the sailing of the liner America, idled over a union dispute since Sept. 15.

> The Senate resumes Saturday sessions on the embattled civil rights bill today *with* Southern Senators talking of boycotting

a Democratic caucus Tuesday where amendments proposed
by the bipartisan leadership will be considered.

wont to is archaic; say *used to* or *usually:*

As the years sped by, Berenson dropped, one by one, the
public faces he had been *wont* (used) to wear—the non-
pareil art connoisseur, the scintillating conversationalist, the
must-be-seen "character."

The network moguls *are wont to* (usually) say at this point
that they haven't decided exactly which shows will not be
renewed for next season.

worthwhile is much overused. Try instead *worth, worthy, good:*

"The Last Savage" was *worthwhile* (worth) writing and it
was *worthwhile* (worth) producing.

Many *worthwhile* (worthy) groups that provide activities
for children and youth, the handicapped, ill and aged are
very short-handed because so many able women have gone
to work.

Now is an especially *worthwhile* (good) time to·sample a
short trial membership in the Literary Guild.

would appear, would seem are often used by timid writers who
don't want to be responsible for what they're saying. Sometimes
would seem or *would appear* should be changed to plain *seem*
or *appear,* but usually it should be left out entirely:

The pianist's style *would seem* (seems) to shine in other
kinds of music and the solo recital he will give here next
month may bear this out.

It *would even seem* (even seems) conceivable that the United
States might persuade the Soviet Union to cooperate in such
an endeavor or at least not to block it.

Recent events (*would seem to*) indicate that the President is
going to bring Mr. Shriver into the limelight more often . . . .

It *would appear that nothing* (Nothing) is more important
now for the United States government than to have a clear-
cut understanding with the Soviet Union as to what it in-
tends to do in the area around Berlin.

Thus (*it would seem that*) after a family of a reasonable
size has been produced, the intelligent use of contraceptives
has much to offer in the prevention of defective babies.

The Royal Philharmonic's prize *would seem to be* (is) the silken tone of its string section.

would that at the beginning of a sentence sounds old-fashioned; say *I wish:*

> *Would that* (I wish) he were representative either of the left or of the right.

> *Would that* (I wish) it had also been written with greater care.

WRONG FACTS. There can't be any good writing without accuracy. If your facts are wrong, even the best words and sentences won't help:

> The play is spoken in Hebrew but *hearing aids* are provided at each seat in the theater, so you can listen to a simultaneous translation into English. (Those were not hearing aids but earphones.)

> The mission took him to *the little Italian island of Lago Maggiore* in January, 1937, at the request of Gen. David Sarnoff of RCA. (Lago Maggiore is not an island but a lake.)

> The influence of Kafka is unmistakable and, coming from a *fellow-Viennese*, understandable. (Kafka didn't live in Vienna but in Prague.)

> In *Ouagadougou, the capital of the Ivory Coast,* they were asked by an "ashen-faced" U.S. Consular officer if they were sure they had checked "every alternative" to their route. (Ouagadougou is not the capital of the Ivory Coast but of Upper Volta.)

Xmas. It's never good style to use the abbreviation *Xmas.* Say *Christmas.*

Y

yclept is a stale joke. Say *called* or *named*.

yea sounds phony. Say *yes:* "I have just concluded reading 'The Pseudo-Ethic' with the greatest enthusiasm. I can say '*Yea*' (yes) to every word of it."

yes doesn't need quotation marks when used as part of a sentence:

ROCKEFELLER SAYS '*YES*'. (YES)

yet at the opening of a sentence isn't used in ordinary English but only in pompous rhetorical prose. Change it to *but:* "*Yet* (But) public concern, already rising, is sure to grow stronger if Congress fails to make a conscientious effort to expose whatever rottenness may exist in its own establishment."

you can sound very pompous when used instead of *I* (as in this columnist's description of a De Gaulle press conference): "Then after an hour and 40 minutes of Chinese history, European economics, French and American constitutional theory, political geography, diplomacy, he ends with a neat clicking sentence, the huge class is dismissed, and *you go* (I went) out again into the Paris drizzle."

young lady always sounds patronizing: "The second *young lady* (girl) to come along last week was Inge Swenson."

youngster sounds just as bad and artificial as OLDSTER. Stick to *child, boy, girl, young man, young woman, young people*— or follow the general usage and say *kids:*

When parents make their child the be-all and end-all of their lives, *the* youngster (he) stops developing a life of his own.

For the past 10 years these jobs have been evaporating as automation has condemned scores of thousands of middle-aged Negroes to discard, and scores of thousands of their *youngsters* (children) to a future that holds nothing.

Thirteen of the *youngsters* (boys and girls, young people) accused of turning the party-after-Fernanda's party into a house-wrecking session were summoned to Suffolk County Court yesterday.

". . . and yet, a large number of suburban kids go to hell

Why? Well, I think it's because *youngsters* (kids) mirror adult society—and then exaggerate it."

See also KID.

youth, in the sense of *boy* or *young man,* is even worse than *youngster:*

Dr. Salber told a meeting on smoking that schoolboys who smoke in grades seven to 12 have lower IQ's and lower scholastic achievement levels than non-smoking *youths* (boys).

Brooklyn's Hasidic Jewish community appeared to be stirred but unremorseful yesterday over the arrest on Monday of five of its *youths* (young men, boys).

Yule, Yuletide is ugly journalese. Stick to *Christmas:*

AT MUSIC HALL *YULE* (CHRISTMAS) TREE
AN ENTERTAINING PACKAGE

Mr. Johnson put off his *yuletide* (Christmas) trip to his Texas ranch while the battle raged.

Z

zenith is often too rhetorical: "As an example of '*hypocrisy at its zenith,*' (utter hypocrisy), Rep. Miller charged that House Democratic leaders merely 'pretended a deep desire to see the civil rights bill enacted' immediately following Mr. Kennedy's death."

ziggurat is one of those words that are unknown to most people but have become a fad among a few. It means a Babylonian temple built like a pyramid. Example: "Tower East departs brashly from the established *brick-ziggurat* (brick pyramid) pattern of post-war apartment buildings here, and has thus caught the eye of layman and critic alike."

046008

870657

WITHDRAWN

Plainfield Public Library
Eighth St. at Park Ave.
Plainfield, NJ   07060